Chichester Excavations IV

EDWARD JAMES, ESQ.

This volume is dedicated to Edward James Esquire, of West Dean, founder of the Edward James Foundation, in grateful acknowledgement of his contribution to the archaeology of the region.

Chichester Excavations IV

by

Alec Down

with specialist contributions by

F. G. Aldsworth, B.A.   Richard Bradley, B.A., F.S.A.
Prof. B. W. Cunliffe, M.A., Ph.D., F.S.A.   G. Dannell, B.Sc., F.S.A.
K. Jane Evans, B.A.   B. R. Hartley, M.A., F.S.A.   K. Hartley, F.S.A.
Dr. M. Henig, M.A., D.Phil., F.S.A.   R. Lintott.   D. F. Mackreth, B.A., F.S.A.
A. Outen.   Dr. D. J. Smith, Ph.D., F.S.A.   R. M. Tittensor, M.A., M.Sc., M.I.Biol.
Prof. J. M. C. Toynbee, M.A., D.Phil., F.B.A., F.S.A.
Dr. C. J. Young, M.A., D.Phil., F.S.A.

Published for

Chichester Excavations Committee
by

Phillimore

Acknowledgements

The Committee wish to thank the undermentioned organisations and individuals whose generous donations have made this publication possible:

Anglia & General Developments Ltd.
Chichester District Council
Chichester Museum Society
Council for British Archaeology
Dexam International
Messrs. Raymond Dobson & Co.
The Edward James Foundation
C. Howard & Sons
The Marc Fitch Fund
A. Olby & Sons Ltd.
Sussex Archaeological Society, Margary Fund
West Sussex County Council
Whiteheads Ltd.
John Wiley & Sons Ltd.

ISBN 0 85033 344 X

Published by
PHILLIMORE & CO. LTD.,
Shopwyke Hall, Chichester, Sussex.

Printed by
UNWIN BROTHERS LTD.,
The Gresham Press,
Old Woking, Surrey.

Author's Note

In an operation lasting nearly 14 years, the number of people who contributed in one way or another to the project grew from less than a dozen in 1963 to many hundreds by 1976. Our first thanks must go to Mr. Edward James to whom this volume is dedicated and whose generosity in allowing the land to be taken out of farming use meant that the excavations on the Chilgrove sites could proceed unhampered and at a pace which could be varied to suit the rescue situation in Chichester. Our grateful thanks are also due to Mr. and Mrs. Huxham of Pitlands Farm, Upmarden who kindly allowed excavations on their farm and showed the liveliest interest in our progress. Other landowners who have helped us over the years are Mr. H. P. Renwick of Chilgrove House, his son, Mr. Michael Renwick of Crowshall Farm and Mr. R. C. Court of White Lodge Farm, who allowed us to trial trench their fields and walk their land after ploughing. The West Dean Estate gave us every facility during the summer vacations, when the Chilgrove sites were invaded, not only by a small army of diggers, but also by large numbers of the general public who were attracted to the excavations by the press reports of our finds. We owe a great debt of gratitude, first to Mr. E. Jermy, and secondly to Mr. M. Heymann, past and present Agents to the West Dean Estate (now the Edward James Foundation), and to the Manager of Brick Kiln Farm, Mr. John Mills, for their help at all times. Special mention must be made of our old friend, Mr. Alf Tribe, now retired, but still active at the age of 79, without whose keen observation neither of the Chilgrove villas would have been discovered.

Our thanks are also due to the Director of the Weald and Downland Open Air Museum, Mr. C. Zeuner, who kindly gave us permission to investigate the small area of the Museum where Roman finds were made in 1974.

The number of people who dug at Chilgrove and Upmarden exceeds five hundred, and it is regretted that they cannot all be mentioned by name. At the time that the project commenced in 1963 we were in process of organising a regular force of volunteer diggers to deal with the ever-increasing problem of rescue work in Chichester. If the battle for Chichester has been won it can be truthfully stated that it was won on the Chilgrove and Upmarden sites, as they not only provided an ideal training ground for new diggers, but gave us a series of base sites to which we could return in between emergencies. Inevitably, Chichester had to have priority, which is why it all took so long.

At Chilgrove 1, supervision was successively the responsibility of Keith Lintott, Brian Boddy, Elizabeth Betts, Helena Ginns (Dr. H. Barnes), and Malcolm Lyne, while Chilgrove 2 was supervised by Jeffery Collins, Janet Hinde (Mrs. R. Upton), R. Maskelyne, and F. G. Aldsworth. The Assistant Supervisors were E. Crossland, J. Eschbaecher, Chris Walker, Roger Hammond, Pauline Carder, and Wilf Shannon. At Upmarden, the work was supervised throughout by Roy and Sheila Morgan, who also carried out the documentary research on the farm and village, only a part of which is published with this first volume.

During the first season, the photography was carried out by David Baker (loaned to us from the Fishbourne excavations), and thereafter by Geoffrey Claridge, Thelma Westmore, Janet Hinde and John Adams, with Jerome O'Hea carrying out the aerial surveys. Mr. T. P. Lees, the Chief Chemist of the Cement and Concrete Research Association, visited the site and took samples of the various mortars from Chilgrove 1 and 2 for analysis. His report is attached to the excavation papers in archive and we are most grateful to him for his interest. We are indebted to a number of other specialists for reports on specific aspects of the finds and these are all mentioned on the title page.

It is appropriate at this point to acknowledge with gratitude the encouragement and help given to us in the early years by Miss Jean Cook, F.S.A., then the newly-appointed Curator of the new Chichester City Museum, and to our old friends Norman Cook, F.S.A., and Ralph Merrifield, F.S.A., at that time Director and Deputy Director respectively of the Guildhall Museum in London.

Max Wholey drew all the published small finds; John Piper, Ann Leyland and the writer and pottery, maps and sections; and Fred Aldsworth the *Gazetteer* maps. Cedric de la Nougerede produced the colour drawings of the mosaics and the reconstruction drawings of the villas; Pauline Castle typed the whole manuscript; and Susan Eeles and John Piper assisted with the final preparation of the book. I am most grateful to Professor Barry Cunliffe, Dr. K. M. E. Murray, Rosamund Hanworth, and Dr. Richard Reece who read various sections of the report and kindly commented upon them. Any errors which persist are mine and not theirs.

Compared with the rescue excavation budgets today, the whole project was managed very cheaply indeed, largely because no-one was paid. Our modest expenses were met each year by small grants from the Chichester Rural District Council and the old West Sussex County Council, and by what we could raise from our visitors. It is a fact of life that the publication of the results has cost over five times the total expenditure on excavation.

Finally, my personal thanks are due to all those people who took part in the excavations and who cannot, for reasons of space, be mentioned here. They came from all over England and from places as far away as Australia, Canada, U.S.A., France, Germany, Italy, Sweden, and Madagascar. Many returned again and again; some met their fate on site and now visit us with their children, whom we hope will grow up to carry on the tradition of voluntary work that brought their parents together.

The outstanding beauty of the sites, the tremendous interest and enthusiasm of the diggers, and the golden late summer weather we almost always enjoyed, made our seasons at Chilgrove pleasant occasions, long to be remembered.

ALEC DOWN

December 1978

vi

Contents

The Mosaics of Chilgrove by D. J. Smith, 109; The Animal Bones by Alan Outen, 113; The Roman Coins from the Sites compiled by Roger Lintott, 132; The Brooches by D. F. Mackreth, 145; The Finds—Bronze and Silver, 149; The Finds—Iron, 151; The Finds—Bone, Shale and Jet, Glass, 163; The Finds—Objects of Stone, Masonry Fragments, 168; The Finds—Flue Tiles, Stone Roofing Tiles, 175; The Stone Axe from Pit 1, Trial Trench 2, Chilgrove 1 by K. J. Evans, 178; The Worked Flints from Site 1 by Richard Bradley, 179; The Statuette of Fortuna by J. M. C. Toynbee, 181; The Iron Age Pottery from Chilgrove 1 by Barry Cunliffe, 184; The Mortaria from Chilgrove by Katherine F. Hartley, 186; Chilgrove 1, the Pottery from the Bath-house Fill, 187; Chilgrove 1, the Fine Wares from the Bath-house Fill, 189; Chilgrove 2, the Pottery from the Boundary Ditches, 189; Chilgrove 2, the Fine Wares, 191; Grogged Wares, 192; Post-Roman Pottery from Upmarden, 193; The Roman Fine Ware by Christopher J. Young, 194; The Samian Stamps from Chilgrove by B. R. Hartley, 199; The Samian Ware by G. B. Dannell, 200.

Key to Figures

List of Plates

ACKNOWLEDGMENTS TO PLATES

Vanessa Simon, Frontispiece; J. R. Boyden, plates 1, 2; Geoffrey Claridge, plates 3–5, 7–11, 14–17, 20; J. Adams, plate 18.

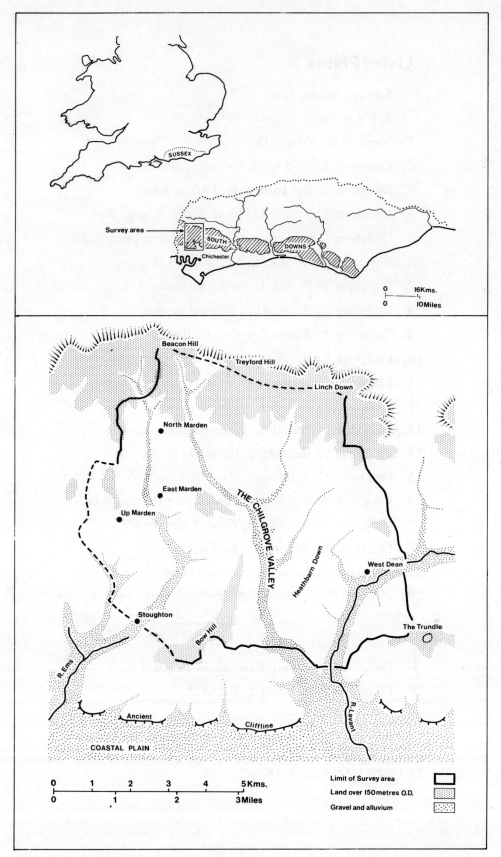

Fig. 1. Location Map.

1

The Evolution of the Landscape

by Ruth M. Tittensor

SECTION 1—THE STUDY AREA

Location

The study area of the Chilgrove Valley Landscape Project, of which this ecological survey is a part, consists of several large parishes on the South Downs of western Sussex, from the Mardens in the west to West Dean in the east (Fig. 1).

PHYSICAL FEATURES

The study area is dominated by steep hills up to about 200 metres high, and deep valleys (coombes) with few watercourses, the typical topography of chalk. Chalk is a soft and very pure form of calcium carbonate, which today carries a thin, basic and well-drained soil called a rendzina, capable of bearing both woodland and grassland. Chalk is a spongy material and holds much water in its aquifers. It was traditionally known for its chalk downland turf, but today is mainly a mosaic of woodland and cereals. Over the plateaux of the South Downs there are often areas of 'clay with flints', geological deposits which produce a contrasting soil type, an acid, clayey, and often deep soil. This may bear heathlands as on the summit of Bow Hill on the western edge of the study area. This clay deposit was probably very much more common over the chalk hills in prehistoric times, before widespread cultivation eroded it away. A few river valleys pass in a north to south direction through the chalk hills, and they contain recent gravel and alluvial deposits. Today, the rich, silty soils of these deposits support good pasture, once managed as 'water-meadows', though a willow and alder woodland with sedges was the likely natural vegetation. The River Lavant is the only watercourse of the study area (Fig. 1). For a detailed assessment of chalk landscapes in southern England consult *Sankey* (1966) and *Smith* (1978).

The equable climate of the South Downs in western Sussex is modified by the maritime influence of the nearby English Channel. A ridge of cloud commonly remains over the crest of the hills, and mist often hangs in the valleys when adjacent areas are clear. There are, on average, 25 to 30 inches of rainfall a year, long hours of sunshine, and little snow. Today, the area supports thriving agricultural and silvicultural industries.

The physical landforms have been largely unaffected by man. But to understand the significance of early man on the vegetation, fauna and soil components of the study areas (Sections 3 to 7), it is necessary to consider the landscape as it was before the arrival of prehistoric man (Section 2). A description of the modern Chilgrove landscape in the final section (Section 8) allows an evaluation of the impact of prehistoric man, compared with that of 'historic' man in the post-Roman period.

1

SECTION 2—BEFORE MAN

In order to assess the landscape changes produced by man's activities it is necessary to define a starting date before which man's activities were negligible. Because even the physical landforms were utterly altered by the Pleistocene Ice Ages, an instant in the post-Glacial period (the last 14,000 years) has been chosen because the landscape, flora and fauna had become typically north temperate in the modern sense. The most appropriate instant is the time at which Britain became an island separated from continental Europe by the English Channel. This occured at about 5,500 B.C., and corresponds with the palynologists' transition zone from Boreal to Atlantic periods when the climate gradually changed from warm and dry to warm and wet, that is, more oceanic (*Pennington* 1969). The separation of Britain and the climatic transition at about 5,500 B.C. are significant for two reasons. Firstly, the flora and fauna of this time was NATIVE; any terrestrial species arriving in Britain subsequently would almost certainly have been brought by man because of the new water-barrier preventing natural spread from Europe. Such species, whether brought accidentally or deliberately, are regarded as INTRODUCED or ALIEN. Secondly, 5,500 B.C. is archaeologically the later Mesolithic period when human artefacts can be dated, but before any great influence by man on the vegatation or fauna can be *detected*.

The natural landscape of 5,500 B.C. is therefore taken as the starting point.

TECHNIQUES

The major tool for studying the natural and prehistoric landscape, apart from the purely human archaeological artefacts, is *pollen analysis*. This consists of taking sample cores from sites where peat has accumulated during the 14,000 years of the post-Glacial period, and then determining the types and relative abundance of plant pollen at successive intervals in the chronologically stratified sequence (*Godwin* 1975). This gives a fairly accurate picture of the vegetation of the vicinity of the core sample at any given period (which can be dated by a variety of means), though interpretation of the pollen analysis results must take many factors into account. Larger remains of plants such as leaves, roots or wood in the peat can also provide data on the vegetation of successive periods.

Nowadays pollen analysis is a sophisticated tool, but it has one major drawback: pollen preservations needs waterlogged or acid conditions, so the well drained soils over chalk mean that peat is not formed and pollen not preserved. It is therefore vary rare to find sites on the South Downs where peat containing pollen is present. Thus pollen analysis data is relatively unavailable for the area in general and the Chilgrove study site in particular. We have to rely upon nearby studies from river-valleys cutting through the chalk, and other low-lying areas. Several applicable pollen-analysis studies are available from two sites close to the South Downs further east, and two sites adjacent to the Kentish Downs. There is also some pollen analysis data for other parts of southern England which gives an overall picture of the natural and prehistoric landscapes.

Analysis of pollen from acid soils buried beneath prehistoric barrows is a technique being widely used in southern England, especially in sandy areas. The amount of pollen in these 'fossilised soils' is small, however, so results are less reliable. The actual chemical and physical composition of a buried soil, its flora and fauna may also be investigated, if suitable remains occur. It is also possible to extrapolate a great deal from knowledge of the composition of a soil alone.

Biological remains at archaeological sites can give information about domestic stock and wild animals, crops and wild plants. Apart from pollen, biological remains which may be investigated include bones, hair, feathers, scales, invertebrate skeletons; wood, charcoal, seeds, fruits, and leaves. Indeed, wood and timber may be integral parts of archaeological remains as at the lake settlements of the Somerset levels. Until recently, pollen analysis, soil studies and analysis of biological remains have not been important archaeological tools, but because biologists as well as archaeologists now need the information, results from such analyses are becoming more readily available. Soil pollen studies and analyses of biological remains have been made both within the Chilgrove study area and at nearly localities on the sandy soils to the north. A recent excavation on the South downs at Bishopstone in East Sussex has provided biological remains from periods from the Neolithic to post Roman (*Bell* 1977). Interpretation of such data should be done with caution because specimens found at residential sites do not necessarily reflect the general environment.

THE NATURAL WOODLAND LANDSCAPE

There is now incontrovertible evidence that the vegetation covering lowland Britain, including the chalk hills, was mixed-deciduous-woodland at 5,500 B.C. Innumerable pollen analyses over the past half century have confirmed this (*Godwin* 1975, *Pennington* 1969). It is likely that at least 90 per cent. of the landscape was woodland, the only open areas being above 600 metres altitude, river flood-plains, very steep slopes, seashores and areas devastated by natural fire or windblow. *Yates* (1972) agreed with this concept of a wooded landscape for the parish of Harting (on the north-west boundary of the Chilgrove study area), while *Thorley* (1971) provided pollen-analysis evidence from a river-valley through the East Sussex chalk; arboreal pollen (oak, hazel, elm, lime, pine, alder, and birch mainly) predominated over non-arboreal pollen. *Godwin* (1943) provided a similar picture from the peat-bog on Amberley Wild Brooks below the Downs near Storrington (10 miles east of the study area), though alder, oak and birch were commoner than pine, lime and elm. At Minsted (on the sandy outcrop two miles north of the study area) *Dimbleby* (1975) found soil-pollen evidence that at about 6,000 B.C. the vegetation was dominated by hazel, with a variety of other woody species in lesser amounts, including pine, oak, lime and heather (Latin names are given in Table I). *Bell* (1977) found 45 tree and shrub root holes in the chalk beneath the Bishopstone site, dating from the Neolithic period and earlier.

There is other local evidence for the natural woodland of the western South Downs. Fossilised soils under prehistoric barrows on the chalk and sand are very different from the present, adjacent soils. Many people mistakenly think that the shallow rendzina over much of the chalk today is incapable of bearing woodland and use this as an argument against a natural vegetation of woodland. However, the deeper, acid soils beneath barrows indicate that in earlier times a soil most definitely capable of bearing woodland was present over wide areas. *Collins* (1974) working at many sites in the study area provided a variety of evidence that the widespread deep, acid soils of the South Downs were eroded away by centuries and millennia of cultivation, to be replaced by the development

3

of shallow and permanently immature rendzinas. Modified versions of the original soils exist under barrows and under ancient woodlands, both sites where the forces of erosion have had little effect.

Studies of 20th-century maps, aerial photographs, consultation with local people, and observations of post-myxomatosis changes on the western South Downs do, however, show that the shallow rendzina soil is quite capable of bearing a full woodland cover (*Tittensor* 1975, 1976), even on extremely steep slopes. Finally, data from elsewhere on the chalk hills adds to the weight of evidence for a natural woodland landscape. For instance, the types of land molluscs (snails) found in hillwashes from Wiltshire chalk downs suggest a well-developed woodland soil once occurred on the slopes and plateaux (*Evans* 1975).

COMPOSITION OF NATURAL WOODLAND

Godwin (1975) and *Pennington* (1969), assessing the evidence for lowland England, agreed that the natural woodland of 5,500 B.C. was MIXED-DECIDUOUS-FOREST (or WOODLAND). The dominant tree species may have been oak, but other important species include lime (a warm-summer-loving species), alder (especially in damper places), and elm. The elm was not the common hedgerow species we are familiar with today, but a typical woodland species. Birch and pine were present but uncommon in the south. Our two other native conifers, yew and juniper were extremely rare in this natural woodland. Hazel was the major shrub species. Beech was present in only minute quantities, suggesting localised patches of it in the vicinity, but sufficient pollen has been found to show that it is native in southern England. Cereals, of course, were absent; grasses, 'weeds' and all the species we nowadays associated with meadows, pastures, downland-turf, and man's dwelling were either very uncommon or absent, showing the scarcity of open habitats in the natural landscape.

The local studies of *Dimbleby* (1975), *Godwin* (1943, 1960), and *Thorley* (1971) agree with the general picture for the south, though each site has its own minor peculiarities. Yew and juniper were absent from the pollen diagrams for all these sites.

STRUCTURE OF NATURAL WOODLAND

It is not generally realised that ALL our English woodlands have been managed for many centuries, if not millenia (*Rackham* 1976, *Reynolds* 1976, *Tittensor* 1975), providing communities with a multitude of materials, nor that many have been planted—and therefore that all are utterly different in structure, as well as (often) in species composition, from the natural woodlands. The same is true for most of Europe, so it is difficult to find a 'virgin' woodland from which to extrapolate to prehistoric times. Bialowieza Forest in Poland is less affected by man than many European woodlands; studies done here and in 'virgin' woodland outside Europe do give clues. In Sussex itself, 'The mens' woodland near Petworth has been shown to be as near 'virgin' or 'natural' as any woodland in southern England due to its millenium as a woodland-common, and a century of silvicultural neglect (*Tittensor* 1977). Ecological studies of 'The Mens' by the Horsham Natural History Society (*Tittensor* and *Tittensor* 1977), and other studies mentioned above make it possible to suggest that the following were structural features of natural woodland in Sussex:

1. It was 'high-forest', i.e., tall timber-sized trees without 'coppicing' or 'pollarding' (terms describing how trees can be cut and harvested) except as would occur after windblow, fire, or the activities of beavers.

2. Trees, shrubs and other plants would be distributed haphazardly, without straight rows, or other regular patterns of distribution except as caused by wet hollows, particular soil types or conditions fitting particular species' requirements.

3. Each tree and shrub species would have a population containing at least some individuals of all ages from young seedlings to mature trees and over-mature dying and decaying specimens. It is man who removes trees at maturity to use for himself, thus eliminating the old and decaying (dead) stages of the tree populations.

4. About one-fifth of the tree population would be dead, undergoing the decomposition stage which returns nutrients to the soil for succeeding generations.

5. Tree and shrub shapes would have been irregular and varied. The extremely narrow crowns of today's plantation conifers and the wide-spreading crowns of long-established parkland trees are the extremes of physical form that can be produced merely by spacing arrangements. In the natural woodlands, all gradations from narrow to wide crowns, as well as gradations in other morphological characters (e.g., height) would have been present.

6. There would have been several vertical strata, with at least the following:

i. soil layer.	iv. shrub and sapling layer.
ii. ground vegetation layer.	v. main canopy layer.
iii. bush layer.	

Numbers iii and iv are usually missing from a man-managed high-forest woodland, and numbers iii and v from a man-managed coppice woodland, for instance.

7. As a result of layering, there would have been a great variety of woodland niches available for fauna.

8. There would have been a large variety of different plant species present also, though the number of individuals of each species may not have been high. Studies of 'The Mens' suggest, in an area of 150–200 hectares at least:

> i. 400 species fungi.
> ii. 100 species lichens.
> iii. 100 species bryophytes.
> iv. 300 species flowering herbs and ferns.
> v. 40 species shrubs and trees.

As a result of the large percentage of the land-surface covered with woodland at 5,500 B.C., the local climate within the woodland would have had the following characteristics:

> i. little wind at ground level.
> ii. little light reaching the woodland floor in summer or winter.

iii. an even temperature regime between summer and winter; modification of seasonal extremes.

iv. an even rate of precipitation reaching the ground due to filtering effect of many strata of vegetation.

Considerable woodland cover would also have had effects on natural processes within the landscape such as regulating water run-off after violent storms due to the filtering effect of the soil, or maintaining a balance of gases within the atmosphere.

Section 8 describes comparable features of the modern Chilgrove landscape and shows how different the natural woodlands, and the landscape they produce, were from today.

NATURAL WOODLAND FAUNA

It is likely that detailed studies of invertebrates will produce most biological knowledge of early landscapes because these animals indicate local conditions accurately. However, there is no date yet available on the invertebrates of pre-Neolithic Sussex and only little information from archaeological sites. Archaeologists have concentrated on larger, more obvious faunal remains, especially birds and mammals, often with their cultural rather than their ecological significance in mind (*Ryder* 1969).

A body of evidence has built up, showing that the following native mammals were present in the natural woodland of southern England—but became extinct in later prehistoric or historic times (*Corbet* 1964):

Latin Name	English Name	Date of Extinction
Equus ferus	Wild horse	not known, but very early
Bison bonasus	European bison	not known, but very early
Felis lynx[1]	Lynx	by Neolithic[2]
Rangifer tarandus	Reindeer	by Neolithic[2]
Bos primigenius	Wild ox (Urus)	by Neolithic[2, 3]
Castor fiber	Beaver	by 9th or 10th century[2]
Ursus arctos	Brown bear	by 9th or 10th century[2]
Canis lupus	Wolf	by late 15th century[2]
Sus scrofa	Wild boar	by late 17th century[2]
Cervus elaphus	Red deer	by early 19th century[4, 5]
Felis silvestris	Wild cat	by 1850[5]
Mustela putorius	Polecat	by 1920s[5]
Martes martes	Pine marten	by 1920s[5]
Sciurus vulgaris	Red squirrel	by 1950s[5]

1. Doubtfully native—no bone evidence, and other evidence inconclusive.
2. Date of extinction in England.
3. The only species in this list that is now completely extinct in Europe.
4. Now present only in parkland herds with feral deer from escapes.
5. Date of extinction in Sussex.

To these can be added the following list of species thought or known to be native, known to favour well-wooded conditions, and still present in the modern Chilgrove landscape:

Latin Name	English Name
Erinaceus europaeus	Hedgehog
Talpa europea	Mole
Sorex araneus	Common shrew
S. minutus	Pygmy shrew
Pipistrellus pipistrellus[1]	Pipistrelle
Plecotus auritus	Common long-eared bat
Vulpes vulpes	Fox
Mustela erminea	Stoat
M. nivalis	Weasel
Meles meles	Badger
Capreolus capreolus[2]	Roe deer
Muscardinus avellanarius	Dormouse
Apodemus sylvaticus	Wood mouse
Clethrionomys glareolus	Bank vole

1. And at least eleven other species of woodland bat.
2. Extinct in Sussex by 18th century; present population descended from escaped park roe deer in the 19th century, e.g., Petworth Park.

The significance of these lists is that all are species adapted to *dense woodland conditions* unlike many of the species introduced later by man (see Section 8). About one-fifth of our native woodland mammals have become extinct in Sussex as a result of man's changes in the landscape.

SUMMARY OF NATURAL LANDSCAPE

It can be seen from this survey of the natural woodland and its fauna, that the pre-Neolithic landscape of Chilgrove was utterly different from today. It is extremely difficult to visualise a landscape dominated by mixed-deciduous woodland, in which large mammals that we rarely see even in zoos were living, where no domestic stock or crops existed, and where no 'tidiness' (e.g., removal of dead trees) had been imposed by man. It is fundamental to bear in mind these basic features of the natural landscape in order to appreciate the effect early man had from 5,500 B.C. to about 400 A.D. The most important part to bear in mind is that the natural vegetation was mainly woodland, that the native fauna was adapted to woodland conditions, and that habitats available to—for instance—grassland orchids or lapwings was severely restricted. In ensuing millenia, woodland species have had to adapt to changing habitats in order to survive, while non-woodland species have been able to expand their ranges.

Table II summarises the natural Chilgrove landscape.

SECTION 3—MAN'S FIRST IMPACT

Mesolithic Period: 5500—4000 B.C.

It used to be thought that man had no noticeable effect on the landscape of the new island of Britain until Neolithic times at the earliest. However, there is increasing evidence from pollen analyses at Mesolithic sites beneath Bronze Age barrows a few miles to the north of Chilgrove (and elsewhere in southern England) that pre-agricultural man produced quite marked effects on the vegetation.

7

Keef et al (1965) showed that on the sandstone at Iping, three miles north of the Chilgrove study area, the natural woodland was dominated by hazel, with oak, birch and pine in lesser quantities; ling (heather) was a major constituent of the bush layer. But around 4,300 B.C., in a layer associated with a mesolithic flint industry, there was a striking change in dominance from hazel to heather, a change which does not seem to have been reversed in later millennia, and which was undoubtedly produced by man's activities such as tree and shrub clearance, fire, and subsequent grazing by herbivores. Thus at Iping the first (and main) phase of woodland clearance was very early.

Under a nearby barrow at Minsted, Dimbleby (1975) found that at an undetermined Mesolithic date a woodland similar in composition to the Iping site (dominated by hazel) showed a great increase in the abundance of ivy, which he attributed to its use by man for feeding the native red deer. At neither of these localities did grasses show any change in abundance associated with man's activities, but at a site below the chalk near Lewes, *Thorley* (1971) showed that there was a gradual increase in the abundance of grasses among the dominant arboreal pollen, at about 4,000 B.C. Grasses are significant because they suggest meadow and pasture conditions associated with domestic stock.

No recognisable Mesolithic sites have yet been discovered within the Chilgrove study area. However, detailed archaeological surveying by *Cunliffe* (1973b) five miles to the west on the South Downs at Chalton, has produced a number of Mesolithic sites on the edge of plateaux deposits of acid clay-with-flints; and at Slindon, six miles east of the study area, Robin Upton has found a number of Mesolithic sites alongside dry river valleys, in an area which is topographically and geologically similar to the Chilgrove valley. These sites are suggestive of a woodland fringe situation where the earliest man-made clearings would have been formed.

Thus, local data provides evidence of some anthropogenic effects on the Chilgrove landscape by about 4,000 B.C.

**Neolithic Period:
4000—2000 B.C.**

SECTION 4—NEOLITHIC LANDSCAPE

Between 4,000 and 2,000 B.C. the landscape of the South Downs remained predominantly woodland, although considerably more man-made changes took place. These were the result, as excavations throughout Britain have shown, of the appearance in the landscape of *agricultural man*. In contrast to the mainly hunting and gathering activities of Mesolithic peoples, Neolithic man introduced farming : that is, the growing of crops and the keeping of domestic livestock for food. The commonest livestock of these early times were domestic sheep and cattle, while on the South Downs barley and wheat were introduced and cultivated (*Cunliffe* 1973a).

Pennington (1969) brought together pollen analysis evidence from all over Britain, to show that by the end of the Neolithic and beginning of the Bronze Age, large stretches were converted from the natural woodland cover, to non-woodland habitats, mainly by initial felling and burning of trees and subsequent cultivation of crops and grazing of stock. Experiments have shown that relatively small numbers of men can clear woodland with flint tools on the scale suggested. As woodland clearance proceeded, pioneer tree species such as birch and ash formed 'secondary' woodlands when agricultural activities ceased; Neolithic agriculture was typically 'shifting' so large areas of derelict farmland must have become available for colonisation by secondary woodland. As birch and ash increased, so elm and lime declined, possibly because of their selective use by man. Cereal grains, charcoal, weed seeds and pollen in peat deposits and at archaeological sites show how widespread farming was in the Neolithic period as a whole.

The available evidence suggests that Chilgrove may not have entirely conformed to this overall pattern, in that it probably remained wooded until the Late Bronze Age. There is considerable archaeological evidence of Neolithic man in the Chilgrove area; for instance, the long barrows at Compton and on Stoughton Down, the flint mines on Bow Hill and Stoughton Down, and the flint-working sites at Linch Down and Binderton. There is a Neolithic causewayed camp on The Trundle just to the east, and at Chalton *Cunliffe* (1973b) found 'prodigous' flint waste at several Neolithic sites. Thus Neolithic people must have produced some change in the Chilgrove landscape, if only to make clearings for barrows, enclosures and trackways. *Cunliffe* (1973b), who found no evidence of Neolithic *farming* activities at Chalton, also concluded that the landscape was still mainly wooded at 2500 B.C., though he suggested large clearings would have been made for temporary autumn and winter settlement.

Pollen analysis from the Lewes site (*Thorley* 1971) showed a still predominantly woodland landscape, only small traces of grasses and weeds were detectable in the pollen samples. *Godwin* (1943) came to the conclusion that the South Downs at Storrington, 10 miles to the east of the Chilgrove area, were covered by woodlands in which beech was still only a minor component. Although the function of the enclosure is still not clear, Neolithic finds from The Trundle (*Curwen* 1931) included bones of domestic cattle, pig and sheep, but not horse; this is the only agricultural evidence as yet from close to Chilgrove. Charcoal of nearly a dozen deciduous tree species suggests a prevalence of wooded conditions, however. At Bishopstone (*Bell* 1977), the Molluscan fauna suggested closed vegetation, probably woodland, early in the Neolithic period. Charcoals of oak, ash, yew, hazel, and hawthorn suggested the composition of that woodland.

The picture on the sandstone at Iping is somewhat different because major deforestation had already occurred. Heather remained dominant throughout the Neolithic period, although latterly deciduous trees were increasing again. Cereal, grass and weed pollen suggest cultivation in the vicinity though not at the site itself (*Keef et al* 1965).

To summarise: Neolithic Chilgrove would have been predominantly woodland, but with changing proportions of tree species resulting from temporary clearing for settlement, communication and, probably, agriculture. Alien animals (domestic stock) and plants (crops) had appeared in the landscape, but its natural appearance was not greatly altered.

SECTION 5—MAJOR LANDSCAPE CHANGES

The Early Bronze Age on the South Downs was really a continuation of the Late Neolithic economy, with evidence of settled agriculture, cultivation and pasture. At Minsted (*Dimbleby* 1975), the pollen of Bronze Age times suggests pastoral, but not arable, farming in the vicinity; however, immediately adjacent to the Minsted Early Bronze Age barrow itself (1800–1100 B.C.) the vegetation consisted of a light cover of deciduous woodland with an abundance of heather, suggesting persistent use of fire to maintain open areas, probably for grazing. At Chalton, Early Bronze Age sites include a few hut sites as well as barrows, mainly on the upper slopes of the chalk hills.*Cunliffe* (1973b), stated that the variety of archaeological evidence at Chalton suggested significant social organisation, the isolated homesteads or small nucleated settlements having field-systems adjacent, but with pastoral activities on the upper areas which also contained the communities' cemeteries. Grain storage pits as well as bones of domestic ox, sheep or goat, pig and dog, testify, however, to the settled agricultural pattern. The Early Bronze Age landscape can be visualised as similar to Neolithic times, with woodland still a major component of the landscape, but agricultural grassland slowly spreading at the expense of trees.

The local pollen analysis studies all point to the Middle and Late Bronze Age being the period of greatest change in the Chilgrove landscape (*Dimbleby* 1975, *Godwin* 1943, 1960, *Keef et al* 1965, *Thorley* 1971). At Wingham in Kent, large-scale deforestation had begun about 1700 B.C., when a drop in the abundance of arboreal pollen coincided with an increase in bracken, grasses, weeds (e.g., *Artemisia,* plantains), and cereals, indicating both arable and pastoral farming on an extensive scale. At Frogholt, also on the Kentish chalk hills, the same pattern occurred at 1100 B.C. In the Lewes area it took place about 1200 B.C., and coincided with an increase in beech as well as birch and ash. At Storrington, there was not such a dramatic period of deforestation, but at Iping beech pollen appeared, along with further indications of nearby cultivation.

There is further evidence that the Bronze Age barrows of the Sussex chalk were built in an open environment. *O'Connor* (1976) showed that the Molluscs of a brown soil from a Late Bronze Age barrow near Alfriston were very similar in species to those found on the chalk grasslands of the area today. *Bell* (1977) also found a Molluscan fauna of dry, open conditions subsequent to the Neolithic and right through to the post-Roman period.

Middle and Late Bronze Age settlements are common along the South Downs, for instance Itford, near Beddingham (*Burstow* and *Holleyman* 1957) and Amberley Mount, near Storrington (*Armstrong* 1974). A site at the head of Kingley Vale on the southern edge of the study area has been interpreted as a Bronze Age farmstead and field-system (*Curwen* 1934); similarly with a 19th-century discovery on Stoke Down (*Harcourt* 1854). Within the Chilgrove study area the earthworks on the summit of Bow Hill are thought to be a Middle or Late Bronze Age pastoral enclosure (*Cunliffe* 1973a). There are many Bronze Age barrows in the Chilgrove study area and nearby, mostly on the plateaux, silhouetted against the skyline when viewed from the valleys; a total of about 1,000 on the crest of the South Downs has been interpreted as evidence of an open landscape (*Brandon* 1974). Thus the archaeological and biological evidence indicates the South Down landscape of the second millennium B.C.

was more open than wooded, with widespread (if not dense) settlement, and permanent (rather than shifting) agriculture, both pastoral and arable. Within woodland areas themselves there was the beginning of an expansion of beech, and a greater relative abundance of birch and ash compared with other deciduous species. Cultivation may have been restricted to the chalk itself, with light woodland and heathland characteristic of the sandy areas just to the north.

By the end of the Bronze Age quite a variety of anthropogenic habitats had come into existence in the landscape. There were the heathlands initiated in Mesolithic times; the fragmentation of the woodlands into small areas provided great lengths of 'woodland-edge' and glades; Neolithic temporary clearances would have become permanent pasture grasslands maintained by continuous grazing by domestic stock; arable fields become a permanent feature of the landscape, prevented from reverting to woodland by continuous cultivation. These and other more minor habitats are listed in Table IV. It is not possible to guess to what extent Bronze Age man also altered the structure of the remaining natural woodlands, but *Reynolds* (1976) has extrapolated from archaeological evidence for Iron Age times (see below).

With the decrease in woodland cover from its original 90 per cent. or more, woodland species of plant and animals would be on the decline while species of heathland, grasslands and the other open habitats would be extending their ranges. As far as the large fauna was concerned, the wild ox (*urus*) was probably extinct in England, while the house mouse (*Mus musculus*) had become an introduced member of the fauna (*Corbet* 1964). A variety of domestic mammals were now a common and permanent feature of the landscape. Along with cereals, introduced 'weeds' had become established, notably charlock and cornflower. There had, indeed, been considerable evolution of the Chilgrove landscape since 5500 B.C.!

Pre-Roman Iron Age: 700 B.C. — A.D. 43

SECTION 6—CHANGES ACCELERATED

From 700 B.C. onwards considerably more archaeological evidence, both from Chilgrove and nearby localities, allows a comprehensive picture of the landscape to be built up. There is less pollen evidence, however, as most of the studies discussed above do not include this period. The trends from 700 B.C. were the same as in the preceding Bronze Age, but more extensive and rapid.

Drewett (1978) and the *Archaeological Gazetteer* (pp. 31-39) list and discuss in detail the innumerable archaeological sites and evidence of Iron Age Sussex detected so far. It is now becoming clear that early Iron Age agriculture was a continuation of the Middle and Late Bronze Age system, but that as time went on it had advanced sufficiently to support a large (and presumably still predominantly 'rural') population that was 'prehistoric' rather than 'historic' only in the sense that as a civilisation it left us no written records. Long-term settlements suggest permanent agricultural systems with crop and animal rotation; use of iron tools and widespread grazing by domestic stock caused further and probably semi-permanent loss of woodland cover. Peter Reynolds suggests that there was probably considerably less woodland on the South Downs during the Iron Age than now. Certainly agriculture was extensive; field-

11

systems are being discovered almost wherever they are sought on the western South Downs, even under present woodland cover. Their absence from valley bottoms is probably only the result of medieval and 20th-century ploughing and downward soil-wash. Iron Age cultivation was not restricted to the chalk hills; indeed, the steeper chalk slopes may have been of marginal quality then (as later), but the extensive field-systems are easier for us to locate here because they are now part of permanent grasslands and are less tree-covered than the Weald, for instance. For a detailed interpretation of Iron Age agriculture relating to the western South downs, based on archaeological, biological and modern experimental evidence as well as eloquent speculation, consult *Reynolds* (1976).

At Chilgrove, as elsewhere, over huge areas of downland and arable, and under forestry plantations, Romano-British field-systems are being discovered and mapped (e.g., Winden Woods, Monkton Woods, Westdean Woods, Preston Down, Chills Down, High Down, Heathbarn Down) showing that many modern woodland situations were agricultural sites in the Iron Age. In the Chilgrove valley itself there is a large stock pound (Goosehill Camp) with a 'Celtic roadway' linking the enclosed field-systems below with the pastoral enclosure along the summit.

Other types of Iron Age sites are also very numerous in the vicinity of Chilgrove. For example, a major hill fort on The Trundle produced bones of domestic sheep, pig, dog (and possibly cat), abundant cattle, and the earliest horse remains in the vicinity. There is a less obvious hill fort on Torberry Hill, near Harting, containing hut shelters. Entrenchments between Chichester and Chilgrove have been described as later Iron Age earthworks protecting the rich agricultural Manhood Peninsula. At Chalton, the Iron Age was a period when single homestead settlements proliferated and field-systems spread over the landscape.

Thus archaeological evidence indicates a basically agricultural landscape modified from the previous natural woodland cover. Biological evidence tells us something about the composition of the agricultural habits and the remaining woodland. *Godwin* (1943) showed that at Storrington birch increased in its usual rapid manner, followed later by a significant increase in beech. Lime, once frequent, was becoming quite rare. The rise in birch, and the later rise in beech may have been associated with the abandonment of some cultivated areas, or with climatic change. The fullest pollen evidence for the chalk hills comes from the two Kentish sites. *Godwin* (1960) described 'massive agricultural effects' in the pollen diagram, both pastoral and arable (a great rise in pollen of grasses, cereals, bracken, weeds, with a decline in hazel, lime and alder, but a rise in birch and pine). A considerable increase in beech came at about 200 B.C. Large areas of Iron Age fields are still evident nearby.

The Iron Age Molluscan fauna at Bishopstone (*Bell* 1977) indicated a very open and dry environment, probably mainly arable. No species suggestive of woodland or semi-woodland conditions were identified. However, Iron Age charcoal was identified, and included hornbeam and poplar as well as the Neolithic species mentioned above. More Iron Age data would be very helpful.

Pollen analysis from all over England has shown that with the Iron Age came a change in climate from the warmth of the Sub-Boreal period to the cooler, wetter conditions of the Sub-Atlantic (*Pennington* 1969). This climatic change may have been one factor favouring the expansion of beech. In the north and

12

west it led to a spread of peat bogs whose presence had been initiated by Bronze Age deforestation.

Table III summarises the pre-Roman Iron Age landscape of Chilgrove. Some more or less natural woodland, little altered in species composition, was probably still present, but *Reynolds* (1976) argues that at least some of the remaining woodland was modified structurally by positive management (that is—*silviculture* comparable by *agriculture*) to provide coppice materials, for instance. There is certainly no reason why silviculture rather than mere exploitation should not have been practised by Iron Age times; agriculture had, after all, taken over from mere exploitation in Neolithic times. More evidence from wood and timber artefacts is required, but meanwhile it is interesting to note that the introduction of the first 'domestic' tree species comparable with the introduction of domestic animals and cereals, awaited the Roman period.

Apart from the accelerating trends involving a decrease in woodland cover, an increase in cultivated areas, in the numbers and types of introduced plants and animals and the relative changes in abundance of tree species, the landscape of Iron Age Chilgrove had new habitats such as woodlands with beech, steep grassy ramparts (hill forts) and large stock and human enclosures that could be regarded as 'urban' and would have provided sites for many plants characteristic of man's dwelling area (Table IV).

Tables II, III and IV show that the Iron Age landscape was as different from the natural setting as is the present landscape (but in different ways). Man had by now made his greatest impact, and the subsequent 2,000 years has been merely an alteration of the proportions of the man-made habitats, the creation of new man-made habitats and the extinction of any remaining natural vegetation. The Roman period cannot be envisaged as a period of great landscape advancement in quite the same way as previous periods, but the Romans made a contribution in their own peculiar way.

Roman Period:
A.D. 43—400

SECTION 7—LANDSCAPE OF THE CHILGROVE VILLAS

Most of the evidence for the Roman landscape comes from archaeological remains, but we have to look to the South Downs in general, and indeed Sussex as a whole for a comprehensive picture of the rural landscape; *Cunliffe* (1973a) gives an admirable summary. A few relevant archaeological finds in the Chilgrove area provide specific details for the locality. Biological remains provide evidence about new, non-agricultural habitats.

The Romanisation of Sussex did not have immediate or devastating effects upon the landscape. The western Weald remained mostly wooded, as before, and native ('peasant') settlements, on the South Downs especially, continued in existence as they had done since Late Bronze Age times. Native farming settlements varied from tiny clusters of dwellings (e.g., Park Brow) to sizeable villages (e.g., Chalton). Their agriculture also continued much as before, though a new design of plough allowed proper furrows to be formed, and so produced longer fields than the previous square fields formed by cross-ploughing with the scraping ard. Some native settlements were replaced on the same site by Roman settlements. The larger ones, such as Chalton, could be considered as Romano-

13

British 'villages'; there may have been a similar situation in the Chilgrove valley, but not yet recognised.

Superimposed upon the peasant landscape were the villas and their estates. The flush of first and second century superior villas (*Cunliffe* 1973) each in a district topographical block of country, suggests a rise in affluence of a Romanised aristocracy whose farming techniques allowed considerable agricultural surpluses which provided for acquisition of imported Roman goods on a large scale. On the South Downs wheat production was the basis of the expanding economy, but in poorer arable areas, local industries such as stone-quarrying or salt extraction were more important.

The villas were located in good positions, generally where a variety of soil types allowed mixed farming, and where a spring-line provided a water supply. The two Chilgrove villas are examples of this, being at the base of the South Downs where chalk meets the valley deposits and spring—and river—water is available. The Chilgrove villas, like most others, were initially built of timber, but flints held by mortar, with roofing-tiles above, became general later in the third and fourth centuries A.D.

The complicated systems of elongate Romanised fields and square Celtic fields can be traced round many of the villas, including Chilgrove. *Holleyman* (1935), in a now classic study, showed what a densely settled and farmed landscape existed on the South Downs between the Adur and Ouse rivers (east of Chilgrove). At Chalton, just to the west of Chilgrove, *Cunliffe* showed there was a complex use of landscape involving hilltop pasture served by trackways, immense arable areas on the slopes and valleys, and many settlements of varying sizes.

Archaeological description and excavation thus provides an overall picture of a densely-settled and heavily-used landscape on the chalk downs (and also the coastal plain and sandy ridge), with the Weald still providing a general barrier between the coast and London, penetrated only by roads, and in the east, industrial workings. But there is enough biological evidence to show that wheat was the main crop in the predominantly arable downs, while barley, oats, rye and legumes were of lesser importance. Animal bones (pp. 113–131), plus structural evidence, show there was pastoral farming too: Chilgrove 1 and 2 have large, enclosed stockyards ('farmyard'), while the Bignor villa had a huge barn presumed for over-wintering and for feeding stock as well as storage. Pigs may have fed in the woodlots, hangers, or Wealden woods (where nearby), while cattle and sheep grazed the grassland areas. Enclosed 'parklands' may have been provided for the introduced fallow deer.

At the end of the fourth century A.D., a political and social decline of Roman civilisation coincided with a massive decline in the birth-rate. Additional loss of manpower was caused by fighting elsewhere in Europe. Much archaeological evidence shows that peasant settlements as well as villas went into decline and were abandoned. Inevitably, the patterned, farmed landscape of the last 1,000 to 1,500 years must have gradually altered, with a decrease of arable areas, encroachment of secondary woodland, escape of domestic stock into the feral state, and the naturalisation of cultivated plants. The landscape would have become more 'untidy' as active agricultural and silvicultural management ceased when people moved from rural to urban settlements. By 500 A.D. the peasant population was again under imposed rule, this time the Saxons, and a completely new pattern of landscape management was to emerge: another story!

The essence of the Chilgrove and South Downs Roman landscape was thus the intensification of management and settlement in an area where fundamental changes from the natural state had already occurred. But the Romans inserted a new feature of their own: URBAN surroundings which introduced minor and small-scale habitats into the landscape. These habitats were of little importance in themselves, but the species that were brought to inhabit them had considerable effects upon the subsequent way of life. The sort of urban-type habitats we know (from archaeological evidence) to have been produced in the Chilgrove area itself, or nearby (as at Fishbourne) were:

STONE-BUILDINGS: dwellings (villas, etc.), farm-buildings, military buildings.

STONE-ROADS: the Chichester to Silchester road passes through the study area.

GARDENS AND SIMILAR: As at Fishbourne.

These urban-type situations would have provided habitats for a particular group of native fauna and flora, as well as those species introduced especially for them. Stone-buildings are a 'pseudo-cliff' habitat suitable for nesting and roosting birds, lichens and mosses, invertebrates, such as spiders, normally found in cracks of bark, and cave-dwelling species like bats. Dwellers of natural caves and cliffs would have been scarce previously on the South Downs and indeed Sussex as a whole due to scarcity of habitat. Stone-roads and gardens would probably have formed extensions of the open habitats first created by settled agriculture, and these would be suitable for weeds, grasses and many small mammals. However, it is the gardens that are particularly relevant to plants introduced purposefully by the Romans. Typically Mediterranean species became a feature of the urban landscape: pot-herbs such as rosemary, fennel, dill and alexanders; sweet herbs like lavender and bay; medicinal herbs like gout weed. And trees bearing edible fruits were introduced: walnut, fig, medlar, vine, sweet chestnut—as well as vegetables such as the pea and radish. Most of these species have remained severely restricted to their urban-type habitats ever since.

In addition, some forms of hedgerows may have been used to define land-tenure boundaries, and woodlands may well have been managed for coppice-rotation for the first time. Waste-heaps from bloomeries and stone quarries were not a feature of Roman Chilgrove, but were certainly newly-created habitats in Sussex as a whole.

There is little evidence concerning introduced fauna. There is no bone evidence for fallow deer (*Dama dama*) at Roman Chilgrove, but it is quite likely they were kept enclosed as domestic animals in an agricultural situation, rather as were rabbits (*Oryctolagus cuniculus*) in medieval times. However, they became extinct at the end of the Roman period and were reintroduced in the late 11th century.

The discussion of the Roman landscape so far has referred to Sussex as a whole, and to the western South Downs in particular. However, detailed field and aerial surveys of the whole Chilgrove valley and its environs, excavations of two of the known villas (Chilgrove 1 and 2) with some preliminary analysis of soil, bones and invertebrate remains does give some evidence at least for the specific locality.

Aerial surveys and field-walking have shown that there are enormous areas of Romano-British fields still detectable throughout the Chilgrove study area, on valley sides down to valley-bottoms. These are in the process of being accurately mapped. The sites of further villas have been located, and the distribution of field-systems suggests more may yet be discovered. This evidence all suggests the Chilgrove valley was intensively settled and farmed in Roman times.

Stone-free soil up to a metre deep below Chilgrove 1 suggests this area was not arable, immediately prior to the building of the villa; but a plough-furrow in the chalk below the floor of Chilgrove 2 shows that site certainly was arable immediately before. Unfortunately there was not enough soil in the furrow for detailed analysis. Two lines of soil evidence verify the theory that major forest clearance had taken place long before Roman times. Firstly, the Roman soil horizons are very similar to today's, i.e., any soil changes resulting from land-use changes had already occurred. Secondly, there seems to be a widespread soil deposit in the Chilgrove valley which is a red-brown silty-clay containing many flints, and it is very similar to the remaining hill-top acid soils often formed from clay with flints. It is thought to be an accumulation of the natural soils (described in Section 3 above) eroded down into the valley after Neolithic and Bronze Age forest clearance. However, there is as yet no definite evidence to date it (*Collins*, pers. comm.).

Thus soil evidence shows there was arable before and during Roman times. Bones of domestic ox, horse, sheep or goat, pig, and dog testify to stockfarming, as do the structural remains of large, enclosed farmyards at Chilgrove 1 and 2. As yet, not enough field-systems and tracks have been mapped to determine the exact spatial distribution of arable and pastoral farming in the study area. It seems likely, on present evidence, that trackways were the routes for cattle and stock from the lower-lying settlements through the cultivated hillsides to the hilltop pastoral areas. Red deer bones suggest possible nearby woodland conditions, as do bones of birds of rook or crow size (tree nesters). Shells of the snail *Hygromia striolata* and other species of damp conditions also suggest there may still have been some woodland in the vicinity. Many shells of the introduced Roman snail *Helix aspersa* show that large mammals like fallow deer were not the only fauna introduced for food (*Outen*, pers. comm.).

Small archaeological finds provide a similar picture, with a variety of carpenters' tools suggesting use of timber and wood (as would be expected for any later prehistoric or historic period) for many purposes; ploughshares are additional evidence for arable farming, and shears for pastoral activities (see below, p. 156).

We would perhaps conclude that, despite differences in architectural detail of buildings, and in actual field-shape and size, the landscape of Roman Chilgrove would not look alien to our 20th-century eyes, but would appear quite similar to what we know, at least in overall pattern. It was an intensively man-managed landscape with enclosed fields, scattered buildings, trackways, similar cultivated plants and domestic animals; woodland was present, but not in large amounts. We would feel at home in such an environment.

SECTION 8—THE LANDSCAPE TODAY

The location and main physical features of the Chilgrove landscape were described in Section 1, but it is worth summarising the biological features of this area today, because it is these that have undergone most modification by man. Table IV lists the man-made habitats of western Sussex in approximate chronological order; Table V lists the introduced mammals; and Table VI summarises the landscape of Chilgrove today.

The study area today is characterised by a great variety of habitats, the prominence of introduced plants and animals, the absence of any wholly natural vegetation whatsoever, and the highly technical way in which most of the habitats are managed for productive purposes. About half the study-area is woodland, mainly high-forest plantations of beech and conifers, and the now old-fashioned sweet chestnut and oak-hazel coppices; there are naturally-regenerated yew woodlands on North Marden Down, Bow Hill and Chilgrove Hill, which date only from the last century and a half (*Tittensor* 1976). Semi-woodland habitats include hedgerows, parkland, scrub, and arboreta (as at West Dean). If silviculture takes up about half of the study area, agriculture takes up much of the rest, as there is little built-up land. Some areas of the now obsolete chalk-grassland pasture still exist nearby as in Kingley Vale National Nature Reserve, but much of the grassland is either temporary cereal crops or short-term, sown pasture ('leys'). Rich water-meadows along the River Lavant have recently been drained and converted to monoculture grassland. Other semi-aquatic habitats are more-or-less non-existent, though dew ponds are being renovated, as in Kingley Vale. Semi-agricultural habitats include gardens, orchards and vineyards. Obviously man-made habitats include churches, churchyards, and road-verges.

With such a variety of vegetation and habitats, the fauna is equally varied. Despite the general notion that intensive agriculture and silviculture destroy wildlife, studies over the past decade by M. Boxall, E. C. M. Haes, A. M. and R. M. Tittensor, and R. L. C. Williamson show that the flora and fauna of this area is particularly rich. Although many mammals, for instance, have become extinct (Section 2), equally large numbers of introduced species have replaced them (Table V) (*Tittensor* 1974).

Collins (1974) studied soils throughout the western South Downs and found that a deep and red-brown, acid, silty soil, probably akin to the soil of the natural landscape occurs over some areas, especially on the plateaux between Cocking and Harting (within the Chilgrove study area). The shallow, black, alkaline rendzina soil, which probably developed after erosion of the natural soil was accelerated by woodland clearance, is particularly associated with areas of long-standing arable. Other soil types do occur: gravelly alluvium occurs along the valley of the Lavant, while certain plateaux, such as Bow Hill, bear an acid soil developed from the clay-with-flints geological deposits.

SUMMARY OF MAN'S IMPACT

Comparison of Tables II, III and VI summarises the considerable impact of man on the Chilgrove landscape. It has been turned from a uniform, wooded landscape into a varied mixed woodland—grassland landscape that is totally

17

artificial except for some native plants and animals that still remain. Most of the changes had already taken place before the Romans arrived, and subsequent changes were merely a continuation of earlier changes on a smaller scale. It is not generally realised that this countryside is so artificial and highly managed, and that there is little 'natural' or 'unspoilt' about it. This has significant connotations for present-day conservation of habitats within the countryside.

CONSERVATION FOR ARCHAEOLOGIST AND ECOLOGIST

The retention and conservation of ecological and archaeological sites is essentially similar, because both are man's artefacts produced at successive periods, used for a while, and then discarded as obsolete or converted to a new use. Just as the archaeologist chooses which of 1,000 round barrows to excavate, designate and preserve, so the ecologist chooses which areas of chalk downland are most suitable for scientific study, designation and preservation as nature reserves. The only difference is chronological—some ecological artefacts (e.g., heathland) are older than any existing archaeological site. Ecological artefacts in the landscape are also more difficult to work with. If left unmanaged, they alter into something else (e.g., heathland becomes invaded by woodland), so now old-fashioned management such as burning or sheep-grazing (done as a matter of course and survival in prehistoric and historic times) has to be instigated. Study of ecological sites also presents more problems because of seasonal change, or movement of fauna.

Thus the basic principles of ecological conservation are the same as archaeological conservation. Similar questions are raised: what is to be achieved by preserving an artefact, which sites are worth keeping, what conservation measures are required, what legal protection is available for sites, should a farmer or forester be recompensed for loss of income due to retention of an archaeological or ecological monument?

TABLE I

Latin Names of Plants Mentioned in the Text

Alder	*Alnus glutinosa*
Alexanders	*Smyrnium olusatrum*
Ash	*Fraxinus excelsior*
Barley (primitive)	*Hordeum vulgare*
Bay	*Laurus nobilis*
Beech	*Fagus sylvatica*
Birch	*Betula pendula, B. pubescens*
Bracken	*Pteridium aquilinum*
Charlock	*Sinapis arvensis*
Cornflower	*Centaurea cyanus*
Dill	*Anethum graveolens*
Elm	*Ulmus glabra*
Fennel	*Foeniculum vulgare*
Fig	*Ficus carica*
Goutweed	*Aegopodium podagraria*
Hazel	*Corylus avellana*
Heather	see Ling
Ivy	*Hedera helix*
Juniper	*Juniperus communis*
Lavender	*Lavandula sp.*
Lime	*Tilia cordata*
Ling	*Calluna vulgaris*
Medlar	*Mespilus germanica*
Oak	*Quercus robur, Q. petraea*
Oats	*Avena sativa*
Pea	*Pisum sativum*
Pine	*Pinus sylvestris*
Plantains	*Plantago spp.*
Radish	*Raphanus sativus*
Rosemary	*Rosmarinus officinalis*
Rye	*Secale cereale*
Sweet chestnut	*Castanea sativa*
Vine	*Vitis vinifera*
Walnut	*Juglans regia*
Wheat (primitive)	*Triticum spelte, T. dicoccum*
Yew	*Taxus Baccata*

TABLE II

Summary of Natural Chilgrove Landscape

1. Over 90 per cent. woodland cover: 'mixed-deciduous-forest'.
2. Little grassland.
3. No beech woods, yew woods, or chestnut woods.
4. Oak, lime, hazel, alder common; birch and ash relatively uncommon.
5. All habitats natural.
6. Landscape relatively uniform in appearance.
7. Deep, acid soil widespread.
8. Watercourses untamed.
9. Seasonal extremes of local climate modified by prevailing woodland cover.
10. Few people.
11. No man's artefacts such as roads, tracks, fields, buildings.
12. No domestic animals or livestock.
13. No cultivated plants.
14. No alien plants or animals.
15. Native flora and fauna all present (by definition).

TABLE III

Summary of Pre-Roman Iron Age Landscape

1. Woodland cover probably about 30 per cent.; some 'mixed-deciduous forest' possibly present.
2. Much grassland.
3. Beech woods present; no yew or chestnut woods.
4. Oak, lime, hazel, alder, relatively uncommon; birch and ash common on 'neglected' areas.
5. Natural *and* man-made habitats present; man-made predominate.
6. Landscape varied in appearance.
7. Natural soils partly eroded.
8. Watercourses untamed.
9. Local climate little modified by woodland.
10. People present in large numbers.
11. Man's artefacts on a modest scale, e.g., tracks, wooden buildings, stockades, banks.
12. Domestic animals common.
13. Extensive areas of cultivated plants in fields.
14. Alien plants and animals present.
15. Some native fauna extinct; pine possibly extinct.

TABLE IV

The Creation of New Habitats in Western Sussex

Habitat	Period First Formed
Heathland*	Mesolithic
Woodland edge Chalk grassland pasture Grassy trackways Arable fields 'Waste' ground Mineral spoil heaps (flint mines) Animal enclosures Wooden buildings 'Secondary' woodland	Neolithic and Bronze Age
Steep grassy ramparts Large urban and animal enclosures Beech woodlands Meadow (cut) grasslands? Coppice woodlands?	Iron Age
Stone-buildings Stone-roads Gardens Vineyards Orchards? Fish-ponds?* Hedgerows Road verges	Roman

TABLE IV (*continued*)

Dew ponds
Water meadows
Gravel pits*
Reservoirs*
Parklands
Yew woodland
Conifer woodland
Chestnut woodland
Mixed conifer—deciduous woodland } Post-Roman
Churchyards
Parks*
Hammer ponds (lakes)*
Canals*
Railway cuttings
Arboreta

*Not present actually within Chilgrove study area

TABLE V

Introduced Mammals in Sussex

Latin Name	English Name	When introduced to Britain
Mus musculus[1]	House mouse	Neolithic
Bos taurus[2]	Domestic cattle	Neolithic
Ovis (domestic)	Domestic sheep	Neolithic
Capra (domestic)	Domestic goat	Neolithic
Sus (domestic)	Domestic pig	Neolithic
Equus (domestic)	Domestic horse	Iron Age?
Canis (domestic)	Domestic dog	Prehistoric
Felis (domestic)	Domestic cat	
Dama dama[3]	Fallow deer	late 11th–early 12th century
Rattus rattus[4]	Black rat	12th century
Oryctolagus cuniculus[5]	Rabbit	12th century
Rattus norvegicus	Brown rat	by 1730
Apodemus flavicollis[6]	Yellow-necked mouse	19th century
Sciu rus carolinensis	Grey Squirrel	19th century
Mustela vison[7]	American mink	20th century
Muntiacus reevesi[8]	Chinese muntjac deer	about 1900
Macropus rufogriseus	Red-necked wallaby	about 1908

1. Recorded by Roman times, but probable date of introduction given.
2. Domestic derivatives of *B. primigenius,* and feral forms of this primitive breed present in England until 12th century.
3. A domestic (park) species until 19th century; Chilgrove population derived from Uppark escapes.
4. Now extinct—last local record 1956, Portsmouth.
5. A domestic (warren) species until 18th century, when widespread escape occurred.
6. Possibly present earlier and overlooked.
7. Escaped from farms 1930 onwards, now feral.
8. Not recorded within Chilgrove study area, but present nearby.

TABLE VI

Summary of 20th-Century Chilgrove Landscape

1. 30–50 per cent. woodland cover: no natural 'mixed-deciduous forest'.
2. Much grassland.
3. Beech woods, yew woods, chestnut woods common.
4. Oak and hazel common in some managed woodlands; alder rare; native lime absent; birch and ash uncommon.
5. No natural habitats remain: all are man-made.
6. Landscape very varied in appearance.
7. Variety of soil types present; deep acid soil restricted in distribution.
8. Watercourses tamed; water-table lowered by considerable extraction.
9. Possibly some climatic modification by woodland.
10. People present in large numbers.
11. Man's artefacts common and widespread, e.g., roads, stone buildings, fields, fences, reservoirs, telegraph poles.
12. Domestic animals prominent.
13. Most vegetation consists of cultivated plants in fields and woods.
14. Alien plants and animals prominent.
15. Many species native fauna and some native flora extinct.

Acknowledgements

    I gratefully acknowledge assistance from the following people in the preparation of this account: Fred Aldsworth, Michael Boxall, Caroline Cartwright, Margaret Collins, Alec Down, Alan Outen, George Peterken, Oliver Rackham, Peter Reynolds, Frank Sheridan, Ann Thorley, Andy Tittensor, David Tittensor.

References

ARMSTRONG 1974 — Armstrong, J. R., *A History of Sussex,* Phillimore, Chichester, 1974.

BELL 1978 — Bell, M., 'Excavations at Bishopstone', *S.A.C. 115*, 1–299, 1978.

BRANDON 1974 — Brandon, P., *The Sussex Landscape,* Hodder and Stoughton, London, 1974.

BURSTOW and HOLLEYMAN 1957 — Burstow, G. P., and Holleyman, G. A., *Late Bronze Age Settlement on Itford Hill, Sussex*, P.P.S. *23*, 167–212, 1957.

COLLINS 1974 — Collins, M. A., 'History and Soils on the Chalk'. Typescript report, King's College Field Station, Rogate, 1974.

CORBET 1964 — Corbet, G. B., 'The Identification of British Mammals'. British Museum, London, 1964.

CUNLIFFE 1973a — Cunliffe, B. W., *The Regni*, Duckworth, London, 1973.

CUNLIFFE 1973b — Cunliffe, B. W., 'Chalton, Hants.: the Evolution of a Landscape', *Ant. J. 53*, 173–90, 1973.

CURWEN 1931

Curwen, E. C., 'Excavations in the Trundle', *S.A.C.* *72*, 100–49, 1931.

CURWEN 1934

Curwen, E. C., 'A Prehistoric Site in Kingley Vale, near Chichester', *S.A.C.* *75*, 209–15, 1934.

DIMBLEBY 1975

Dimbleby, G. W., 'Pollen Analysis in: The Excavation of a Turf Barrow at Minsted, West Sussex, 1973', ed. P. Drewett, *S.A.C.* *113*, 61–2, 1975.

DREWETT 1978

Drewett, P. (ed.), 'The Archaeology of Sussex', C.B.A. Research Report, 1978.

EVANS 1975

Evans, J. G., *The Environment of Early Man in the British Isles,* Elek, London, 1975.

GODWIN 1943

Godwin, H., 'Coastal peat beds of the British Isles and the North Sea', *J. Ecol., 31*, 199–247, 1943.

GODWIN 1960

Godwin, H., 'Vegetational History of the Kentish Chalk Downs as seen at Wingham and Frogholt', *Veroff. Geobot. Inst., Rubel, 37*, 83–99, 1960.

GODWIN 1975

Godwin, H., *A History of the British Flora*, 2nd ed., Cambridge University Press, 1975.

HARCOURT 1854

Harcourt, L. V., 'Site of British Village at Stoke Down', *S.A.C. 7*, 32, 1854.

HOLLEYMAN 1935

Holleyman, G. A., 'The Celtic Field-system in South Britain', *Antiquity 9*, 443–54, 1935.

KEEF, WYMER and DIMBLEBY 1965

Keef, P. A. M., Wymer, J. J. and Dimbleby, G. W., *A Mesolithic site on Iping Common, Sussex, England*, P.P.S. *31*, 85–92, 1965.

O'CONNOR 1977

O'Connor, T. P., 'The Excavation of a round barrow and cross-ridge dyke at Alfriston, East Sussex', *S.A.C. 114*, 151–63, 1977.

PENNINGTON 1969

Pennington, W., *The History of British Vegetation*, E.U.P., London, 1969.

RACKHAM 1976

Rackham, O., *Trees and Woodland in the British Landscape*, Dent, London, 1976.

REYNOLDS 1976

Reynolds, P. J., *Farming in the Iron Age*, Cambridge University Press, 1976.

RYDER 1969

Ryder, M. L., *Animal Bones in Archaeology*, Blackwell, Oxford, 1969.

SANKEY 1966

Sankey, J., *Chalkland Ecology*, Heinemann, London, 1966.

SMITH (in press)

Smith, C., *The Ecology of the English Chalk*, Academic Press.

THORLEY 1971

Thorley, A., 'Vegetational History in the Vale of the Brooks', in R. B. G. Williams (ed.), *Guide to Sussex Excursions,* I.B.G. Conference, 1971.

TITTENSOR 1974

Tittensor, A. M., *Sussex Mammal Report, 1970 and 71,* Sussex Trust for Nature Conservation, Henfield, 1974.

TITTENSOR and
TITTENSOR 1977

Tittensor, A. M. and R. M., *Natural History of 'The Mens', Sussex,* Horsham Natural History Society, Horsham, 1977.

TITTENSOR 1975

Tittensor, R. M., 'A Survey of South Downs Woodlands'. Typescript report, Monks Wood Experimental Station, Huntingdon, 1975.

TITTENSOR 1976

Tittensor, R. M., 'The Ecological History of Yew (*Taxus baccata* L.) Woodlands on the South Downs'. Typescript report, Royal Society, London, 1976.

TITTENSOR

Tittensor, R. M., 'A History of "The Mens": A Sussex Woodland Common', *S.A.C. 116* (forthcoming).

YATES 1972

Yates, E. M., *A History of the Landscapes of the Parishes of South Harting and Rogate,* Phillimore, Chichester, 1972.

2

The Chilgrove Valley Landscape Project
The Archaeology of the Study Area
by F. G. Aldsworth

The area which is the subject of this study covers about twenty square miles (forty-eight square kilometres) on the dip slope of the South Downs, and its centre is six miles (nine kilometres) north of Chichester, in West Sussex. The northern limit is the top of the scarp slope of the Downs which rises up to over 230 metres O.D. at Beacon Hill, Treyford Hill, and Linch Down. The southern limit is marked by the parish boundaries of West Dean and Stoughton which occupy a position close to the southern margin of the chalk, where it gives way to the gravel of the coastal plain, at about sixty metres O.D. The eastern limit is the east boundary of West Dean parish, and the western boundary extends along a dry valley through Stoughton and Compton to the western boundary of the parishes of Marden and Elsted.

This particular area was selected for several reasons. It contains a sufficient number of known sites to indicate that a detailed study might provide a typical section through the South Downs. It is large enough to examine the relationship between the Prehistoric, Roman and later landscapes, but remains sufficiently small to be manageable.

The chalk, which is capped by clay-with-flints in some places, is bisected by three main valleys which extend from north to south through the study area. That to the east carries the River Lavant which, as its name implies, flows only when the water table has reached a certain level, normally only during the winter months. That to the west carries a tributary of the River Ems, which today commences a little south of Stoughton, but its now dry valley extends further north for about three miles as far as North Marden. It is the central of these three valleys, the Chilgrove Valley, that dominates the study area, extending from the east side of Beacon Hill, Harting, down through Chilgrove to join the Lavant valley south of Binderton House. It is joined on its eastern side by dry valleys at Chilgrove and near Brick Kiln Farm.

The evidence from a series of late Saxon land charters for Hampshire indicates that in the 10th century A.D., the water table on the Hampshire Downs was much higher than at present, and this evidence does appear to confirm that the lowering of the water table was specifically a medieval or late occurrence (*Aldsworth* 1973). If this is so, then we must consider that water was much more freely available to those living on the Downs than at present, but that during the medieval period this supply may have been reduced, causing the excavation of deeper wells and some migration of settlement. At the time of writing (1978), the Roman well at Chilgrove 2 has been excavated to a depth of 122 feet (37 metres), without reaching the bottom, approximately 43 feet (13 metres) above the water level reached near Chilgrove 1. In 1975, the Water Authority sunk a borehole near to the valley bottom opposite Chilgrove 1, and

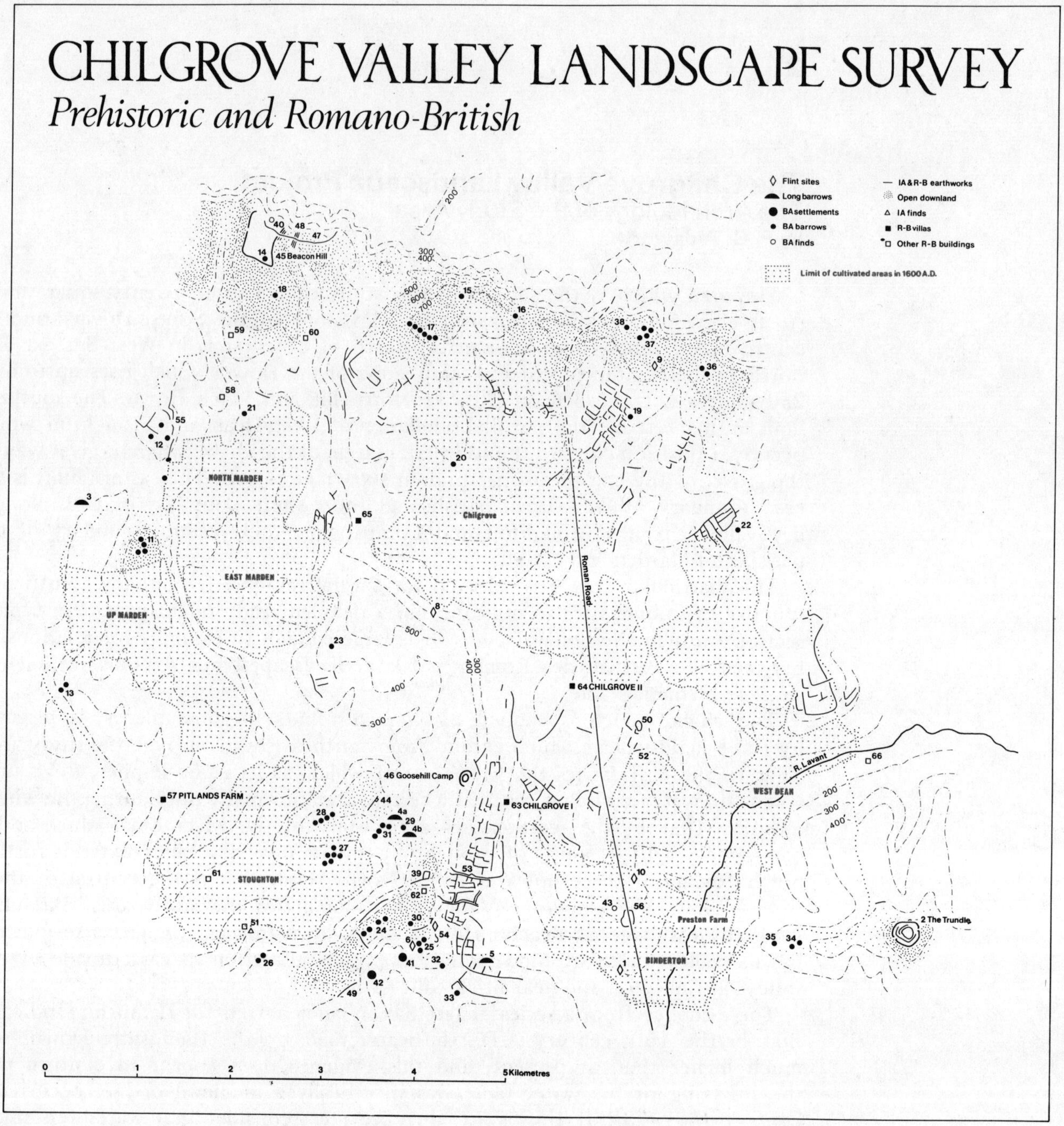

CHILGROVE VALLEY LANDSCAPE SURVEY
Prehistoric and Romano-British

Legend:

◇ Flint sites
▬ Long barrows
● BA settlements
• BA barrows
○ BA finds

— IA & R-B earthworks
▒ Open downland
△ IA finds
■ R-B villas
□ Other R-B buildings

▒ Limit of cultivated areas in 1600 A.D.

NORTH MARDEN

EAST MARDEN

UP MARDEN

Chilgrove

Roman Road

45 Beacon Hill

58

55

12

3

11

13

23

8

65

20

18

59

60

21

40 48 47

14

15

16

17

38

37

9

36

19

22

64 CHILGROVE II

50

52

R. Lavant

66

46 Goosehill Camp

57 PITLANDS FARM

63 CHILGROVE I

WEST DEAN

28

29

4a

4b

31

44

27

61

STOUGHTON

39

62

53

10

43

56

Preston Farm

BINDERTON

35

34

2 The Trundle

51

30

6

24

25

54

5

26

41

32

49

42

33

0   1   2   3   4   5 Kilometres

Fig. 2

26

water was reached at a depth of 75 feet (23 metres), approximately 110 feet (33 metres) O.D. Nearby wells, dug in the 19th century at Stapleash and Chilgrove were eventually taken down to a depth of 200 feet, but have in recent years been abandoned in favour of mains water, due to the fact that they frequently ran dry in dry years. The bottom of the well at Chilgrove 2 must lie at some point between the depth reached at present and the modern water table, unless there is some abnormal factor local to the villa which is affecting the water table there. There has certainly been a lowering of the water table in the valley since the introduction of the first water undertaking in this century, but there is insufficient evidence at present to show whether the table has been affected by factors other than higher extraction rates in the period between Roman times and the present. More work needs to be carried out before all the reasons for a lower water table are isolated. Ruth Tittensor has discussed the early vegetation of the study area, and there is little to add to this from the archaeological evidence except to say that intensive fieldwork on the South Downs, particularly at Slindon (*Aldsworth* 1977), is demonstrating that substantial areas, especially alongside valley bottoms, were occupied during the Mesolithic and Neolithic periods.

THE PREHISTORY

When considering the archaeological evidence for settlement in and immediately adjoining the study area, we are faced with the problem of not knowing whether the remains which have so far been discovered are representative of the original situation, or whether they are even representative of what actually survives but has yet to be found. The distribution of the surviving Prehistoric and Roman field-systems for example, clearly reflect the extent to which they have been destroyed by intensive ploughing in later periods. It is, therefore, not possible to completely reconstruct the picture, and for this reason a study has been commenced of the situation in the post-Roman period which, it is hoped, will form a supplementary volume to this report. The two surveys have demonstrated that there are virtually no prehistoric earthworks remaining within the areas of the medieval common fields or the later extensions to the arable in the late medieval period (Fig. 2). Further sites appear to have been almost completely destroyed by the expansion in arable which replaced open downland at the end of the 18th century. Thus, it is only within the parts which survived as open downland or woodland into the 19th century (i.e., Heathbarn Down and Bow Hill) that extensive areas of prehistoric and Roman earthworks are seen.

Over much of the study area the evidence has been reduced to surface scatters of flints, pottery and bone, and to features buried below the ploughsoil. No doubt if all the fields and woodlands were walked and photographed from the air at all seasons of the year other sites could be located, but for the present we must accept the information that has come to light during several years of casual walking and an examination of the air phorographs provided by the County Planning Officer, the Air Ministry, and Mr. Jerome O'Hea of Chichester.

The earliest evidence for occupation is in the form of a number of *Paleolithic* implements found near Binderton House by a Dr. Higgins before 1950 (Site 1).

No details are known, but we must assume that these finds are probably roughly the same date as those found recently at Eartham and Slindon, about four miles east of Chichester, by Andrew Woodcock of Chichester Museum. At Eartham, a series of stratified paleolithic working floors have been found near the foot of a buried chalk cliff beneath the gravel of the coastal plain. The top of the cliff lies approximately on the 61 metre O.D. contour line, and probably extended on this line a little south of the study area through Lavant and West Stoke, representing the coastline during one of the interglacial periods of the Ice Age (Fig. 1). At Slindon a working floor has been found on a raised beach alongside a now dry valley which once opened out on to the coastline represented by the cliff at Eartham. No recognisable finds have been made for the *Mesolithic* period, which commenced at the beginning of the present Interglacial through to the beginning of the Neolithic, somewhere between 4000 and 3500 B.C. The problem is that sites, usually indicated by scatters of flintwork, are only discovered as the result of intensive field walking, and even when they are found it is not easy to differentiate between material of the Mesolithic and Neolithic periods. The transition from one to the other is not clearly defined in the artefacts; indeed, it is the economy that is probably the most important factor in landscape studies. Little is known at present about the economy of the Mesolithic, although at Iping Common, on sandy heathland north of the Downs, man appears to have been responsible, either by deliberate act or accident, for modifying the landscape to the extent that hazel woodland was replaced by heather (*Keef et al* 1965). Mesolithic sites are frequently found on the Downs, and at Slindon Robin Upton has found a number of flint-working floors alongside dry stream beds which almost certainly carried water in the Mesolithic (*Aldsworth* 1977).

Neolithic, c.3500—2000 B.C.

Three types of Neolithic field monument survive in the Chilgrove Valley. A causewayed enclosure (Site 2), long barrows (Sites 3, 4 and possibly 5), and flint-working areas (Sites 6, 7, 9 and 10), but a further type, frequently found in other parts of the country, the henge, is not represented in the study area, nor, indeed, in Sussex. The survival of these features allows some reconstructions to be made, but the function of some of them is obscure.

The causewayed enclosure on The Trundle was the subject of trial excavations in 1928 and 1930. The discovery of pottery and animal bones has long been taken to indicate that this and other contemporary causewayed enclosures were occupation sites, but a recent consideration of their function, bearing in mind that several have produced complete and disarticulated human remains, suggests that they may have been primarily areas defined for burial (*Drewett* 1977a). If the enclosure of The Trundle was not an occupation site there is little evidence for permanent settlement elsewhere in the study area, although the occurrence of contemporary burial mounds suggest habitation somewhere in the vicinity. It seems likely that during the Neolithic, settlements may have been 'open' and that these survive only as scatters of flint flakes (Sites 9 and 10), which elsewhere, as on Bullock Down, near Beachy Head, have produced pottery (*Drewett* 1977b). Elsewhere on the South Downs Neolithic man mined for flint, but in the Chilgrove area there is evidence to suggest that he may have obtained his source material from surface workings on Bow Hill (Sites 6 and 7), and the valley gravels.

Since no recent excavations have been undertaken on Neolithic sites in the study area there is insufficient evidence to reconstruct the economy, but what little information there is from elsewhere on the Downs suggests that the late Neolithic was a period of nomadic pastoralism activity within an area which remained predominantly woodland.

Bronze Age, c.2000—700 B.C.

The end of the Neolithic and the commencement of the early Bronze Age is marked by the arrival of the Beaker folk, who introduced a new method of burial, but they appear not to have altered other aspects of life, especially the economy. They are normally regarded as practising individual inhumation burial under a round mound, but cremation burials are also found. In the Chilgrove area, over sixty burial mounds are known (Sites 11-38), and most of these probably date from the Early Bronze Age, but only one (Site 14), has been properly excavated. The group of four on Bow Hill were the subject of trial trenches in 1859, when two were found to contain urned cremations, and a third appears to have contained 'a large deposit of grey ashes and charcoal' which may have been the remains of a cremation not placed in an urn.

Four barrows were excavated on Linch Down (Site 37) by Miss P. A. M. Keef in 1955, but the results of her work have not been published. The small barrow on Beacon Hill, Harting (Site 14), was excavated by the Sussex Archaeological Field Unit in 1976, and this had apparently been previously dug, but a few pieces of human bone suggest that it may have been a Beaker grave. Few early Bronze Age settlement sites have so far been found, and their elusiveness has been taken to indicate that they were nomadic pastoralists like the late Neolithic. But whereas there is ample evidence for burial in the Early Bronze Age, but little for occupation, the reverse is true for the Middle and Late Bronze Age. There was a considerable expansion in agricultural activity with the establishment of basic patterns of permanent settlement, which persisted into the Romano-British period.

Several settlements are known in the study area (Sites 40-43), and it seems likely that some of the field-systems also originated in this period, but in some parts of the study area evidence for arable cultivation is notably absent. It is within two of these areas, apparently laid to permanent pasture, on Bow Hill and Stoughton Down, that small rectangular enclosures with accompanying dykes occur (Sites 39 and 44), and it seems likely that these, like other examples at Highdown and Thundersbarrow, date to the Late Bronze Age. They presumably functioned as animal pounds and may have been used in association with cross-ridge and spur dykes in a ranch-style economy.

Iron Age,
c. 700 B.C. — A.D. 43

During the Iron Age and Romano-British periods the intensive agricultural use of the Downs continued, with areas laid variously to permanent pasture and arable. Farmsteads remained the basic unit of settlement, but large enclosures are also known. Defended hill-top enclosures were constructed on The Trundle (Site 2), Beacon Hill (Site 45), and at Goosehill Camp (Site 46), but, although they are all often referred to as hill forts, their true nature is not known. Excavations on The Trundle provided evidence for the nature of the defences of the surrounding earthwork, but little is known of its true economic function, although it does appear to have been in use throughout most of the Iron Age.

At Beacon Hill a comparatively large area is enclosed by a feeble bank and ditch, which has recently been dated to the early Iron Age. Contemporary occupation is represented by several pits and four-post structures, but the extent of this occupation is not known. At Goosehill Camp in 1953–5, Boyden examined the defences and a small area within a hill-slope enclosure formed by a double concentric bank and ditch. At least one hut-site was examined, and this indicates that there was some occupation within what is probably best seen as a cattle enclosure (Site 46).

At Binderton, Jerome O'Hea has recently discovered a ditched enclosure from the air, measuring about 170 metres by 120 metres (Site 56). It is bisected by the Roman road from Chichester to Silchester and appears to contain a small rectangular enclosure in its western half. Its date is not known, but in form it is similar to Iron Age enclosures known in Wessex.

References

ALDSWORTH 1973 — Aldsworth, F. G., *Towards a Pre-Domesday Geography of Hampshire: A Review of the Evidence.* Undergraduate Dissertation, Depts. of Archaeology and Geography, University of Southampton, 1973.

ALDSWORTH 1977 — Aldsworth, F. G., 'Some recent discoveries on the Slindon Estate', *Sussex Archaeological Collections,* 114, 1976, pp. 327–8.

DREWETT 1977a — Drewett, P. L., 'The excavations of a Neolithic Causewayed enclosure on Offham Hill, East Sussex, 1976', *Proceedings of the Prehistoric Society,* 43, 1977, 201–241.

DREWETT 1977b — Drewett, P. L., pers. comm. 1977.

KEEF 1965 — Keef, P. A. M., Wymer, J. J., and Dimbleby, G. W., 'A Mesolithic Site on Iping Common, Sussex, England'. *Proceedings of the Prehistoric Society,* 31, 1965, pp. 85–92.

Gazetteer of Sites and Finds: Pre-historic and Roman

compiled by F. G. Aldsworth and Alec Down

1. *Palaeolithic Implements*   SU 8465 1066
Found by a Dr. Higgins before 1950.
(*O.S.* 1971)

2. *The Trundle*   SU 8774 1107
A prominent hill top which was occupied by a Neolithic causewayed enclosure, a late Bronze Age plateau hill fort, and an Iron Age Hillfort.
(*S.A.C.,* 70 [1929] 33–85 E. C. Curwen; and *S.A.C.,* 72 [1931] 100–149 E. C. Curwen.)

3. *Neolithic Long Barrow* (Bevis's Thumb)   SU 7876 1551
About sixty metres long, and up to one and a half metres high.
(*S.A.C.,* 75 [1934] 219 and 244 L. V. Grinsell.)

4. *Two Neolithic Barrows* (Stoughton Down)   (a) SU 8217 1219
About forty metres and twenty metres long respectively.   (b) SU 8234 1205
(*S.A.C.,* 66 [1925] 173–5 E. and E. C. Curwen: and *S.A.C.,* 75 [1934] 219 and 144 L. V. Grinsell.)

5. *Possible Neolithic Long Barrow*   SU 8320 1072
Oval mound, oriented east-west, about fifty metres long and fifteen metres wide, which appears to have flanking ditches.
(*W.S.C.C.,* 1977.)

6. *Neolithic/Bronze Age Flint Workings*   SU 8241 1091
A series of hollows once thought to be flint mines, but excavations in 1933 showed that they were only surface flint workings.
(*S.N.Q.* 4 [1933] 246–7; and *Archaeology of Sussex,* 1954, 120, E. C. Curwen.)

7. *Neolithic/Bronze Age Flint Workings*   SU 8264 1109
A series of depressions which may represent the remains of workings.
(*O.S.,* 1971.)

8. *Neolithic Axe*   SU 8250 1430
Polished axe found on Chilgrove Hill.
(*Joint Archaeological Committee Bulletin* 9 [1962], 4.)

9. *Neolithic Flint–Working Site*   SU 8494 1702
Found by P. L. Drewett in 1975.
(*W.S.C.C.,* 1975.)

10. *Neolithic Flint-Working Site*   SU 8480 1160
Found by a Dr. Higgins before 1961, and scatters of waste flakes still visible over a wide area.
(*O.S.,* 1971; and *W.S.C.C.,* 1977.)

11. *Barrow Cemetery* (Apple Down)   SU 7945 1500
Four round barrows, now ploughed out.
(*S.A.C.,* 75 [1934], p. 244, L. V. Grinsell.)

12. *Barrow Cemetery* (Fernbeds Down)   SU 7960 1620
Four round barrows between eleven and eighteen metres in diameter.
(*S.A.C.,* 75 [1934], p. 244, L. V. Grinsell; and *O.S.,* 1971.)

13. *Barrow Cemetery* (Grevitts Copse)   SU 7861 1355
    Two round barrows each about twelve metres in diameter.
    (*O.S.*, 1971.)

14. *Barrow* (Beacon Hill)   SU 8071 1804
    Small ditched barrow about ten metres in diameter, excavated by the Sussex
    Archaeological Field Unit in 1976 when fragmentary remains of an inhuma-
    tion were found.
    (*S.A.C.*, 75 [1934], 244, L. V. Grinsell; and *Drewett*, 1977.)

15. *Barrow* (Treyford Hill)   SU 8267 1770
    Small bowl barrow, nine metres in diameter, enclosed by a square ditched
    enclosure which is presumably of a later date.
    (*S.A.C.* 75 [1934], 245, L. V. Grinsell.)

16. *Barrow* (Didling Hill)   SU 8347 1750
    A bowl barrow, about ten metres in diameter, now reduced by ploughing.
    (*S.A.C.*, 75 [1934], 245, L. V. Grinsell.)

17. *Barrow Cemetery* (Devil's Jumps)   SU 8247 1731)
    A group of five large bell barrows and two small bowl barrows.
    (*S.A.C.*, 75 [1934], 223, 232, and 245, L. V. Grinsell.)

18. *Possible Barrow*   SU 8086 1765
    A mound, about twenty metres in diameter, and less than one metre in
    height.
    (*O.S.*, 1971.)

19. *Barrow* (Linchball Wood)   SU 8473 1646
    Twenty-seven metres in diameter.
    (*O.S.*, 1971.)

20. *Barrow*   SU 8281 1594
    Twenty metres in diameter.
    (*O.S.*, 1971.)

21. *Barrow*   SU 8056 1643
    Thirteen metres in diameter.
    (*O.S.*, 1971.)

22. *Barrow*   SU 8588 1529
    Eighteen metres in diameter.
    (*O.S.*, 1971.)

23. *Barrow*   SU 8125 1402
    Eleven metres in diameter.
    (*S.A.C.*, 75 [1934], 245, L. V. Grinsell.)

24. *Barrow Cemetery* (Bow Hill)   SU 8190 1100
    Two bell and two ditched bowl barrows.
    (*S.A.C.* 7 [1854], 51–2; *S.A.C.* 75 [1934], 223 and 247, L. V. Grinsell;
    S.A.C. 82 [1941], 115–119, L. V. Grinsell; and *S.C.M.* 10 [1936], 45,
    L. Faraday.)

25. *Barrow Cemetery* (Bow Hill)   SU 8247 1095
    Three bowl barrows which were the subject of excavations in 1859.
    (*S.A.C.* 22 [1870], 62–5, Rev. H. Smith; *S.A.C.* 72 [1931], 63, L. V.
    Grinsell; *S.A.C.* 75 [1934], 247, L. V. Grinsell.)

26. *Barrow Cemetery*   SU 8075 1074
    Two bell barrows.
    (*S.A.C.* 75 [1934], 223 and 247, L. V. Grinsell.)

27. *Barrow Cemetery*   SU 8159 1179
    Six or more ploughed-out barrows.
    (*S.A.C.* 75 [1934], 247, L. V. Grinsell; *S.N.Q.* 6 [1936-7], 139-40, E. C.
    Curwen; and *S.A.C.* 112 [1974], 158, R. Bradley.)
28. *Barrow Cemetery*   SU 8145 1220
    Four ploughed-out barrows.
    (*S.A.C.* 75 [1934], 247, L. V. Grinsell.)
29. *Barrow* (Stoughton Down)   SU 8224 1209
    Thirteen metres in diameter.
    (*S.A.C.* 75 [1934], 247, L. V. Grinsell.)
30. *Barrow*   SU 8240 1114
    Seven metres in diameter.
    (*O.S.* 1971.)
31. *Barrow Cemetery* (Stoughton Down)   SU 8202 1202
    Remains of at least four barrows.
    (*O.S.* 1971.)
32. *Possible Barrow*   SU 8272 1663
    Now ploughed out.
    (*S.A.C.* 75 [1934], 247, L. V. Grinsell; and *W.S.C.C.* 1977.)
33. *Possible Barrow*   SU 8290 1039
    Mound, about eleven metres in diameter, which may be a barrow, but may
    be spoil from a pond immediately to the south.
    (*O.S.* 1971.)
34. *Barrow Cemetery*   SU 8650 1092
    Two bowl barrows each about twelve metres in diameter.
    (*O.S.* 1971.)
35. *Barrow*   SU 8621 1092
    Thirty metres in diameter.
    (*O.S.* 1971.)
36. *Barrow Cemetery*   SU 8548 1697
    Two bowl barrows, thirteen and eighteen metres in diameter.
    (*S.A.C.* 75 [1934], 245, L. V. Grinsell.)
37. *Barrow Cemetery*   SU 8482 1735
    Four bowl barrows excavated in 1955.
    (*S.A.C.* 75 [1934], 245, L. V. Grinsell; and *Sussex Archaeological Society
    Research Committee Minutes, No. 42* [1955], P. A. M. Keef.)
38. *Barrow*   SU 8466 1745
    About seventeen metres in diameter.
    (*S.A.C.* 75 [1934], 245, L. V. Grinsell.)
39. *Late Bronze Age pastoral enclosure and boundary ditches*   SU 8256 1164
    (Bow Hill)
    (*S.A.C.* 59 [1918], 49-50, E. and E. C. Curwen; *Antiquity* 2 [1928],
    50-55, F. Wagner; *S.N.Q.* 13 [1950-53], 134-7, S. Coffin; and *Antiq. J.*
    51 [1971], 8-29, R. Bradley.)
40. *Bronze Age 'hut platforms'* (Beacon Hill)   SU 8090 1834
    Excavated near north-east corner of hill fort by P. A. M. Keef in 1940s. Two
    Bronze Age gold ornaments were found at the west entrance of the hill fort.
    (*S.N.Q.* 6 [1936-7], 243-4.)
41. *Late Bronze Age Settlement* (Kingley Vale)   SU 8221 1074
    Four shallow depressions enclosed by a bank appear to represent the remains

41. (*continued*)
of a farmstead which was partially excavated in 1932.
(*S.A.C.* 75 [1934], 20g–215, E. C. Curwen; and *Archaeology of Sussex* 1954, 183–4, E. C. Curwen.)

42. *Late Bronze Age Settlement*   SU 8205 1059
A 'D'-shaped enclosure and associated lynchet.
(*O.S.* 1971.)

43. *Late Bronze Age Occupation*   SU 8461 1129
Fragments of a saddle quern found.
(*O.S.* 1971.)

44. *Late Bronze Age pastoral enclosure and cross dyke*   SU 8190 1230
(*Antiq. J.* 51 [1971], 21, R. Bradley.)

45. *Iron Age Hill fort* (Beacon Hill)   SU 8069 1826
An early Iron Age univallate hilltop enclosure. The west entrance was excavated by Miss P. A. M. Keef in the 1940s, and in 1976/77 the Sussex Archaeological Field Unit re-excavated this entrance and examined an area within the south-east corner.
(*S.N.Q.* 6 [1936–7], 243–44; *Antiq. J.* 33 [1953], 204–6.

46. *Iron Age enclosure* (Goosehill Camp)   SU 8297 1265
An enclosure, defended by two concentric lines of banks and ditches, which was partially excavated between 1953 and 1955.
(*Archaeological Journal*) 109 [1952], 22, A. Fox; and *S.A.C.* 94 [1956], 70–99, J. R. Boyden.)

47. *Linear Earthwork* (Pen Hill)   SU 8073 1846 & 8152 1837
This appears to be later in date than the early Iron Age enclosures on Beacon Hill (Site No. 45), and the cross-dykes (Site No. 48), but its precise date has yet to be ascertained. It may be Iron Age, Romano-British, or Medieval.
(*W.S.C.C.* 1976.)

48. *Cross-Dykes* (Beacon Hill)   SU 8106 1827
A series of three banks and ditches extending across a ridge. Their precise date is uncertain.
(*W.S.C.C.* 1976.)

49. *Cross-Dyke*   SU 8161 1036 & 8181 1051
About 250 metres long.
(*O.S.* 1949 and 1971.)

50. *Enclosure* (Lodge Hill)   SU 8484 1323
An oval enclosure, about sixty-three metres by thirty metres, defined by a bank and ditch existed here until about 1950, but it has now been destroyed by ploughing. Its date is uncertain.
(*O.S.* 1949 and 1971.)

51. *Iron Age/Romano-British site*   SU 8056 1100
Pottery of this date found.
(*S.N.Q.* 14 [1955], 133, E. C. Curwen.)

52. *Cross-Dyke* (Warren Down)   SU 8480 1297
A bank and ditch, about 125 metres long.
(*O.S.* 1971.)

53. *Iron Age/Romano-British earthwork*   SU 8308 1166
A field way with an oval depression surrounded by a bank appears to be the remains of a 'circus' for the protection of cattle overnight. It was excavated in 1924.

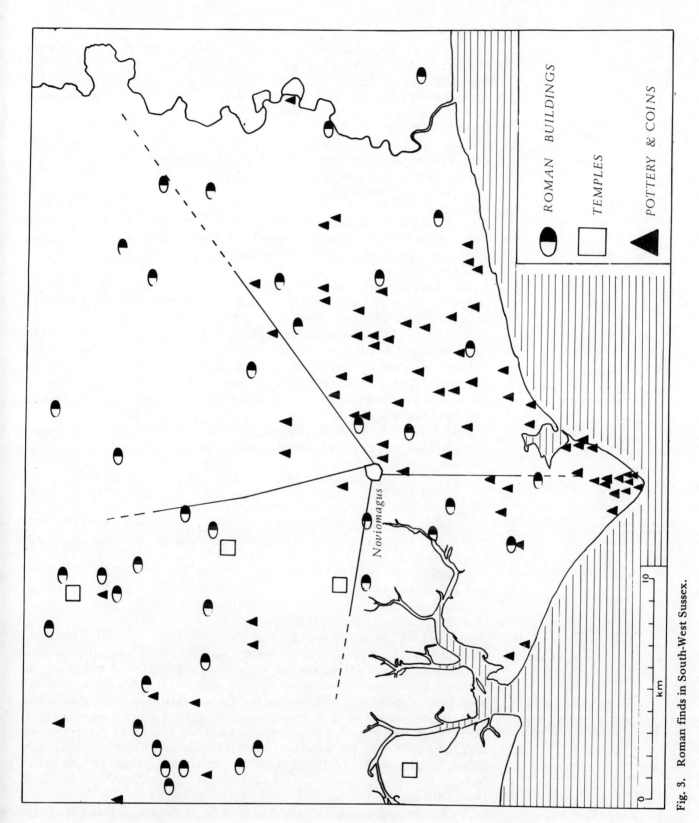

Fig. 3. Roman finds in South-West Sussex.

53. (*continued*)
(*S.A.C.* 66 [1925], 163–172, E. and E. C. Curwen; and *Prehistoric Sussex* [1929], 96, E. C. Curwen.)

54. *Iron Age/Romano-British earthwork*   SU 8267 1100
An oval depression with a surrounding bank, which is entered from the north by a field way, may be the remains of a 'circus'.
(*W.S.C.C.* 1976.)

55. *Field-System* (Fernbeds Down)   SU 7960 1620
Late Bronze Age/Iron Age/Romano-British field-system which was once thought to be a Roman Camp.
(*Antiquity* 32 [1896], 97–8.)

56. *Iron Age enclosure*   SU 8474 1120
An oval, ditched, enclosure measuring about 125 metres by 115 metres, is visible on aerial photographs taken by Jerome O'Hea and the Ordnance Survey. It is bisected by the Roman Road.
(*W.S.C.C.* 1976.)

57. *Roman Villa* (Pitlands Farm)   SU 7971 1240
One wing of a villa, facing north, with a bath suite at the east end. Excavated between 1966 and 1969 (for full report, see pp. 101–108.)
(*J.R.S.* 57 [1967], 198; *Ibid.* 58 [1968], 231; and *Ibid.* 59 [1969], 231.)

58. *Romano-British Settlement*   SU 8025 1660
Probable villa or farmstead noted by S. E. Winbolt, who found pottery, flint-walled huts, an enclosure bank, and lynchets on the south slope of North Marden Down. This appears to be the site re-discovered in 1976 in a series of small trial holes.
(*V.C.H.* 3 [1935], 70, S. E. Winbolt; *The Times Newspaper,* 10 September 1934; and information from Dr. O'Bedwin, 13 October 1976.)

59. *Romano-British settlement*   SU 8037 1728
Pottery, coins and other objects found before 1894.
(*S.A.C.* 39 [1894], 225–64, D. Gordon; and *V.C.H.* 3 [1935], 57, S. C. Winbolt.)

60. *Romano-British settlement*   SU 8130 1730
A series of hollows, banks and lynchets are thought to be the remains of a settlement.
(*O.S.* 1954.)

61. *Romano-British settlement*   SU 8031 1153
Pottery and other objects found in 1947–8.
(*S.A.C.* 87 [1948], xii; and *O.S.* 1971.)

62. *Romano-Celtic temple* (Bow Hill)   SU 8251 1143
Excavated by Carlyon-Britton between 1926 and 1930, but not published. The structural remains appear to have been scanty, but there were considerable quantities of roof tiles (*tegulae*), nails and wall plaster, and enough postholes to indicate a roughly square timber structure about eighteen feet (5.5 metres) square, with an inner room, an open verandah and tiled roof. There were also a quantity of bricks with a wavy combed pattern which may have been used for flooring. Over 150 coins were found, ranging from Trajan to Theodosius (A.D. 97 to 395). (Information from Lt.-Col. W. D. Shaw, who excavated with Carylon-Britton as a schoolboy, and to whom thanks are due.)
Grinsell: *The Archaeology of Wessex,* 232; *VC.H. Sx.* (iii), 51; E. C. Curwen,

62. (*continued*)
   Archaeology of Sussex, 1954, 288–9; M. J. T. Lewis, *Temples in Roman Britain*, 1965, 124–5.

63. *Roman villa* (Brick Kiln Farm)—Chilgrove 1   SU 8344 1244
   Excavated between 1963 and 1969 by the Chichester Excavations Committee (see pp. 53–70.)
   J.R.S. 54 (1964), 177; *Ibid.* 55 (1965), 219; *Ibid.* 57 (1967), 198; *Ibid.* 58 (1968), 202; and *Ibid.* 59 (1969), 231.

64. *Roman villa* (Brick Kiln Farm)—Chilgrove 2   SU 8415 1364
   Excavated between 1965 and 1976 by the Chichester Excavations Committee (see pp. 80–100.)

65. *Roman building* (Long Bottom Field, Hill Lands Farm)   SU 8180 1534
   First noted in April 1971, when the field was ploughed for the first time for many years. Ploughing was to a depth of 12 inches.
   Several large sandstone blocks, similar to those used for post-bases in the aisled barn at Chilgrove 2 (pp. 88–92), were struck by the plough, and part of the base of a flint wall was seen. Other surface finds include *tegulae*, Horsham stone roofing tile and Roman pottery, much abraded, together with large numbers of flints.
   (*W.S.C.C.* 1977.)

66. *Romano-British building*   SU 873 129
   Found at the Weald and Downland Open-Air Museum, Singleton, in 1974, when the pond adjoining the blacksmith's workshop was being dug by machine.
   Excavation of the remains by the Chichester Excavations Committee showed a fragment of badly eroded wall foundation aligned roughly east-west, with some indication of a hearth. The remains were too slight to permit a conjectural reconstruction, but the absence of large amounts of building material in the vicinity suggests a small building, possibly an outbuilding belonging to a larger complex which has still to be discovered. The Roman pottery recovered as surface finds includes fourth-century colour coated wares, and is in the possession of the Weald and Downland Open-Air Museum.

67. *Roman Coin*   Site unknown
   Coin of Claudius (43 A.D.) found at Binderton.
   (*S.A.C.* 68 [1927], 279, S. E. Winbolt.)

68. *Roman Coin*   Site unknown
   Coin of Maximinus 1 (235–238) found at East Marden.
   (*S.A.C.* 67 (1926), 221, S. E. Winbolt.)

69. *Romano-British cemetery*   Area centred SU 844 136
   Dallaway notes that several small Roman 'Sepulchral urns' were discovered under the Down near Chilgrove in 1812. Harcourt recorded that seven or eight inhumations were found in 1843–5 'not more than two feet below the surface . . . on a bed of chalk'. They were all oriented with head 'a little towards the north of east' and accompanied by glass and pottery vessels, bracelets and finger rings. He noted that 'about six or seven hundred yards from the spot where they were found a large cinerary urn was discovered some years ago . . .' (presumably the 1812 discovery) . . .' and it was remarkable that, supposing a straight line to be drawn between these two spots,

there is a place without vestiges of a building on it, not far from the centre of that line, which is still denominated Castle Corner . . . Drawings of the 1843–45 discoveries were given to the Society of Antiquaries in about 1849.

Castle Corner Copse is at SU 8446 1366. The Rev. Harvourt owned land to the south of this in 1849 and W. L. Woods, on whose estate the 1843–5 discoveries were made owned the copse and land to the north. If a circle of diameter 600 yards is drawn around the copse then the 1843–5 discoveries were probably made within its northern half.

The 1812 discovery should have been made diagonally opposite it.

(*A History of the western division of the County of Sussex* 1), (1915) 168. J. Dallaway: *Archaeologia* 31 (1846), 312–7, and Pl. IX; Rev. L. V. Harcourt: *S.A.C.* 1 (1849), viii; Rev. W. D. Lewis: *Proceedings of the Society of Antiquaries* 1 (1849), 6; Rev. L. V. Harcourt: *S.A.C.* 10 (1857); *V.C.H.* 1 (1905), 329, G. Clinch; *V.C.H.* 3 (1935), 53, S. E. Winbolt; and *Tithe Map for West Dean* 1849.

The villa at Watergate Hanger, West Marden

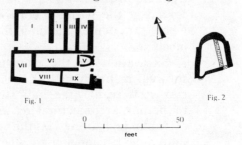

Fig. 1   Fig. 2

0 _____ 50
feet

Fig. 4

70. *The Villa at Watergate Hanger, West Marden.* (Fig. 4)   SU 774 125
Although this site is just outside the study area, it has been included in the Gazetteer because of its proximity to the Upmarden villa. It was partly excavated by Dr. Talfourd Ely, F.S.A. between 1907 and 1911.
(*Arch. Journal* 70 [1913], 11–16; *S.A.C. 40 (1896), 283; V.C.H. Sx 3* (1935), 28–9, 61.)

Commenting on the plan by Ely (Fig. 4), Mr. Roger Goodbourn* suggests that it may represent the western part and one other room, to the east of a range. Rooms VI, VII, VIII, IX and an area east of it may be a bath suite, and Room V might be a later cold bath. The 'road' to the east, and also the 'platform' referred to by Ely in 'Busto' meadow might also be the rubble from other buildings. The 'nymphaeum' could either be a latrine or possibly another plunge bath.

*We are greatly indebted to Mr. Roger Goodbourn for his comments on this and other aspects of the report.

38

References and Abbreviations

Drewett, 1977 'Rescue Archaeology in Sussex 1976'. Bulletin No. 14, Institute of Archaeology, London.

O.S.   Ordnance Survey Archaeological Records.

S.A.C.   Sussex Archaeological Collections.

W.S.C.C.   West Sussex County Council, Planning Department. Archaeological Records.

S.N.Q.   *Sussex Notes and Queries.*

S.C.M.   *Sussex County Magazine.*

V.C.H.   *Victoria County History.*

J.R.S.   *Journal of Roman Studies.*

3

Excavations at Chilgrove and Upmarden

Introduction

In the spring of 1963, Mr. Alf Tribe was ploughing a field called Wellmeadow on Brick Kiln Farm, which is situated in the Chilgrove valley on the B.2141 from Chichester to Petersfield. His plough struck a large stone object which proved to be part of a small column (Fig. 62). Through the good offices of Mr. Ken Knowles this find was notified to the writer some time later, and when the site was visited, a spread of Roman building material was noted in the growing barley. The area was photographed from the air by Mr. J. R. Boyden later in the summer, and a long rectangular building was seen as a crop mark.

By kind permission of Mr. Edward James, the owner of the site, and of the West Dean Estate, trial excavations were carried out in the autumn of the same year and these proved the existence of a Roman corridor villa with at least one mosaic. The West Dean Estate kindly isolated the whole area to allow excavation to proceed and work commenced on stripping the site the following year. At this point it was intended to carry out a purely local examination of the building with a view to preserving it from total destruction by the plough, but by a process of natural evolution the excavations grew into a research project lasting for some fourteen seasons and embracing two villas within a mile of each other and a third a few miles away at Upmarden. By then it had become obvious that the villas could not be satisfactorily studied in isolation, but must be related to their surroundings, and what began as a simple rescue project in 1963 had become the Chilgrove Valley Landscape Project by 1975 with terms of reference which cover not only the Roman period, but the Saxon, medieval and post-medieval developments. This volume is the first of two. The second will deal with the 'origin of villages study' currently being carried out, which has as its main objective the establishment of the date of the earliest Saxon settlement in the valleys north of Chichester, taking up the story where the tale of Romano-British farming leaves off. In recent years, work on the sites had to be confined to a short season each summer, due to the tremendous pressure of rescue excavation in Chichester, but this, while it has delayed the completion of the work and the publication of the report, has in the long term proved an advantage. The villas span the period from *c.* early Flavian to early fifth century; slightly shorter than the Roman occupation in Chichester, and it has been useful to compare the origins, development and decay of the country sites with the same processes in the nearby town. In Chichester, which has been occupied by a succession of cultures for over 1,900 years, the position is much less clear, due to the destruction and robbing of the Roman levels, whereas at the Chilgrove sites (though not at Upmarden), the main enemy has been the plough. Some robbing of the collapsed masonry is certain to have occurred in post-Roman times, but no quarrying of wall foundations has been noted. As a result, the processes of violent destruction and gradual decay can be seen more clearly.

CHILGROVE 1: THE VILLA IN WELLMEADOW (SU 834 125) Fig. 2

The Location
of the Sites

The villa is placed in a small valley running north-south along the east flank of Bow Hill, which thrusts southwards from the main line of the South Downs. The villa and the associated fields which may belong to it (see below), lie in the valley gravel, with the main range of the villa buildings lying just above the spring line. The Early Iron Age enclosure of Goosehill Camp (p. 34) lies just above, near the top of the east flank of Bow Hill, and a mile away to the south and also on the top of the hill, is the site of a Romano-British temple (p. 36).

Today the B.2141 runs through the valley bottom, and it is certain that throughout historical times there has been some form of road or trackway following the valley, connecting the hamlets of Binderton and Chilgrove with North and East Marden. Until fairly recently the road used to flood in wet weather, but the installation of the local water undertaking and a succession of very dry summers has lowered the water table to a point well below what it must have been in the Roman period, when it is likely that the valley bottom supported a small stream in wet weather. Trial borings in 1975 by the water authority indicated that the water table was then some seventy-five feet below the level of the road opposite the villa.

The Roman road from Chichester (*Noviomagus Regnensium*), to Silchester (*Calleva Atrebatum*), runs northwards across the top of Heathbarn Down, to the east of the villa. The line of a trackway (Fig. 7) cuts across from a point just west of the road and aims straight down the slope of the hill towards the gateway of the stockyard. This line is regularly seen as a cropmark in the upper fields and disappears in the meadow nearest the modern road. Some years ago it was noted as a hollow way, then it was estimated to be *c*. five feet deep and *c*. fifteen feet wide. Modern ploughing has now completely destroyed the profile, but it may be a reasonable assumption that the trackway is the original Roman one from the villa to the Roman road.

CHILGROVE 2: THE VILLA IN CROSS ROADS FIELD (SU 842 137) Fig. 2

In 1964 we were again indebted to Mr. Tribe, who noted that the tiles being excavated at Chilgrove 1 were similar to those he was ploughing up a mile away. A visit to the site in company with Mr. E. Jermy, then Agent for the West Dean Estate confirmed that another hitherto unsuspected Roman site was being steadily destroyed by the plough, and with typical generosity the West Dean Estate agreed to isolate the site and allow excavation to proceed.

The villa is positioned on the west slope of a small valley which branches off the main Chilgrove valley and runs north-east. The Roman road to Silchester descends from Heathbarn Down, and its course cuts diagonally across the east slope of the valley and passes within a few hundred metres of the villa, which has its main range of buildings facing towards it.

In the last century Roman burials were reported at Chilgrove (see p. 37), and although the account of the discovery does not provide a recognisable description of the site, the location 'Castle Corner' is referred to by the author, the Revd. Vernon Harcourt. Castle Corner field lies to the north-east of the villa and the south-west corner is only a few metres away from the stockyard.

The Roman road runs across it (Fig. 5), and it may well be that the burials found in the 19th century belonged to the villa cemetery.

In 1975, with the kind permission of Mr. Court of Lodge Hill Farm, Castle Corner—which is a small copse within the north-east corner of the field of the same name— was surveyed and trial trenched. It proved to be a ditched enclosure, probably post-medieval in date and no Roman burials were found within it. The profile of the ditch shows that it was constructed with a steep angle on the inside, which had signs of stone revetment and was clearly designed to keep animals out. It will be discussed in greater detail in the second report on the study area.

In spite of extensive aerial survey work over a number of years it has not been possible to map any of the fields belonging to the villa. There are a number of field banks on the west-facing slope of Heathbarn and Warren Downs, but most of these can be shown to post-date the Roman road.

THE VILLA AT PITLANDS FARM, UPMARDEN (SU 797 124) Fig. 2

The site was first reported when Mrs. Huxham, the wife of the farmer, Mr. G. Huxham, visited Bignor Roman villa and noticed that the Roman roof tiles on display were similar to those she had been digging up in her new kitchen garden. She immediately contacted the Chichester City Museum and a subsequent visit to the site established the presence of Roman building debris in the garden. Permission to excavate in the garden and the adjoining paddock and orchard was kindly given by Mr. Huxham, and the work was carried out over a number of seasons from 1966 to 1969. The villa is halfway up a small valley just below the 250-foot contour line. Chilgrove 1 is two and a half miles to the east and the villa at West Marden (p. 38) is one and three quarter miles to the west.

SUMMARY AND DISCUSSION
CHILGROVE 1

Earliest Periods

Numbers of worked flakes and cores were found during the excavations within the stockyard area, representing transient occupation by the hunter food-gatherers of the Neolithic and Mesolithic. These are briefly reported on by Richard Bradley (p. 179 and Fig. 67).

Period I: Pre-Roman Iron Age, c.2nd to 1st century B.C.

There is evidence for slight occupation during the century or so preceding the Roman occupation. Numbers of potsherds were found in the stockyard area of the later villa, with traces of a hearth and postholes of a rectangular building and a circular hut which might belong to the same period. The pattern of small rectangular fields to the south of the site probably belongs to the small settlement which must have had its nucleus nearby, and to which the ditched enclosure at Goosehill Camp may be linked.

Period 2: Roman, c. late 1st century A.D.

Pits and a number of postholes below the earliest masonry footings indicate an earlier occupation, although no ground plan of a timber building can be seen. The sparse dating evidence includes second-century samian and the total absence of first-century samian from the site may be a pointer to the date when the first buildings were erected.

42

Period 3

At some time later, and there is no evidence of date, a building was constructed with narrow ground cills of flint. Only five rooms can be identified (Fig. 8), but there may have been a corridor along the east side. At this stage there may have been a number of granaries or store-buildings on the north side, and it is possible that the timber buildings at the south end may also belong to this period. The stockyard at this time may have been enclosed by a stockade.

Period 4, Phase A: c. late 3rd to early 4th century

Probably towards the end of the third century the villa was rebuilt on almost the same plan but on a larger scale, with a bath-house at the south end. A new wall was built for the stockyard, with barns of masonry construction built against it on the inside.

Period 4, Phase B

Later on, in the fourth century, there were a number of modifications to the bath-house and a mosaic was added to Room 6, with an additional room being added to the north end of the range. This also had a mosaic, constructed above a cross-flue hypocaust, and the impression is gained of a prosperous farmer equipping himself and his family with the latest modern luxuries.

Period 5: late 4th to 5th century

By some time near to the end of the fourth century a dramatic change had taken place. By then, part of the villa had been burned down; the bath suite was robbed of building stone, and an iron-working forge had been built on the floor in Room 8. Other rooms showed signs of 'squatter' occupation. In the stockyard there is some evidence to suggest that corn drying went on until the end of the life of the villa, which implies that the land continued to be worked. It is not known for how long this period lasted. The coin series ends with Magnentius (363 A.D.), but it is possible that about this time most of the labour force may have been based on Chilgrove 2, with which the villa may have been amalgamated.

CHILGROVE 2

Period 1: Roman, c. 2nd century

As at Chilgrove 1, the earliest period was in timber, and only traces of two buildings could be identified. These were surrounded by a ditched enclosure of which only part could be traced.

Period 2: (undated)

At this stage, one of the buildings was rebuilt as a range of five rooms with a corridor. Another building, possibly a barn, was built on the north side of it.

Period 3: c. late 3rd to early 4th century

The main building (Building 1) was rebuilt on masonry walls of flint and on a larger plan, with modifications to the corridor. The ditched enclosure, which by then had silted up, was replaced by a stockyard wall on a smaller plan.

**Period 4: c. first
quarter 4th century —
mid 4th century**

The villa was again enlarged, with the barn to the north of Building 1 being replaced by a large aisled building of masonry construction. This structure, which was probably a barn, was modified several times during its life. At the south end of the site, a new wing in masonry replaced the earlier timber buildings, and a bath suite was constructed at the east end. Another barn was built against the north-east side of the stockyard wall.

Probably during this period, the rooms of the main house (Building 1) were laid with tessellated floors, with a mosaic in the principal room. Building 2, the aisled barn, had three rooms inserted into the south end, one of which had a tessellated floor with a design of nine circles upon it.

A decline in the living standards is perceptible in the late fourth century. The aisled barn was further modified, and a series of hearths and a large bread oven built within it. The floors in Building 1 became worn and were patched with Horsham tiles and it is possible that the bath-suite may have been partially demolished and turned over to corn drying.

At some stage the aisled barn was destroyed by fire and possibly part of Building 1 also. There is some evidence for makeshift use of some parts of the old bath wing (Building 3). Hearths were built upon floors, a roof with a central post-hole was erected over one room, and hurdle marks in the floors suggest that livestock may have been penned in them. The coin series ends slightly later than Chilgrove 1, with Valentinian 1, but the length of time the latest coins remained in circulation cannot be conjectured.

UPMARDEN: THE VILLA AT PITLANDS FARM

Very little is known of this villa, due to the fact that only one wing of the main building, a small section of the stockyard and part of a ploughed-out structure uphill from the farm could be investigated. Most of the villa and its outbuildings must lie below the present farm, and the garden and orchard to the rear of it. It is remarkable in one respect, in that late Saxon and medieval occupation on the site is noted, but there is no evidence of occupation in the early Saxon period.

The earliest samian ware suggests a date in the Flavian period for its origins and at the other end of the time scale, the presence of fourth-century products from the New Forest and Oxford kilns indicates that it probably functioned at least as late as the two Chilgrove villas. There is no sign of destruction by fire, nor can late 'squatter' occupation be seen in the relatively small area it was possible to excavate, but this is not to exclude the possibility. Within the range of rooms making up the bath suite, at least two phases of alteration can be seen, when the baths were enlarged and altered. This, on the evidence of the pottery, was at some time after the late third century and could easily have been during the early fourth, when similar improvements were taking place at the other two villas.

DISCUSSION

Of the three sites excavated, only Chilgrove 1 can be seen to have any pre-Roman antecedents and even here there appears to be no direct link with the people using the land in the late first century B.C., but this may be misleading. The earliest structures below the fourth-century villa cannot be dated closely, but the date indicated by the earliest samian is late first to early second century.

It is possible that the farm began before that, and that the inhabitants were down on the subsistence level and unable to spare the cash for luxury items. The situation is slightly different at Chilgrove 2, where the total samian is much less than at Chilgrove 1, perhaps implying a smaller and poorer establishment in the early years, and here the earliest samian seems to be of early Antonine date, which suggests a later starting date. On balance therefore, it seems likely that both farms had their origins in the early part of the second century, but this is not to rule out the possibility of an earlier site near to Chilgrove 1 which might have had direct links with the pre-Roman Iron Age. At Chilgrove 1, the shadowy field bank which surrounds three sides of the villa (Plate 2) is intrusive into the Iron Age field pattern, being at a different angle, which is a clear indication that the villa came later than the fields, At Chilgrove 2, no trace of Iron Age occupation was found, nor has field walking in the neighbourhood produced any pottery to date, and as far as can be seen, the villa was erected on a site previously unoccupied.

Any estimates of the extent of the land farmed by the three villas must necessarily be highly speculative. It is possible that they may all have extended their acreage as the owners became more prosperous, but originally the holdings might have had as little as 200 to 250 acres under cultivation, assuming a mixed farming basis. Comparison with several small farms in the same area today suggests that perhaps something in the neighbourhood of 150-200 acres is needed for a family farming unit employing no staff and operating mainly as dairy farmers, growing only a certain amount of cereals for stock. To farm the same acreage in the Roman period, allowing for a high proportion of arable might require in the region of fifteen workers to carry out the seasonal tasks of ploughing, sowing, harvesting and manuring, so as to have something more than mere subsistence after taxes had been paid to the government.

It seems from the evidence of the pottery and buildings that the two Chilgrove villas remained quite modest establishments up to the late third or early fourth century, with the buildings being of timber, sometimes on ground cills of flint, and the impression is gained that the inhabitants were well above subsistence level by the end of the second century, but not yet in a position to make large-scale improvements in their farm buildings. By the early fourth century the position is quite different. At both Chilgrove villas and the Upmarden one there is a significant improvement, with the buildings being replaced in stone, or at least half timbering; with bath suites being added, and mosaics laid in the principal rooms. At this point some comparison between the three villas in terms of material wealth may be possible. The bath suite at Chilgrove 1 was a modest affair, added on to the main range of rooms which made up the living quarters. At Chilgrove 2, where two wings of domestic quarters had developed, the bath suite was of similar proportions, but the total size of the living accommodation if the aisled barn is included is more than twice that of its neighbour. At

45

Upmarden, only the range of rooms connected with the bath suite have been excavated, but the baths are superior in size and construction to the other two and may point to a larger and more prosperous establishment. At this stage in the fourth century it is fairly likely that the two Chilgrove villas were separate concerns, and it is a fair measure of the prosperity of Romano-British farming at this time that the owners should have sufficient surplus from their production to indulge in luxury building. The surplus available to them must have been influenced by a number of factors, such as the type of farming practised, whether mainly arable, or with the emphasis on sheep and cattle, and the size of the undertaking. Above all, there must have been an expanding market.

An attempt has been made to assess the acreage of Chilgrove 1 in the fourth century on the basis of the likely land available for arable, assuming that then, as now, only the lower part of the western slope of Bow Hill was ploughed and allowing for cultivation on the east side of the valley almost up to the Roman road (Fig. 5). It is possible to envisage the northern boundary of the farm as being just north of the road and track junction at Brick Kilm Farm (SU 835128) with perhaps the southern boundary being the track coming down from Bow Hill at the junction between the B.2141 and Binderton Lane. It is likely that the area north of the suggested northern boundary would be within the territory of Chilgrove 2, and south of Binderton Lane there may well be another villa. This conjectured farming unit, occupying the centre part of the Chilgrove Valley, adds up to *c.* 280–300 acres, and it is noteworthy that the acreage of the original Brick Kiln Farm was *c.* 265 acres. If it is assumed that in the early life of the villa the farming was mainly arable, with one-third lying fallow each season, then something in the region of 200 acres would have to be ploughed between the autumn and spring which, estimating a day's work for one ox-team as about half an acre, and allowing for possibly six ox-teams, would require 66 working days to plough the 200 acres once only. In fact, Columella (*Res Rustica*) states that an *iugerum* (about three-fifths of an acre), required four day's labour, which includes three ploughings and the sowing. He was writing about agriculture in Italy towards the end of the first century, B.C., where soil conditions varied widely, but it is possible that in the Chilgrove area the light valley gravels could have been broken up by two ploughings (one each way), which would reduce the task by a third. Even so, a total of *c.* 132 ploughing days would be required which, allowing for bad weather, would take from the beginning of autumn up to the end of the winter if six teams were used, and longer if less than six. The iron ploughshare tips found at both Chilgrove villas were designed for use in stony soils (Fig. 50), but would have been of doubtful value on areas where clay capping survived.

Columella gives no details of the size of ploughing team, but probably two men were required, one to lead and one to plough. In addition to the plough teams, men would be required for hoeing, animal husbandry, and the many maintenance tasks required on a farm, which would support a number of cattle, sheep and pigs. The figure of *c.* 300 acres mentioned above allows only for the arable, and, although the cattle would be grazed on the fallow, it is likely that the sheep grazed the upper slopes of Bow Hill and Heathbarn Down, while pannage for the swine would be had in the coppices in the coombes. In all, it is likely that a farm of the estimated size of Chilgrove 1 would require between 15 to 20 people to

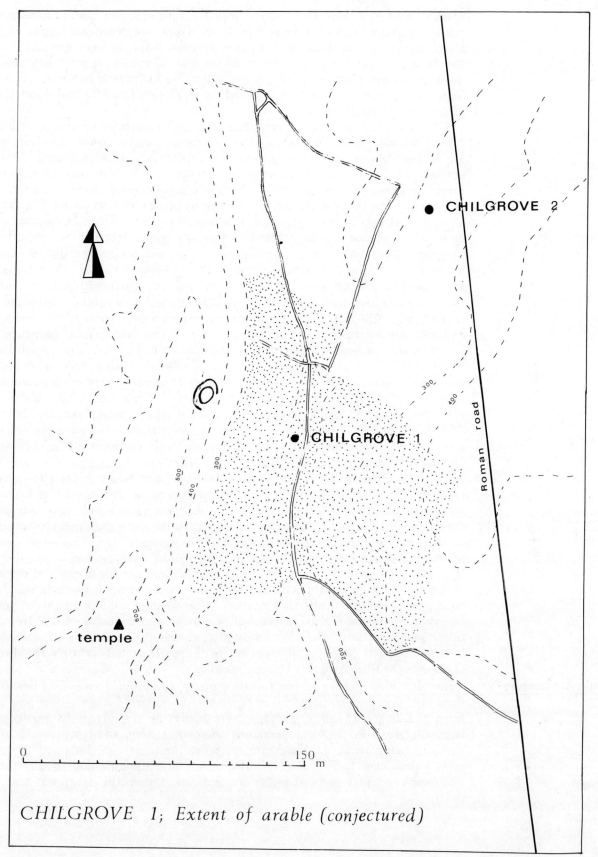

CHILGROVE 1; *Extent of arable (conjectured)*

47

Fig. 5

work it. Some of these would have been the farmer's own family, some possibly poorer relations, and some may have been slaves. Free contract labour might be hired during harvest time. Not all the workers might be accommodated within the farm precincts and the farm workers who were not 'family' may well have lived in a small settlement which has still to be identified, but which may have been very similar to those recognised by Professor Cunliffe and John Budden at Chalton (*Cunliffe* 1973, 182-4).

By the fourth century the emphasis may well have been on sheep, with arable taking second place. The advantages of sheep farming were manifold. It was much less labour intensive, a very important factor in a society that was suffering from a chronic shortage of manpower; it provided meat both for domestic consumption and the market, and a good wool crop. Certainly, in the late third and early fourth century, British woollen products were being exported abroad, and two items figured in Diocletian's edict of 301 A.D. Perhaps significantly, the percentage of sheep bones in the upper levels in the stockyard at Chilgrove 1 is slightly higher, but again it might mean no more than an increase in the amount of mutton being eaten. By the mid-fourth century there is evidence to show that Britain was exporting corn regularly to the Rhineland, and that this was increased during an emergency in 359 A.D. to a total of 600 bargeloads. (*Frere* 1967, 280). These are no more than pointers to some of the reasons for a significant increase in the prosperity of Romano-British fourth-century villas in which the farmers at Chilgrove and Upmarden had a share. For British farmers to be able to export part of their surplus abroad there must have been a steady increase in demand on the home market, and the prosperity of the countryside must have directly reflected the rising prosperity of the towns. The villas reached their maximum prosperity in the first quarter of the fourth century. In nearby Chichester there is clear evidence from recent excavations (*Chichester*, 3, pp. 76-80) that the early fourth century was a period of rebuilding and expansion, with new town houses being built and frontages extended and a spread of urban development outside the East and South gates (*Down*, forthcoming). The Chilgrove and Upmarden farmers were well placed to supply the increased market with meat, corn and wool, and these staple products sold to the town would have helped to provide the cash for the mosaics and bath suites.

This period clearly demonstrates a well-organised rural economy able to produce and market both cereals and the products of animal husbandry on a large scale, a big stride forward from the simple subsistence farming of the earlier centuries. At Bignor, which is not far from the study area, the villa was rebuilt on a grand scale in the fourth century (Fig. 6), and while it might be possible to explain it as the seat of a very rich personage whose wealth derived from some other source, it is much more likely that it was the centre of an estate which became enlarged and very prosperous in the early fourth century for the same reasons as the Chilgrove and Upmarden villas.

The later 4th century

By the third quarter of the fourth century, Chilgrove 1 ceased to be used for domestic occupation, possibly as the result of a fire which affected part of the main building range, but, perhaps more likely, as a result of its amalgamation with Chilgrove 2. The coin series is important here, the last issues found on the site being those of Magnentius, whilst the series at Chilgrove 2 goes on until Valentinian 1 (Fig. 47). The absence of Valentinian coins, usually plentiful on fourth century villa sites, is an indication that the farm was not being

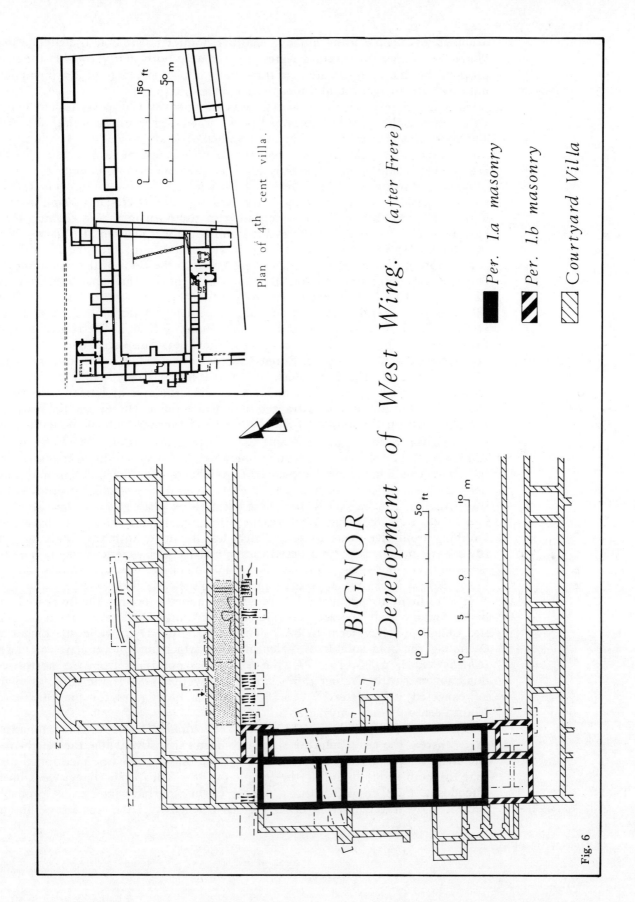

Plan of 4th cent villa.

BIGNOR
Development of West Wing. (after Frere)

Per. 1.a masonry

Per. 1.b masonry

Courtyard Villa

Fig. 6

49

occupied by people using money. Another pointer is the colour-coated wares. While New Forest and Oxford wares are present at both sites in roughly the same proportions, the numbers are over three times greater at Chilgrove 2, which might indicate both a larger establishment and a longer life (p. 197).

At some time after the last coin was dropped at Chilgrove 1, and before Valentinian I, the farm buildings had been turned over to iron working and other activities. It seems evident from the number of finds in Room 14, which was used as the rake-back for the forge, that a wide range of iron tools and other articles were manufactured, possibly for more than one establishment.

While the living quarters were being used in this fashion, with evidence of a rough makeshift roof over Room 7, the land was almost certainly being worked, with small corn-drying ovens functioning in the barn in the stockyard. There may be some evidence that the main labour force was centred at Chilgrove 2 at this time. The very large bread oven in the aisled barn (Building 2), and the concentration of a series of smaller ovens cut into the floor of the barn indicates considerable domestic activity. By then it is likely that the bath suite at Chilgrove 2 had been turned over to corn drying, and the re-flooring of the caldarium with tegulae may be an indication of this. Later still, the aisled barn at Chilgrove 2 burned down, and possibly Building 1 also. The Horsham stone tiles from the roof of the barn covered the floors and bread oven, and were not disturbed again, except in Room 7 where there is evidence for some salvaging of sound timbers. The fire, which might well have stemmed from the activities within the aisled barn, need not have signified the end of human activity on the site, as the attempt to salvage building material might indicate the will to rebuild, even on a makeshift basis. Room 15 at the west end of the bath-house had a central posthole inserted and there were many hurdle stake-holes in the floor, and Rooms 12 and 13 in the same range had been modified to allow carts to enter. This might have happened before the fire, or the building may have been adapted when the others were burnt down; it is incapable of proof either way. All that can be said is that these events took place at some time after the latest coins of Valentinian 1 had reached the site, and the time could have been anything from five years to several decades. By then, both the farms and the town were making do with a deteriorating coinage and were reverting to a barter economy. For the villas, the wheel had come full circle, from subsistence farming in the early second century to the same state in the early fifth.

It is difficult to postulate a time when a money economy finally ceased and barter became again the accepted method of trading. The latest Roman issues in the Chilgrove valley seem to be Valentinian 1 (364–375), while at Chichester, excluding the gold solidus of Valentinian III which may never have circulated (*Chichester*, 2, p. 33, No. 77), the coin issues published from the north-west quadrant end with Gratian (367–383), roughly the same as the villas, as might be expected (*Chichester*, 3, p. 339). Comparable figures for the three sites (fourth-century coins only), are:

Chilgrove 1 (93); Chilgrove 2 (71), N.W. Quadrant; (136), but it is emphasised that, whereas the two Chilgrove sites have been exhaustively dug, the North-West Quadrant sample is from one area of the town only. It must be mentioned here that the coin series found at the temple on Bow Hill (p. 36 above) went on to Theodosius (378–88 A.D.), but a temple might well have later coins, probably deposited by travellers from other regions reached by later coin issues. In any case, on the available evidence it seems that the region around Chichester was using a bronze coinage which was not replenished in the last fifteen years or so of the fourth century. Many of the coins of the fourth century found in and around Chichester show surprisingly little wear, possibly because they may have been hoarded and used only for certain transactions where simple bartering was not possible. The farmers of the prime sites in the Chilgrove valley must always have been self sufficient, and the absence or near absence of a money economy would have made little difference to their basic standard of life other than to deny them the luxuries hitherto obtainable at the local markets. The first casualty of a collapse in the money economy would have been the large pottery factories at Oxford, Alice Holt, and the New Forest, and supplies of the fine colour-coated wares from these regions would have dried up. It is possible that, for a short while, locally-based enterprises might have tried to fill the gap, and the small percentage of colour-coated wares of unknown manufacture which are found in Chichester may be accounted for in this way (*Chichester,* 3, p. 261). The domestic pottery made by local potters might still be traded for agricultural produce on market days, but some, at least, must have been made on the farms. This was a skill which never entirely died out in the country districts and, as our own experiments on site have shown, good hand-made wares finished on a slow wheel can be made from the clay obtainable from the clay cappings surviving on the Downs and fired in a simple kiln or on a bonfire with very little trouble.

It is possible that the amalgamation of the two Chilgrove villas, which is implicit in the coinage and pottery at some time before Valentinian, may have been on a larger scale and involved other villas in or near the valley which have not yet been found. There may be another late-fourth-century 'home farm' which was the focus for farming in the valley, something perhaps on the scale of Bignor, not yet discovered, but this is felt by the writer to be unlikely in view of the intensive ploughing of recent years, unless it exists below woodland which has not been ploughed in recent memory. This, however, is speculation. What *can* be said is that the obvious deterioration in the villa buildings, with the living quarters being converted to industrial use, and one villa being virtually empty of occupants, need not be interpreted as a series of disasters. The amalgamation of a number of farms in the Chilgrove valley, especially if sheep farming was practised on a large scale, would mean a number of redundant farm buildings which would rapidly become run-down. A 20th-century parallel for such a situation exists on the same land today. A study of Warren Farm (SU 841 133), for example, would show that the stockyard became derelict after World War Two, with the farmhouse being used by one of the farm staff (the shepherd), while the rest of the building became overgrown with nettles. It would be easy for an archaeologist excavating the site some centuries later to prove that the house continued in use after the farm buildings fell down, but it would be entirely wrong to assume that the land went out of use. In fact, it was amalgamated with Brick Kiln Farm, which is now part of a larger farming complex of about two thousand acres in extent, and incorporates the following units:

Brick Kiln Farm (SU 835 128). Farm manager's house let, most of old farm buildings demolished, much rebuilding.

Warren Farm (SU 841 133). Farmhouse occupied by shepherd. Stockyard by farm out of use and derelict.

Preston Farm (SU 854 112). Occupied by farm manager and is the focus of the new complex.

Home Farm, West Dean (SU 865 128). Farmhouse occupied by gardens manager; farm building still in use.

Broom's Farm, Chilgrove (SU 832 155). Occupied by livestock manager, most of old farm buildings demolished.

Staple Ash Farm (SU 840 153). Farmhouse occupied by cowman; old buildings demolished.

There is a high proportion of arable farming practised today, with some sheep and dairy farming. Mechanisation and modern transport have firstly reduced the number of people required to work the land, and secondly, enabled many of those who do to live in the villages of Chilgrove and West Dean, with a few of the former farm workers' houses being sold off. Assuming a similar amalgamation of farms in the late fourth century, with sheep farming being the principal activity and an acute shortage of manpower, it is easy to see how the farm buildings would become run-down for lack of maintenance, eventually becoming untenable as living quarters.

The problem, in the twilight years of the province, would have been the replacement of old and damaged buildings, and such repairs as were possible were necessarily rough and ready ones, with apparently no desire or capacity to rebuild to the old standards. The end point for the Chilgrove villas is shrouded in mystery, but it could have been well on into the fifth century, or even later still before they became deserted ruins and the land reverted to scrub. It is at this point that the question must be asked, 'Where did the people go?' Did they flee to the town for refuge? Did they all die of plague? Or did they leave the isolated and run-down villas and live in village communities (perhaps the forerunners of the present hamlets), cultivating as much of the land as was possible and necessary and occasionally using the old villa buildings for penning the sheep and cattle, using the roofless walls for shelter in bad weather, building the occasional ramshackle roof to keep the rain out in lambing time?

In Chichester, which cannot be separated from the countryside around it, the evidence seems to suggest a slow decline, with the public amenities falling into decay (*Chichester*, 3, pp. 82-3), and it is impossible to conjecture how long the decline lasted. But it can be said that the absence of pagan Saxon artefacts of the fifth and sixth centuries, or of any cemeteries of the same date either in or near Chichester, suggests, not a period of abandonment (*Welch* 1978, p. 27, but, much more likely, the survival of a late or sub-Roman town sufficiently strong to dominate the region immediately around it. There is really no reason why this should not be so, as all the while there was sufficient force to man the walls, the taking of the old *civitas* by force would have been an expensive and unprofitable adventure for the Saxons, and it is likely that the town and the countryside around it may have existed for some years as an independent entity within a kingdom otherwise dominated by Aelle and his sons. The problems for the fifth-century inhabitants of Chichester would arise when there were not enough men to defend the walls, when the city would cease to be a refuge and become a trap. If this situation had arisen during the fifth or sixth centuries it is surprising that the news of it did not find its way into the *Anglo-Saxon Chronicle,* and this may be yet another pointer, albeit a negative one, towards the possibility of an enclave where Saxon penetration had not been achieved. It may well have been as late as the early seventh century before the area was finally absorbed, probably quite peacefully.

As far as our present knowledge goes, the earliest Saxon pottery that can be identified in Chichester is likely to be seventh century in date, and nothing earlier can be seen at Pagham or Medmerry, and, discounting the sixth-century small-long brooch from St. Pancras (*Leeds* 1945, 94, Fig. 12), which may well have had a long life before it was lost, there is no metal-work which can point to an earlier date.

It may never be possible to fix the time when the final transition from sub-Roman to Saxon took place, but part of the answer may be found in the date of the earliest Saxon settlements in the Chilgrove, West Dean and Marden valleys, and the origins of villages study, which is the follow-up to the necessarily incomplete study of Roman farming discussed here, may perhaps provide some clues to this fascinating problem.

CHILGROVE 1: THE VILLA IN WELLMEADOW—THE EXCAVATIONS

Period 1: Pre-Roman Iron Age, c. 1st century B.C.

Excavation of the stockyard area in the valley bottom produced a number of sherds of Iron Age pottery together with the remains of a hearth. It is possible that the circular hut just outside the north end of the stockyard (Fig. 13) could also be of Iron Age date. It was cut into the compacted valley gravel and was partly destroyed by a large hole cut into the slope in Roman times (see below). The system of small rectangular fields in the field to the south of Wellmeadow (Fig. 7) could belong either to an Iron Age settlement yet to be discovered and of which the remains noted above were the outliers, or part of the villa field system (see below).

The slight evidence for Early Iron Age occupation probably relates to the earthworks on the east slope of Bow Hill just above the site, and it is possible that Goosehill Camp was the cattle enclosure for a nucleated settlement near the valley bottom (p. 34, No. 46). Professor Cunliffe's discussion of the pottery (p. 184 and Fig. 68) shows that it spans the first century B.C. and has close affinities with pottery from Stoke Clump, two miles to the south (*Cunliffe* 1966, 109–120), the Trundle (*Curwen* 1929, Plates 11, 12), and Castle Hill, Newhaven (*Hawkes* 1939, 269–292). There is no ceramic evidence for continuity of occupation from the Iron Age into the Roman period, although some of the pottery types illustrated might have continued into the first century A.D. The evidence of the samian wares from the villa indicates that occupation on the site may not have started until late first century at the earliest. This does not exclude the possibility of an earlier Romano-British site in the vicinity which does directly descend from the Iron Age, but regular field walking after annual ploughing has so far produced no finds which might support this theory.

The stockyard, which produced most of the Iron Age pottery, was stripped of turf over a wide area and allowed to weather during winter months. Apart from the Iron Age horizon in Trench 0.2 (Fig. 20) and the remains of a hearth, the scatter of pottery suggests no more than slight occupation. No pits were found, but several postholes inside the stockyard were discovered, which did not fit into the Roman pattern of building, and a rectangular building may be postulated (Fig. 8).

The picture suggested by the evidence is of a small settlement nearby in the valley bottom at some time in the late Iron age.

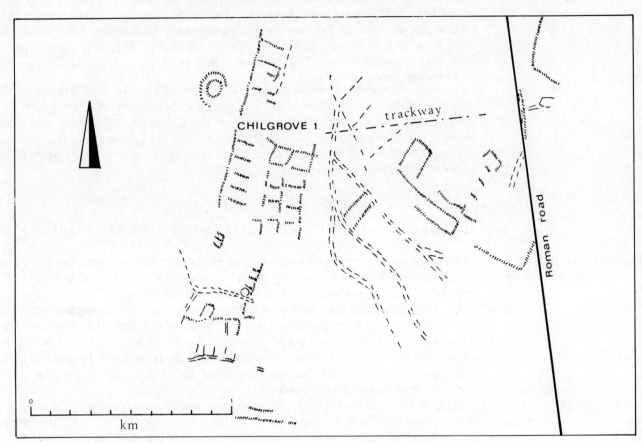

Fig. 7:   The fields around Chilgrove 1

THE FIELDS (Fig. 7)

A scrutiny of the R.A.F. 1947 aerial survey of the area, later confirmed by observations during successive seasons, showed that a group of small rectangular fields covered the field to the south of Wellmeadow. These spread partly up the lower slopes of Bow Hill and also ran around the west and north sides of the villa. Heavy ploughing in recent years has virtually destroyed the field banks, which can now only be seen where they enter the hedgerows, and as slight swellings in the field. The whole system dramatically came to life during the late winter of 1967 when snow, followed by a slow thaw, exposed the tops of the field banks, still marginally higher than the surrounding soil, before the snow had melted within the field boundaries. The resulting brown and white patchwork could be clearly seen from the western slope of Bow Hill. Aerial observation by Mr. John Boyden showed a field bank around three sides of the villa (Plate 2). This does not align with the remainder of the field pattern, and probably delimits the environs of the villa and seems to be later in date.

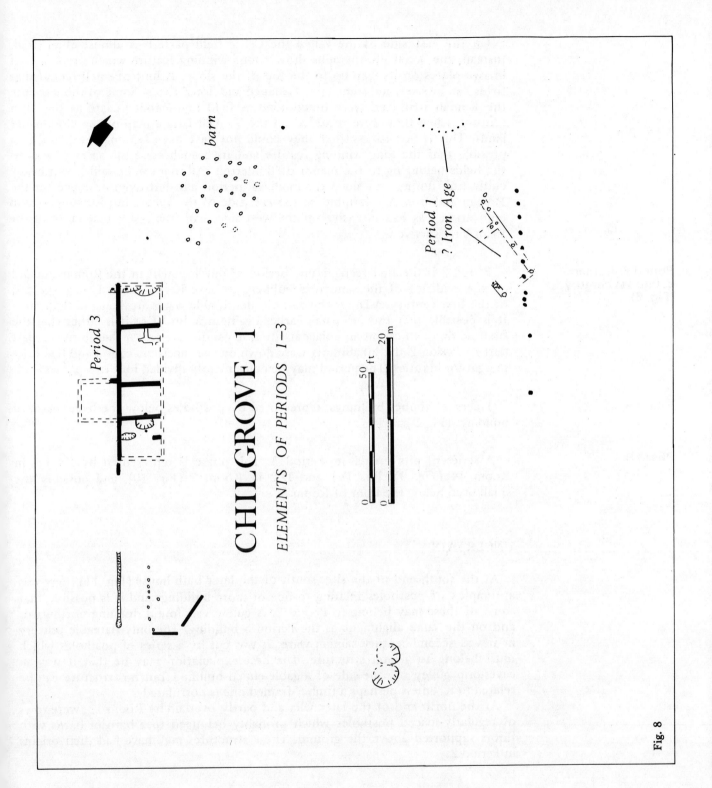

CHILGROVE 1

ELEMENTS OF PERIODS 1–3

Period 3

Period 1
? Iron Age

barn

Fig. 8

55

On the east side of the valley the Celtic field pattern is almost eliminated. Instead, the aerial photographs show a long winding feature which branches off in two places on its way up to the top of the slope. A hint of small rectangular fields can be seen, and some large L-shaped and 'long' fields. Some of these overlie the Roman road and were functioning as field boundaries as late as the 18th century, when they were recorded on the Yeakell Estate map of the Goodwood lands. This is not to say that they could not have been late medieval, and it is possible that the long winding feature and its branches are the access tracks to the fields belonging to the manor of Binderton. All that can be said is that heavy cultivation during and since the medieval period has destroyed evidence for the Roman and Iron Age farming on the east side of the valley, but for some reason cultivation was less intensive on the west side, with the result that more of the fields have survived.

Period 2: Roman, c. late 1st century (Fig. 8)

Period 2 is the first recognisable period of development in the Roman era and on the evidence of the samian is unlikely to have begun much before the end of the first century A.D., as the earliest identifiable wares are Trajanic-Hadrianic. It is possible that the farm had earlier beginnings, but if so it is either that the first buildings stood on an adjacent site not yet discovered, or that in the earliest part of Period 2 the inhabitants were down on the subsistence level and had little margin for luxuries. The period may be conveniently divided into two phases:

Phase A

Traces of timber buildings, represented by postholes below the later masonry buildings (Fig. 9).

Phase B

A series of pits pre-dating Period 3. This phase is represented by Pit L.1 in Room 14 (Fig. 9), Pits D.1 and D.2 in Room 7 (Fig. 10), and possibly the small oven below the floor of Room 8.

UNCERTAIN

At the south end of the site, south of the later bath-house (Fig. 11) there was a complex of postholes relating to one or more buildings and it is possible that some of these may belong to Period 2. A gulley was found draining northwards and on the same alighment as the Period 3 building. The only dateable pottery in it was second-century samian ware. It was cut by a series of postholes which must belong to a later structure. The best explanation may be that it was an eaves-drip gulley on one side of a gable-ended building, but no structure can be related to it, unless perhaps a timber-framed one is postulated.

At the north end of the later villa and partly overlaid by Room 15, were rows of regularly-spaced postholes which probably belonged to a barn or barns with floors supported above the ground. These structures may have had their origins in Period 2.

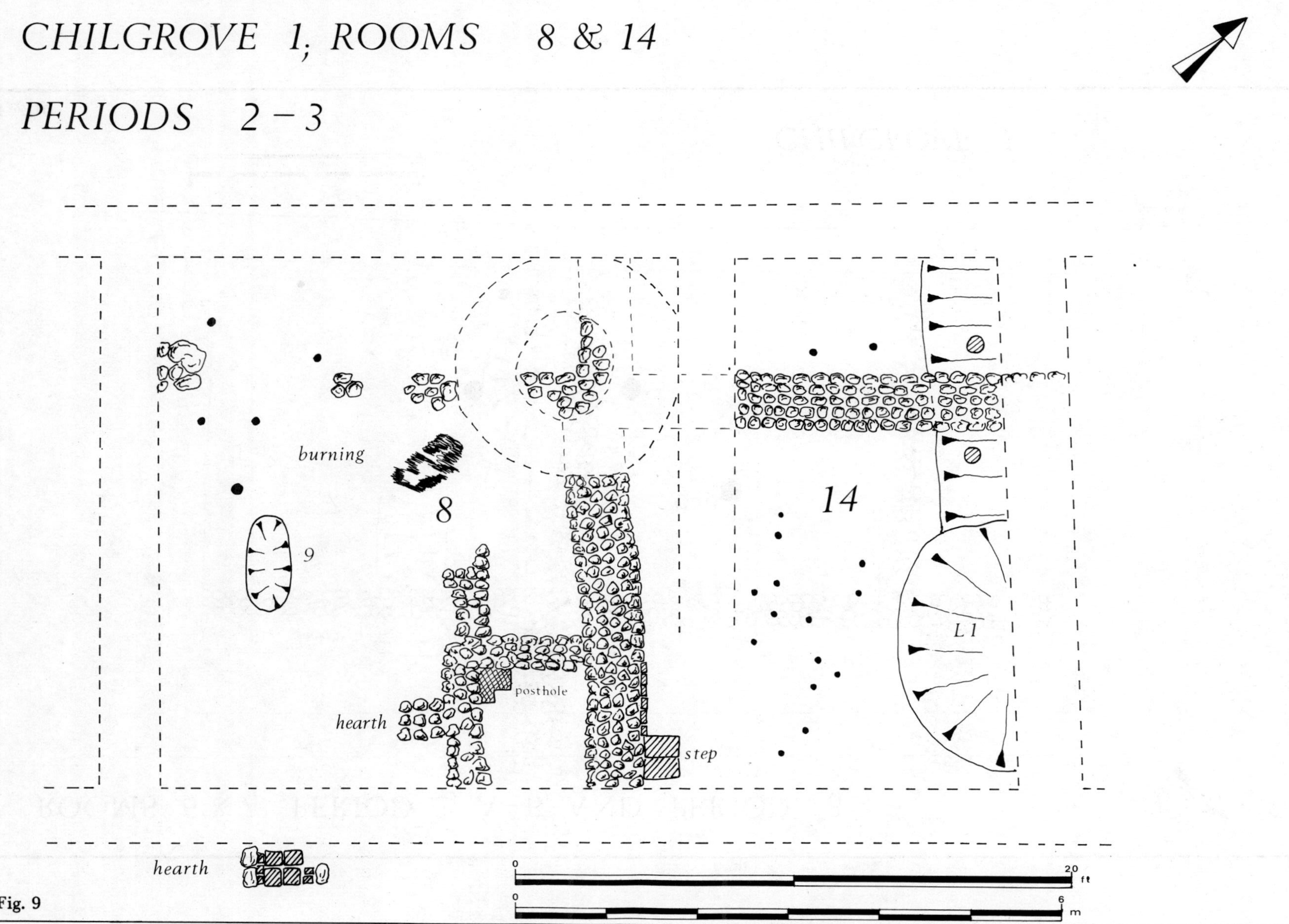

CHILGROVE 1; ROOMS 8 & 14

PERIODS 2 – 3

14

L1

step

posthole

hearth

8

burning

9

hearth

hearth

20 ft

6 m

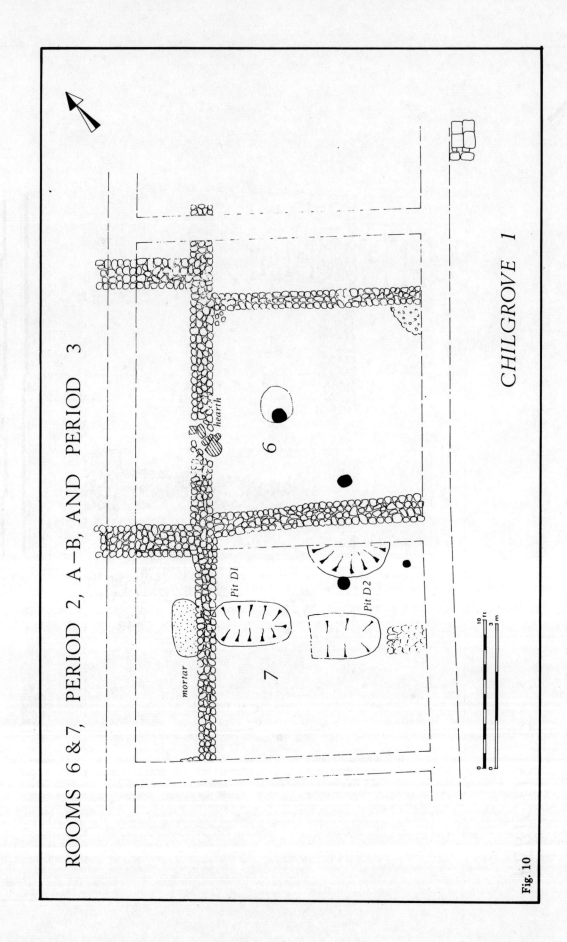

ROOMS 6 &7, PERIOD 2, A–B, AND PERIOD 3

CHILGROVE 1

Fig. 10

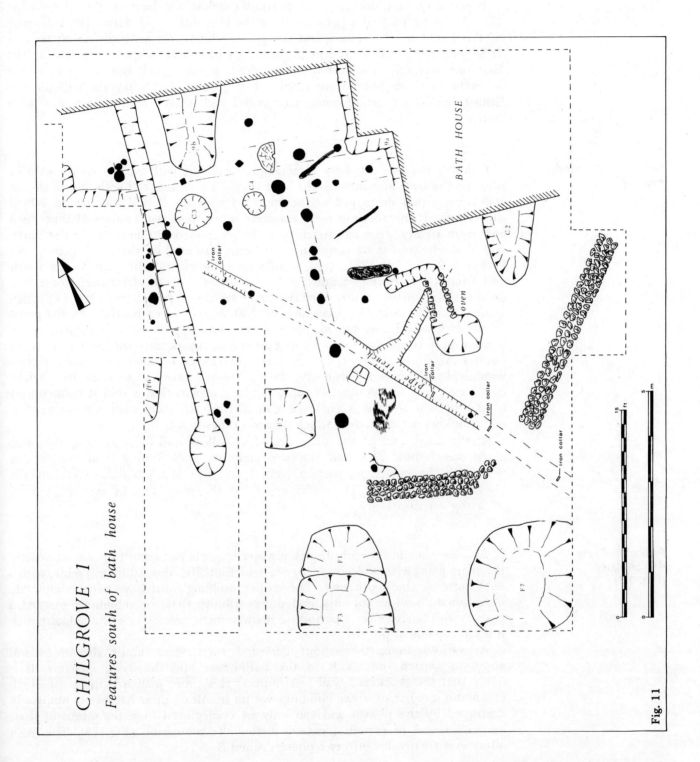

CHILGROVE 1
Features south of bath house

Fig. 11

THE STOCKYARD

It is likely that the deep-cut postholes below the later stockyard cobbling (Fig. 13) were part of a palisade along the east side of the farm. The full range of this could not be traced, but the posts, which were generally about six feet (1.83 m.) apart, had rotted in position, leaving voids in the valley gravel. The first one was only discovered by accident, when a pick was dropped, and it is likely that the posts were sawn off at ground level when the palisade was dismantled, as a crust of compacted gravel had formed across the top of each post void.

Period 3: (undated) (Fig. 12)

Period 3 is represented by a rectangular building with narrow dwarf walls of flint, on the same alignment as the later Period 4 building, and with the south-east wall being either destroyed or incorporated with the Period 4 structure. Where they survived, the footings were nowhere more than two courses of flints high and were clearly designed to carry a timber-framed building. While the north end of the house can be conjectured as being obscured by the north wall of the Period 4 Room 14 (Fig. 12) it is difficult to work out the plan of the south end from the surviving details, and it is likely that the later bath-house had destroyed it. Further south were two sections of wall foundation (Fig. 11) which were set at an angle of approximately 130 degrees to each other. At the point where they would have joined, the wall was cut away by the pipe trench for the water supply to the bath-house and Building 3. Again, only the last two or three courses of flints survived, set in clay and chalk. To have been an effective windbreak, which is a possibility, the wall would have had to stand to a height of at least four to five feet. Possibly the best explanation is that it formed part of the kitchen area, as it enclosed a small L-shaped oven, with a quern nearby, and a number of burnt areas which suggest domestic activity.

At the north end of the site, part of a shallow wall foundation of flint and chalk was found. This had traces of another wall joining it at right-angles and both fragments of walling were later than the postholes provisionally assigned to Period 2. They may represent the rebuilding of one of a series of barns on dwarf walls.

Period 4: Early 4th century (Fig. 12)

At some time in the early fourth century the villa was rebuilt on almost exactly the same plan, with wide masonry walls of flint 2ft. 3ins. (0.69 m.) wide, with a bath suite at the south end. The earlier building must have been completely demolished to allow for this, and the possibility that the rebuilding marked a re-entry to the site after a period of abandonment cannot be excluded, although it is not capable of proof.

At various times throughout Period 4 there were minor alterations and additions carried out, both to the bath-house and the living quarters. It is likely that the stockyard wall was built at this time, with a barn at the north end and a number of other buildings within it. All of these had been completely destroyed by the plough and can only be conjectured from the scraps of floor material found in certain locations below the ploughsoil (Fig. 13). The main alterations are divided into two phases, A and B.

60

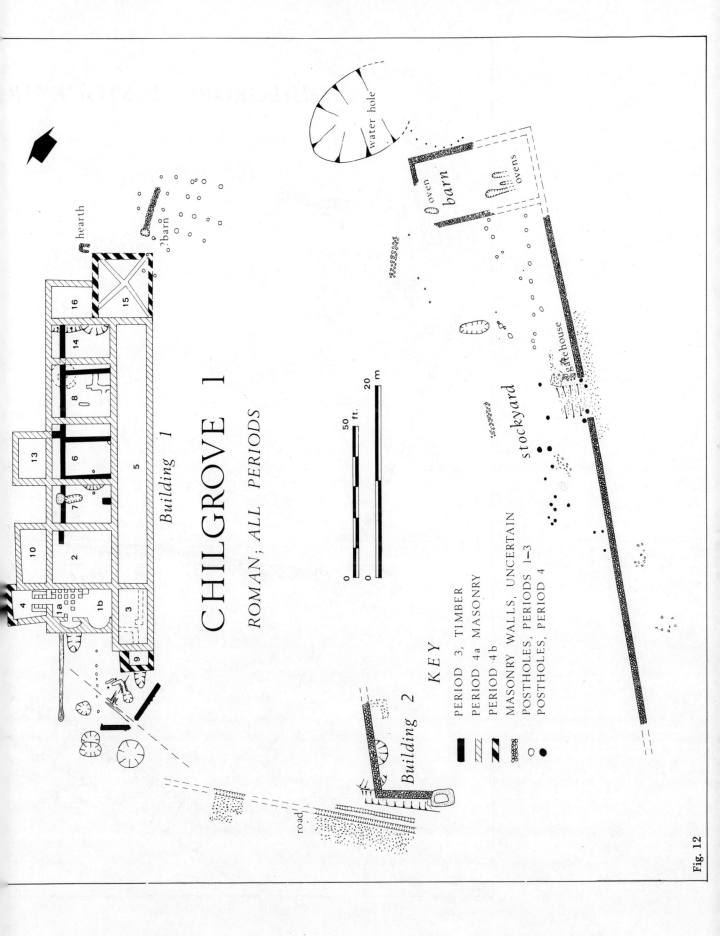

CHILGROVE 1

ROMAN; ALL PERIODS

Building 1

Building 2

hearth

?barn

16

15

14

13

8

6

5

7

10

2

4

1a

1b

3

9

barn

oven

ovens

water hole

stockyard

gatehouse

road

KEY

PERIOD 3, TIMBER

PERIOD 4a MASONRY

PERIOD 4b

MASONRY WALLS, UNCERTAIN

POSTHOLES, PERIODS 1–3

POSTHOLES, PERIOD 4

50 ft.

0

20 m

0

Fig. 12

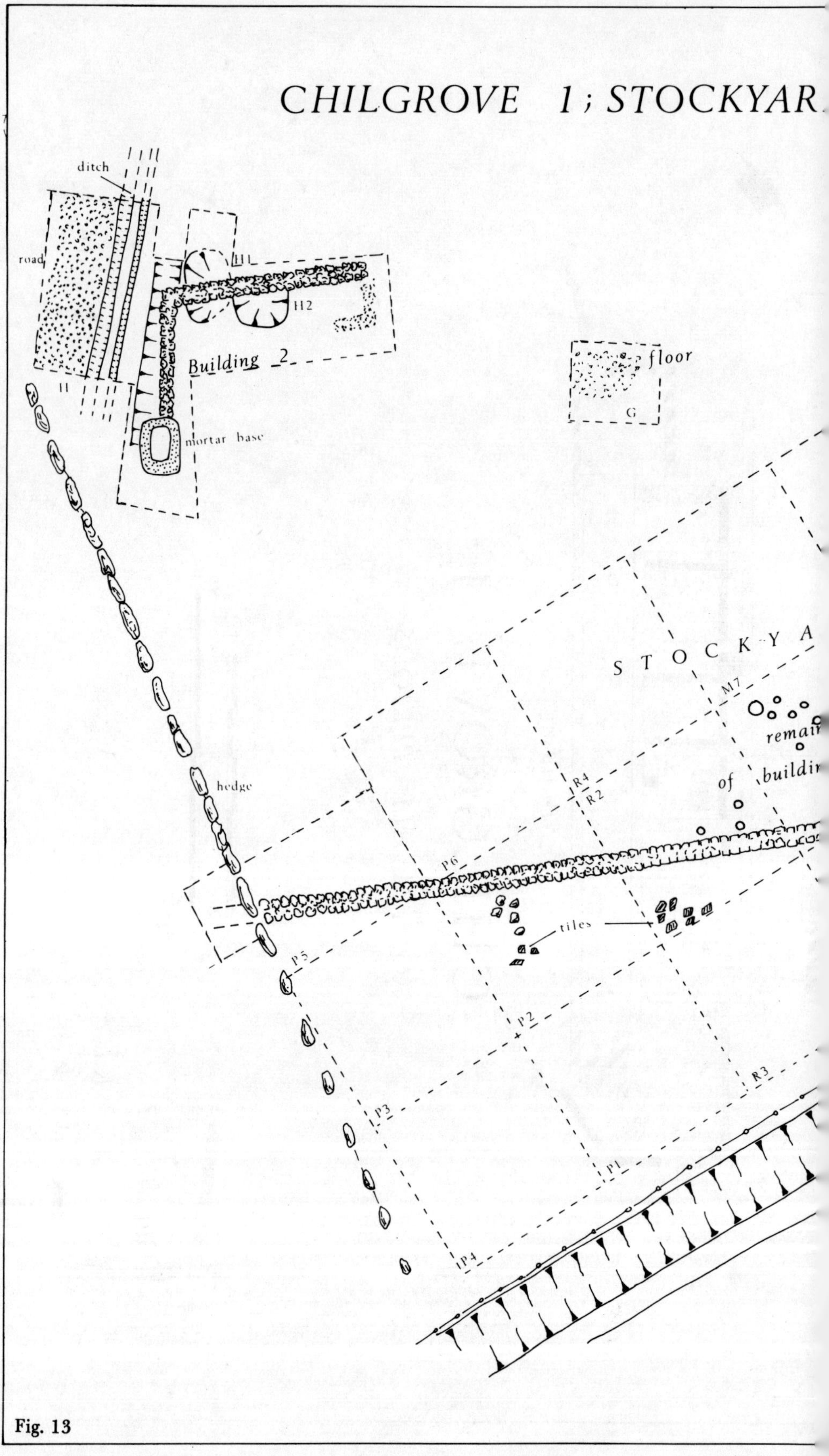

ditch

road

H1

H2

Building 2

floor

G

mortar base

hedge

STOCKYA

M7

remai

R4

of buildi

R2

P6

tiles

P5

P2

R3

P3

P1

P4

62

Fig. 13

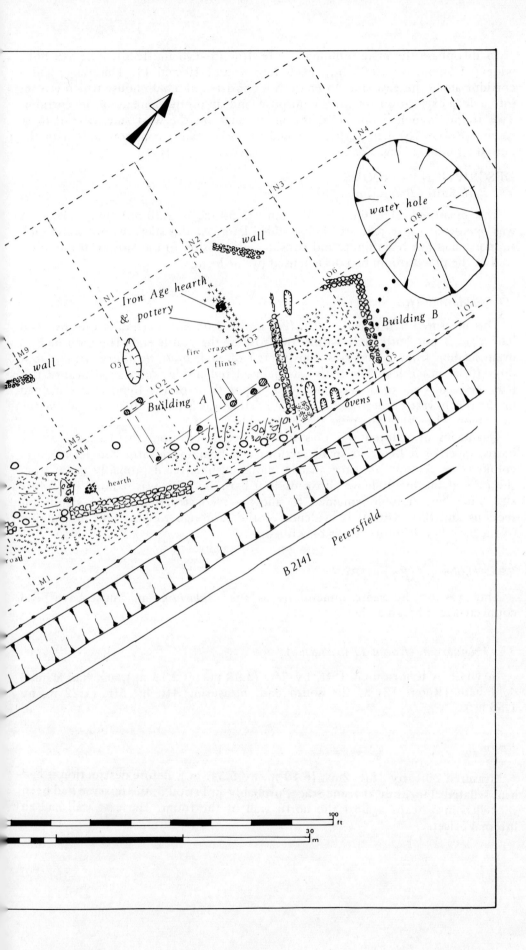

wall

water hole
O8

wall
N4

N3

N2
IO4

N1

Iron Age hearth
& pottery

O6
Building B
O7

M9
wall

O3

fire crazed
flints

IO3

O5

O2
O1

Building A

ovens

M5
M4

hearth

M1

road

B 2141   Petersfield

100
ft
30
m

63

In this phase the main building was re-structured, being 136ft. long and 36ft. wide (41.46 m. by 10.97 m.), excluding Rooms 10 and 11. This range had a corridor along the east side. In Phase A it consisted of a bath-house which was set into a deep excavation cut for the purpose, and six rooms flanked by the corridor. Two rooms branched out from the main range on the west side. One of these rooms (Room 13) had earlier antecedents as it had a common wall with the Period 3 building (Fig. 12).

DESCRIPTION BY ROOMS:
The Bath Suite—Praefurnium (Room 4)

This measured 11ft. 6ins. by 9ft. 6ins. (3.50 m. by 2.90 m.), and in Phase A was open-ended, the rear wall being added later. At this stage the hot-water tank supports had not been built, and considerable erosion of the mortar of the south wall of the praefurnium had been caused by the heat.

The Caldarium (Room 1A)

This measured 9ft. 6ins by 10ft. (2.9 m. by 3.05 m.), excluding the apse, and had a small hot bath built within the apse at the south end. The bath had no drain leading from it and was constructed of pink *opus signinum* with a floor 6ins. (0.15 m.) thick. The bath was painted red inside and a good deal of this had survived. One small section of the upper floor of the hypocaust remained in the north-west corner of the room, and this was 2ft. 4ins. (0.71 m.) above the floor base. Elsewhere, the pilae had been robbed.

Quantities of painted wall-plaster were recovered from the back-fill of the baths, most of it being in small sections and being a uniform Pompeian red in colour. One section of three-quarter moulding recovered probably came from the roof of the small alcove above the hot bath, and this was painted red, white and blue. Not enough remained to allow a reconstruction of any significant sections and this in itself is evidence of the thorough robbing and destruction of the bath-house before it was backfilled.

The Tepidarium (Room 1B)

This was of the same dimensions as the *caldarium* · and must have been connected to it by an arch.

The Frigidarium (Room 11 in Phase A)

In Phase A it measured 13ft. by 7ft. (3.96 m. by 2.13 m.), and had a small cold bath (Room 12) at the south end, measuring 4ft. by 5ft. (1.22 m. by 1.53 m.).

Room 2

Measured 20ft. by 18ft. 2ins. (6.10 m. by 5.54. m.). Before destruction it had a tessellated floor, but at some stage, probably in Period 5, the tesserae had been shovelled into heaps against the north wall of the room. The east wall had an internal offset.

Room 7

This lay to the north of Room 2 and measured 13ft. 6ins. by 20ft. (4.12 m. by 6.10 m.) internally. It had a mortar floor with a coving along the sides. A number of box flue tiles were found collapsed from the south-west corner (Plate 9 and Fig. 15) together with a few roof tiles of Horsham stone. The tiles may have been used as voussoirs for an archway connecting Rooms 2 and 7. Later squatter occupation (see below) had obscured many of the original features, but it could be seen that the Period 4 floor had partly collapsed into an earlier oven below. The same oven had been responsible for subsidence in the Period 3 wall, despite filling the west end of the pit with concrete.

Room 6

North of Room 7, measuring 20ft. by 18ft. 6ins. (6 m. by 5.64 m.). This room was floored with a polychrome mosaic surrounded by a border of red tesserae, probably in Phase B (see below, p. 108 and Plates 1 and 7). It was badly damaged in antiquity, probably during Period 5, and although well designed, was of very poor construction, being laid on no more than a few inches of dirty mortar pitched upon trampled earth.

Room 8

This was north of Room 7, measuring 17ft. 3ins. by 20ft. (5.26 m. by 6.10 m.). It had a floor of red tesserae in Period 4, laid above an earlier mortar floor which may relate to the Period 3 building. The Period 4 floor was randomly patched with greensand tesserae. It ended 1ft. 2ins. (0.36 m.) short of the north wall, and on the line of the earlier Period 3 foundation. It could well be that a beam had been laid as a permanent bench against the north wall and the floor laid up to it.

Room 14

North of Room 8. Internal measurements were 10ft. by 20ft. (3.05 m. by 6.10 m.). No features survived belonging to Period 4 due to the use of the room as a rake-back during Period 5.

Room 16

North of Room 14. It probably originally measured 10ft. by 20ft. (3.05 m. by 6.10 m.), but was either modified or demolished when Room 15 was constructed in Phase B. The most likely explanation may be that it was modified and used as a store for fuel for the hypocaust. Its reduced size was 10ft. by 14ft. (3.05 m. by 4.27 m.). No floor remained.

Room 15

North of Room 14 and constructed in Phase B since it is obviously a later addition to the range and Room 16 was modified and shortened to allow for it. It measured 17ft. by 19ft. inside (5.18 m. by 5.79 m.) and had a cross-flue hypocaust with a patterned mosaic laid above it (Plate 8). No evidence of walls or robber trenches was found, and it is concluded that the superstructure must have been of timber-framed construction. There was no trace of a firing chamber for the hypocaust, although there were signs of heat on the box flue tiles which made up the small central chamber and there was some charcoal present in small quantities within the flues. It is likely that charcoal was used as the fuel and that the hypocaust was fired from one end of the flues, probably the south-west corner.

The mosaic was almost completely destroyed by ploughing, only a few fragments remained which had collapsed into the hypocaust. The design on the surviving fragments is similar to that from Room 6 and the same size and type of stones were used in the work. It is likely that the mosaics were contemporary.

Room 10

West of Room 2 and measuring 18ft. by 8ft. 6ins. (5.49 m. by 2.59 m.). No floor survived and the function is uncertain. It could have been a store-room and might have had a planked floor.

Room 13

West of Room 6 and measuring 9ft. by 13ft. 3ins. (2.74 m. by 4.04 m.). Again, no floor survived. There was a small channel cut through the west wall, with the collapsed debris from what might have been a tiled arch lying above it. The room had its origins in Period 3, as an earlier wall ran below the north wall.

Phase B   *Main Range of Rooms and Bath Suite*

A number of alterations were made to the building during Period 4. The praefurnium had a back wall added and the presence of a tiled sill on the south site suggests that the fuel was loaded in through an aperture at this point. Probably at the same time, a hot-water tank was placed across the flue, being supported on walls surfaced with tegulae. A wall comprising flints set in clay was then built up around the tank, which must then have been accessible from the caldarium only.

The frigidarium (Room 11) was enlarged to 18ft. 6ins. by 10ft. (5.64 m. by 3.05 m.) (re-numbered Room 3), and the old cold bath was filled in and a new one constructed on the south-east corner of the building. This is designated Room 9 on the plan (Fig. 12), and dimensions were 7ft. by 5ft. (2.13m. by 1.52m.) inside. Room 15 was added to the north end and the mosaics were laid in Rooms 6 and 15.

The Water Supply to the Bath Suite

South of the building, a line of iron collars (Fig. 11) were found at a distance of 6ft. (1.83 m.) apart and it could be seen where a pipe trench had been dug with a branch line off to the cold bath. The collars were almost certainly for wooden water pipes laid for a water supply to the bath-house, but the origin of the supply is in some doubt. The spring line, before the recent lowering of the water table, would have been at some point in the stockyard near the valley bottom, and to get it up the slope to the baths would have meant first pumping it up into a water tower. This would be going to a lot of trouble when all that was needed was a well slightly uphill from the bath-house. A well was sought, but not found. Water must also have been supplied to Building 2 in the stockyard, as the pipeline extended downhill past the limits of the bath-house. No iron collars were found further downhill, but these would certainly have been ploughed out.

The Stockyard in Period 4 (Fig. 13)

It was probably in this period that the main stockyard wall was constructed, with a large building 38ft. by 21ft. (11.58 m. by 6.4 m.) at the north end. This was probably a barn. The south end of the wall ran out of Wellmeadow field and was ploughed out beyond the modern field bank, but since no signs of mortar or flints were seen in the ploughsoil beyond this point it is concluded that the wall turned west (uphill) and may have connected with Building 2. There was a gateway with a double set of postholes in the east side of the wall and the roadway into the stockyard had been well used and was worn hollow. There were faint traces of which might have been a small gatehouse on the north side of the gateway.

Other Buildings within the Stockyard

On the south side of the gateway and just inside the stockyard was a scatter of Horsham stone roofing tiles lying above the remains of a mortar floor. There were a number of tesserae of greensand in association, and two of these were in position. No limits could be set to the structure as the few postholes nearby could not be related to the floor, but it does indicate that there were some slightly more sophisticated buidings within the stockyard, and further west, large numbers of red tesserae from a completely ploughed-out floor were found. Here the absence of any posthole bases which might indicate a building may point to a timber structure, perhaps on masonry cills, which would not have survived the ploughing.

Two fragments of masonry wall were found (Fig. 13), but these could not be related to any other features, and at the north end of the main building, a short length of wall 15ft. (4.57 m.) long with a posthole at the south end is seen to be later than the postholes belonging to the earlier barn, and it might relate to Period 4.

Building 2 (Fig. 13)

Only one corner of this building remained. It was well constructed with greensand quoins and this corner *could* be the south-west corner of the stockyard enclosure. There were slight traces of a floor base of fine gravel aggregate, but everything else was ploughed away. The south wall was cut away by a sub-rectangular feature consisting of a weak mortar mix. It might have been the base for some kind of tank and is evidently later than the wall, which disappears

67

completely further downhill. The wall of Building 2 was constructed across two pits (H 1 and H 2). The latest dated sherds in Pit H 1 were two New Forest body sherds in Fabric 1A (*Fulford* 1975, 43–52) which can date from *c.* 270 to 400 A.D. This is a wide date bracket, but these two sherds are likely to fit into the earlier years of it. No dateable material was found in the second pit, and on balance it seems feasible to suggest an early fourth-century date for the construction of Building 2.

On the south side was a narrow road 9ft. (2.74 m.) wide (Figs. 13 and 18). This was bounded by a ditch which later silted up and another timber-lined box drain was built alongside it. This later drain cut through a layer of rubble which can only be interpreted as tumble from the wall of Building 2, and it seems that by the time the second drain was built, this building had fallen into disrepair. The full extent of the road could not be traced; it petered out north and south of the extent shown on the plan, but it is likely that it ran down-hill and along the outside of the stockyard wall down to the gate.

THE WATERHOLE

On the north side of the stockyard was a large oval feature which was first thought to be a well. When it was sectioned it was found to have been cut into the slope of the field in such a way as to form a waterhole. Bearing in mind the probable height of the water table in Roman times it is likely that such a hole, or perhaps pond would be a better description, would retain water for most of the year and would enable cattle to be watered without fear of accident by constructing a 'walk in' on the downhill side.

Period 5: c. late 4th century onwards (Figs. 14 and 15)

It can be said that the villa reached its peak of development in Period 4 (see discussion p. 48). Thereafter a decline set in. At some time which cannot be accurately determined, but which could have been as early as the third quarter of the fourth century, the living quarters of the villa ceased to be used for that purpose. Traces of burnt beams were found on the south end of the corridor (Room 5) where it abutted Room 2. This burning was sealed by the fallen Horsham stone tiles from the roof, and the inference is that part of the main building was damaged by fire and that no repairs took place thereafter. With the exception of the area adjacent to Rooms 8 and 14, the tessellated floor in the corridor was well preserved and protected from the plough by rubble from the walls, below which were the roof tiles. The one area free of rubble and tiles was that against the rooms mentioned above. Here the tesserae had completely disappeared and the floor had been patched with rammed chalk. Within Room 8 a circular foundation had been built upon the floor in the north-west corner and this had what appeared to be a step built against it. The large amount of forge slag present on the floor and in the adjacent Room 14 showed that iron working had been carried on,[1] with the wall between the rooms and the corridor levelled to the foundations; with Room 14 being used as the rake back and carts loaded with fuel and iron blooms fetched in across the corridor. Room 14 was full of slag and soot and had been periodically floored with thin layers of mortar (Fig. 19). The debris contained numbers of iron objects, including knives, latch-lifters, carpenter's tools, brackets, and needles, and it seems that the industry was intended to supply a wide variety of domestic and agricultural items, possibly for a larger unit than one farm.

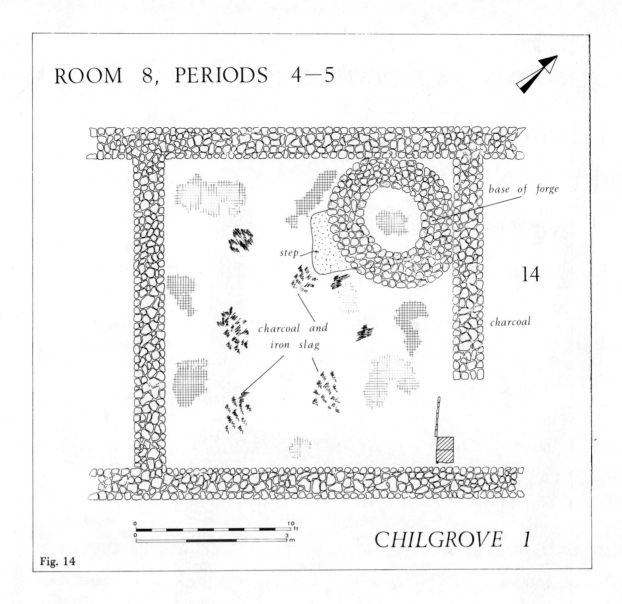

ROOM 8, PERIODS 4—5

base of forge

step

charcoal and
iron slag

14

charcoal

CHILGROVE 1

Fig. 14

In Room 6, a central posthole had been inserted into the floor (Fig. 15) and at some time an infant burial was placed below the floor in the south-east corner. In Room 2, the tesserae from the floor were shovelled up into heaps and a globular amphora inserted into the floor, possibly either as a urinal or a storage jar. By this time the bath-house had passed out of use and the pilae had been robbed from the tepidarium and caldarium. The resulting void may have been partly backfilled immediately after the robbing, and thereafter the depression became filled with a layer of dark loam containing large amounts of occupation debris. This layer (A5 and C3, Fig. 17), produced most of the 140 coins found on the site, with the majority of these being in the fill of the cold bath. The latest dated artefacts are coins of Magnentius and fourth-century wares from the

69

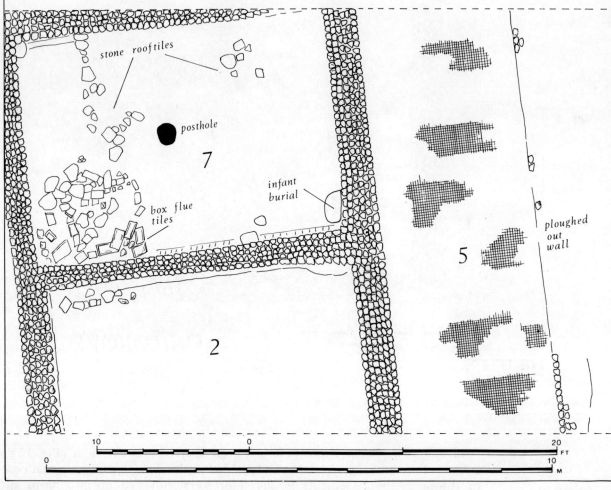

ROOMS 2 & 7, DESTRUCTION LEVELS

CHILGROVE 1

baulk

stone rooftiles

posthole

7

infant burial

box flue tiles

2

5

ploughed out wall

10   0   20 FT

0   10 M

Fig. 15

Alice Holt, New Forest and Oxford kilns (p: 180). The impression gained was that the robbing of the bath-house took place over a short period and probably while the rest of the buildings were still being used for industrial purposes. In the stockyard the position is less clear. The small corn-drying ovens found in the barn may have operated until the land ceased to be worked and the barn went out of use, as rubble from the collapsed south wall had fallen directly on to the tiles bridging the flues, but this is no more than a pointer. The evidence from Rooms 2, 8 and 14 suggests that some of the rooms were being used for iron working and others for living quarters, and the presence of the iron working points to a continuity in the use of the land since there would be little point in setting up such a project in isolation.

It is not certain, nor can it ever be established, whether or not there was a period of abandonment between the time when the last owners of the villa left and the 'squatter' occupation with the iron working started. There are a number of possibilities which can be considered and these are discussed in pp. 45–53 above.

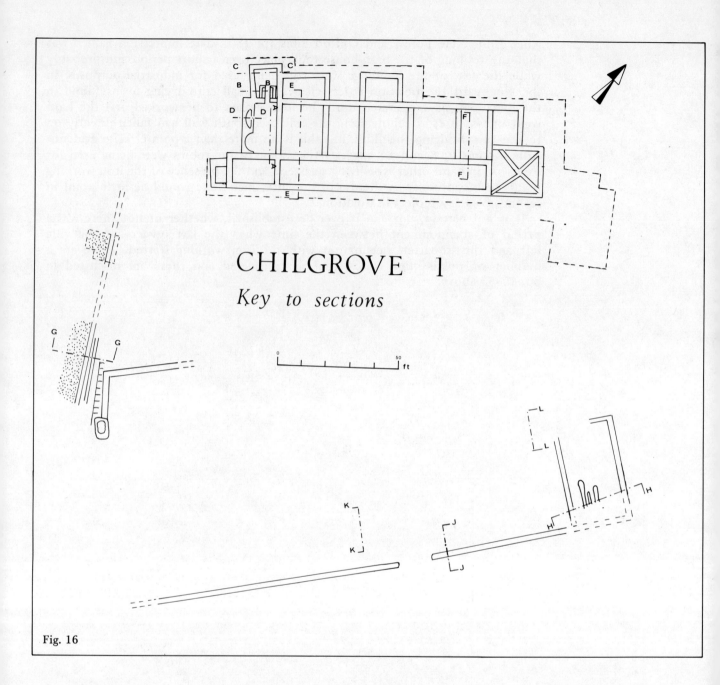

CHILGROVE 1

Key to sections

0   50 ft

Fig. 16

CHILGROVE I, BATH HOUSE

A1–A2, North section, A–A

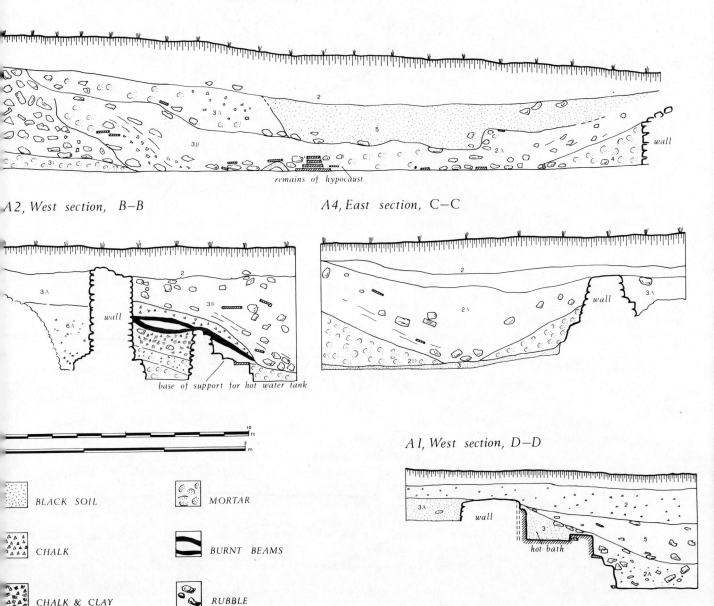

A2, West section, B–B

A4, East section, C–C

remains of hypocaust

wall

base of support for hot water tank

A1, West section, D–D

hot bath

wall

10 ft
3 m

BLACK SOIL

MORTAR

CHALK

BURNT BEAMS

CHALK & CLAY

RUBBLE

Fig. 17

CHILGROVE 1, STOCKYARD

H3 & H7; West section across road   G—G

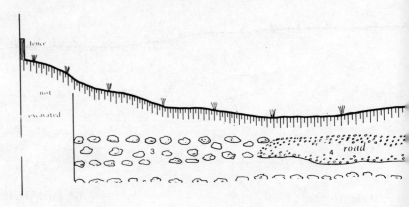

O1 & O3; East section   H — H

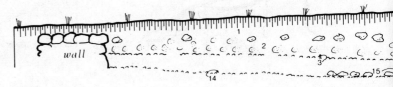

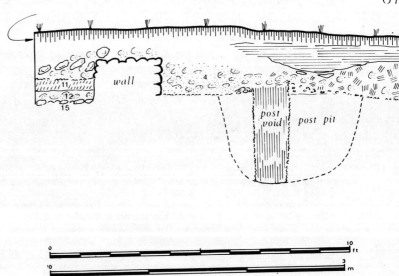

74

Fig. 18

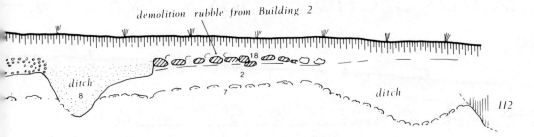

demolition rubble from Building 2

18

2

ditch
8

7

ditch

112

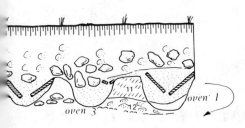

oven 1

11

oven 3

12

 GRAVEL

 COBBLED SURFACES

 DARK SOIL

 BROWN SOIL

 CLAY DAUB & MORTAR

 GRITTY SOIL

75

D1-2, SOUTH SECTION, ROOMS 2 & 5 E—

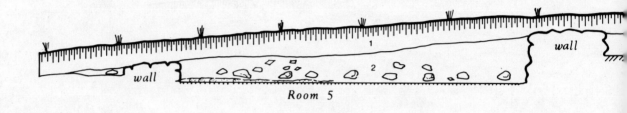

Room 5

△ CHALK   MORTAR   CLAY

L1, SOUTH SECTION, ROOM 14 F—F

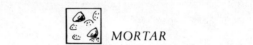

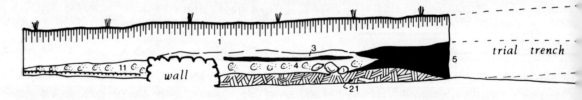

trial trench

Fig. 19

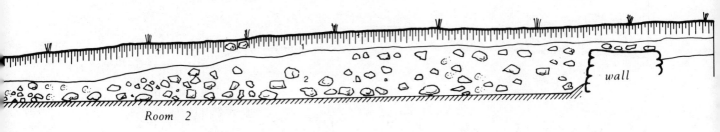

Room 2

CHARCOAL

CHILGROVE 1

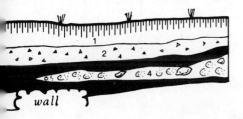

wall

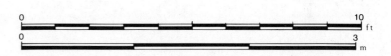

M1 & M3; North section,   J—J

M1 & M3; South section,   K—K

O2; North section,   L—L

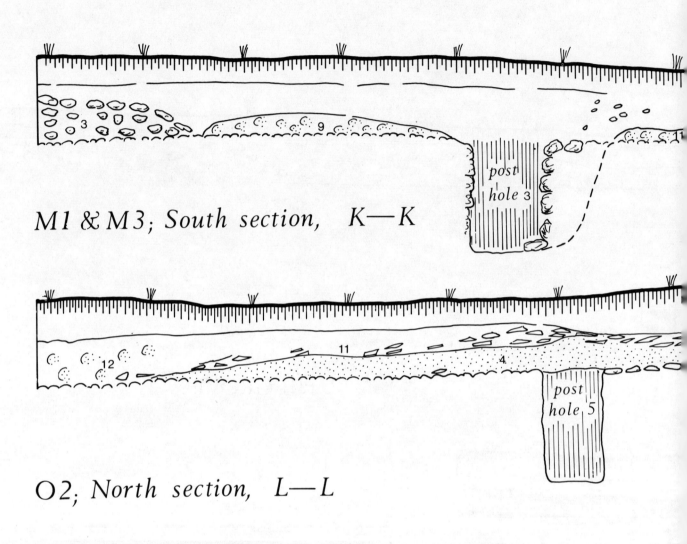

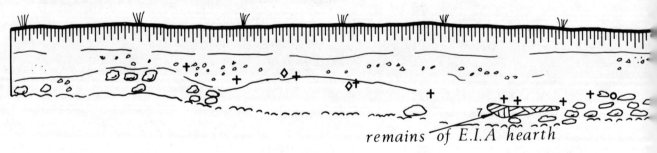

remains of E.I.A hearth

Fig. 20

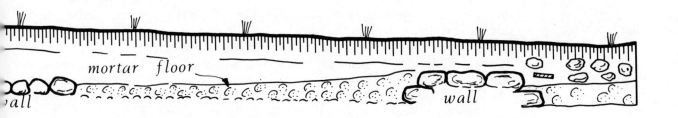

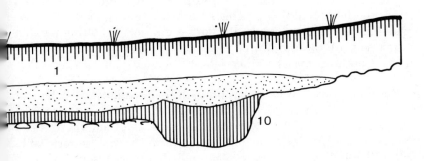

 MORTAR

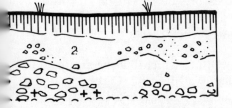

 CHALK & MORTAR

 FLINT FLAKES

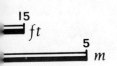

 IRON AGE POTTERY

Work commenced in 1965 on this villa, with only a small amount being done each year until Chilgrove 1 had been completed. Thereafter, a short season in August and occasional weekend work in the summer was all the time that could be spared from the rescue effort in Chichester. As at Chilgrove 1, it was found that the plough had done considerable damage, and it was only on the uphill side of the site, where soil washing downhill had covered the foundations to a greater depth, that the floors and walls survived to any extent.

Period 1: commencing c. early 2nd century (Fig. 21)

The earliest structures on the site appear to have been of timber construction and were surrounded by a ditched enclosure, only part of which has been traced. The date of these first buildings may be earlier than the end of the first century, but the earliest dated samian wares from the site suggest a date of late first to early second century for its commencement.

Two buildings were identified. The first one comprised a short length of beam slot parallel to the lip of Ditch 1 on the uphill (west) side of the site, and a set of postholes at right-angles to this slot may be the south end of the structure. Part of another building was found along the south side at right angles to the other one and below the later Building 3. This comprised timber slots of which only three sections survived, and a length of charred cill beam running parallel to, and on the north side of the structure, which might have been the outside wall of a corridor. This building may have been the living quarters, with the other one being a barn.

Of the ditches, the uphill one (Ditch 1) was quite deep and almost of defensive proportions (Fig. 31). It ended abruptly at the south end and was lost below the foundations of the Period 4 aisled barn on the north side, but there was a hint that it might have turned east (downhill), partly under the modern lane. Ditch 2 on the east (downhill) side was less deep, and there was a series of post- and root-holes along the inside lip which indicated that a fence and probably a hedge also had been placed there to keep stock away. The ditch turned uphill at the north end and was traced by resistivity survey at the south end where it was seen to turn westwards up the hill, although it did not appear to link up with Ditch 1.

Other Features (Fig. 22)

There were a number of post- and stakeholes on the west side of Ditch 2. These may belong to Period 1, but could equally belong to any of the later periods. Heavy ploughing rendered interpretation difficult, but elements of what might be wattle huts or shelters could be distinguished.

Also within the stockyard area was a mass of flints which had been spread by the plough and which seemed to be a demolished wall footing. Careful examination of this feature failed to produce a convincing wall foundation and only a ragged line of flints set in loam were left when the debris had been cleared. It might just have been a rough flint raft to carry a cill beam. A short length of slot joined it at right-angles and this had several posts set in it. It is therefore likely to have been a rough building and is provisionally assigned to Period 1, although it could quite easily have been later.

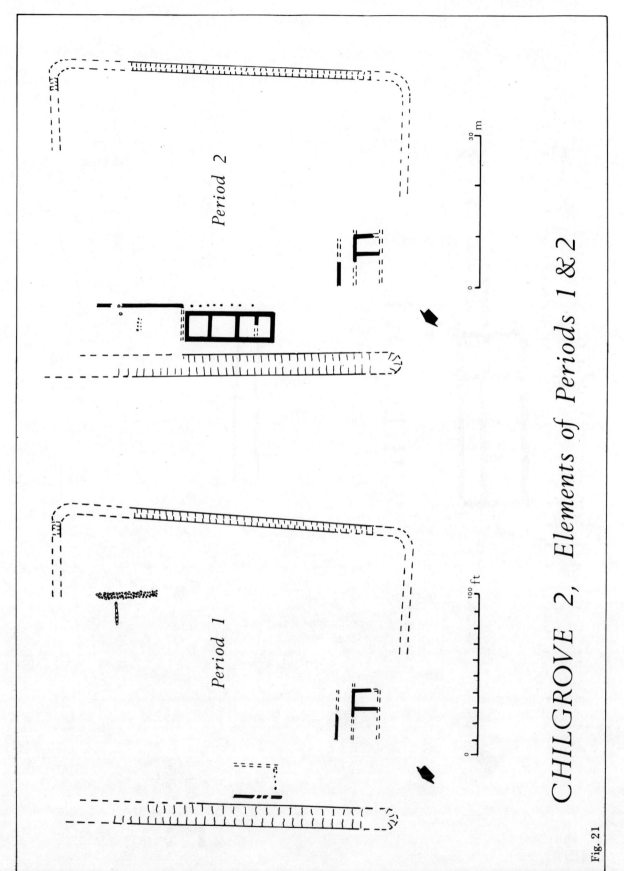

Period 2

Period 1

30 m

100 ft

CHILGROVE 2, Elements of Periods 1 & 2

Fig. 21

81

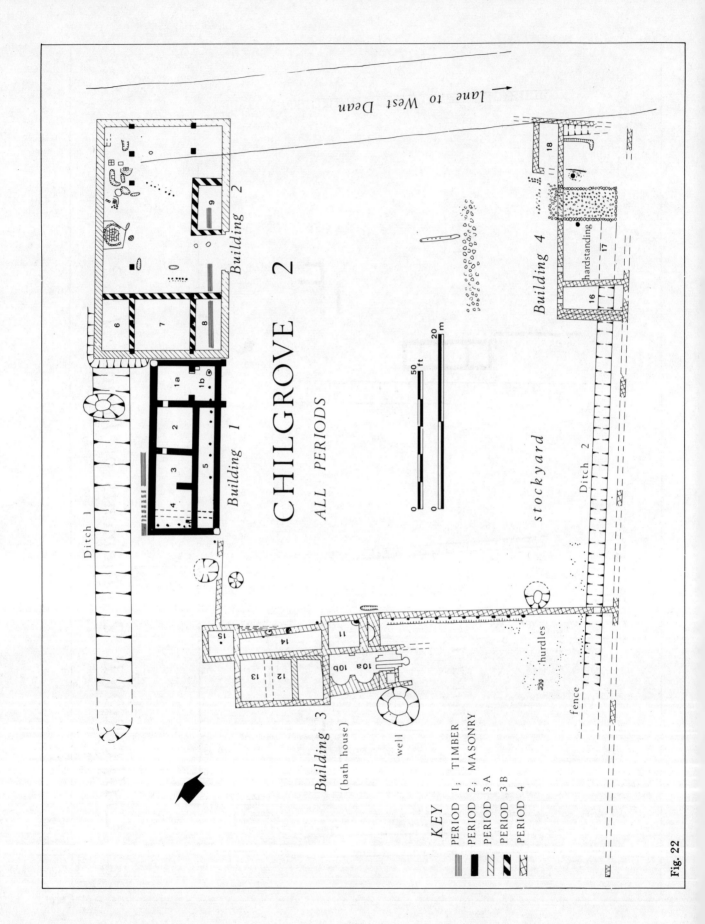

CHILGROVE 2

ALL PERIODS

lane to West Dean

Ditch 1

Building 2

Building 1

Building 3
(bath house)

well

Building 4

hardstanding

stockyard

Ditch 2

hurdles

fence

50 ft
20 m

KEY

PERIOD 1; TIMBER
PERIOD 2; MASONRY
PERIOD 3 A
PERIOD 3 B
PERIOD 4

Fig. 22

At this stage, for which a date cannot be given, Building 1 was rebuilt and probably became the main living quarters. It consisted of a range of five rooms with a corridor along the east side, with the corridor roof being supported by posts set into stone-packed post pits. A second building (Building 2), which may have been a barn, was erected on the north side of it and was probably butted against it, although this possibility is obscured by the foundations of the later barn. The evidence for Building 2 consists of a narrow dwarf wall of flints below the later aisled barn, and the remains of a wattle partition at right-angles to it, together with two tiled post bases which might also belong to the ground plan. One of the postholes belonging to the wattle partition had a coin of Claudius II (after 270 A.D.) in the top fill. The building must have been of timber-framed construction and of slight proportions, and a demolition date of some time after the last quarter of the third century is suggested by the coin.

The structure on the south side of the site may well have continued in use in this period and the ditches had probably silted up. A study of the sections (Fig. 31) show that Ditch 1 gradually filled up with weathered chalk from the sides. Some pottery found its way into the upper silt layers in Trench K (Section C–C), where K9 had one sherd of Trajanic and one sherd of Antonine samian.

Period 3: c. late
3rd century to
early 4th century
(Figs. 23 and 27)

Building 1 was rebuilt with masonry walls of flint and on a slightly larger plan. The walls were 2ft. 6ins. (0.66 m.) wide and post sockets were found in three corners. The building was buttressed on the south side, which may indicate that it had timber framing. Room 1 was modified, being extended across the width of the corridor and divided into two sections by means of an archway supported on tiled buttresses. The corridor was shortened by the width of Room 1 and the rooms south of it were modified to suit the new plan.

Room sizes in Period 3 were as follows:

Room 1A: 12ft. by 12ft. 9ins. (3.65 m. by 3.89 m.).
Room 1B: 7ft. 6ins. by 12ft. 9ins. (2.29 m. by 3.89 m.).
Room 2: 13ft. 9ins. by 15ft. (4.19 m. by 4.58 m.).
Room 3: 10ft. 6ins. by 13ft. 9ins. (3.20 m. by 4.19 m.).
Room 4: 14ft. 6ins. by 14ft. (4.42 m. by 4.27 m.).
Room 5: (corridor), 44ft. by 6ft. (13.41 m. by 1.83m.).

Building 2 may have remained unchanged at the time that Building 1 was rebuilt, as the aisled barn assigned to Period 4 was built after the masonry footings of Building 1 were constructed. Building 3 may also have remained unaltered at this stage, but the presence of a line of postholes set in a trench extending eastwards from it to the stockyard wall (Fig. 23), suggests that a palisade was constructed. It is possible that a palisade ran south from Building 1 to the north-west corner of Building 3, as one posthole was found on the alignment, the others possibly being masked by the later curtain wall.

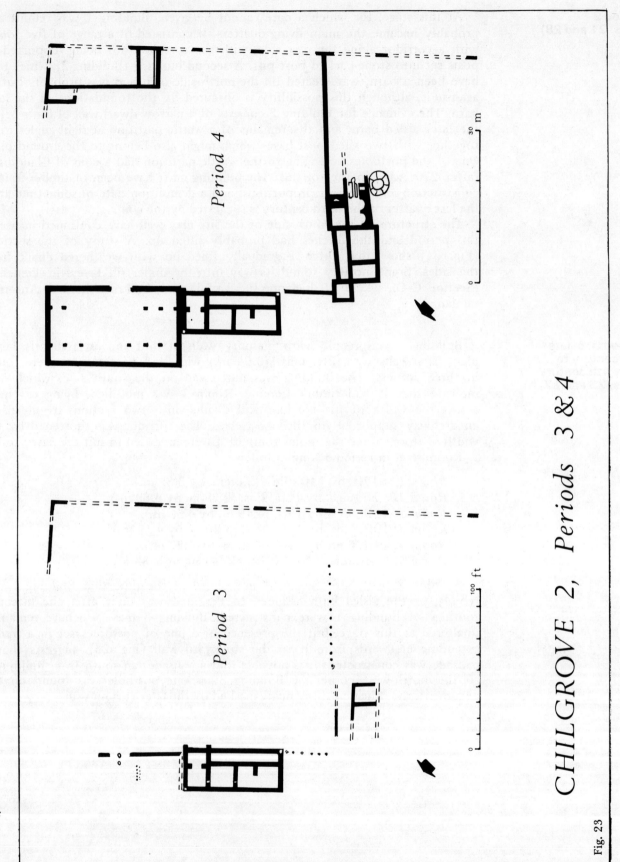

84

CHILGROVE 2, Periods 3 & 4

Period 4

Period 3

Fig. 23

Stockyard

It was probably in Period 3 that the stockyard wall was built along the north and east sides of the farm complex. The wall on the east side, which lay partly outside the area reserved for excavation, was traced by selective trial trenching for a distance of 250ft. (77 m.) southwards, where it appeared to end abruptly and was not seen to turn westwards up the hill.

The area enclosed by the farm buildings and the palisade running down to the stockyard wall would give a stockyard of smaller size than that enclosed by the earlier ditches. By the end of Period 3 the partially silted up Ditch 1 was being used as a refuse tip by the people using Building 1. Whether Period 3 represents a rebuilding after a period of abandonment or whether the establishment of a smaller enclosure signified a change of function is not clear, but it is perhaps possible to envisage the smaller enclosure as being more strictly concerned with storage, corn-drying and threshing activities, with the animals being penned elsewhere, on the south side of the southern range of buildings.

Period 4: first quarter of 4th century—mid 4th century (Fig. 23)

At some time in the early fourth century, probably in the reign of Constantine, the villa was further enlarged. Building 1 remained unaltered, except that it is likely that the mosaic in Room 1 was laid at this time, and possibly the tessellated floors in the other rooms. One of the floors sealed a coin of Tetricvs 1 (270-273 A.D.). It was probably also at this time that the large aisled barn (Building 2) was constructed. This is seen to be later in date than the final version of Building 1 (but how much later is uncertain), as the foundation trench at the south end of the barn avoids the footings of Building 1, which must have already been there, and the builders simply butted the south wall up against the existing building. The west wall of the barn was built into the bottom of the earlier Ditch 1 which ran underneath the west side.

The barn had walls of up to 3ft. (0.92 m.) wide and the roof supports were set upon large sandstone pads, one of which was a partially carved column base rejected by the mason. They may well have been quarried near to Midhurst, where this type of stone outcrops, and similar pad stones were ploughed up at another site a few miles away (p. 37, No. 65). There were a number of phases of development within the barn, and these are discussed below.

At the south end of Building 1 the timber buildings were replaced by a masonry structure (Building 3), with a bath-house at the east end. The range was connected to Building 1 by a curtain wall, and another curtain wall replaced the palisade on the east side of Building 3.

Whether Building 4 at the north end of the stockyard wall was built at this time is uncertain. It might have been built earlier, in Period 3 when the stockyard wall was built; there is no evidence either way.

The Bath Suite (Fig. 24)

It is not clear whether the four rooms on the west side of the bath suite proper were part of the suite, or whether they were living quarters as in the earlier periods. The south wall of Room 10A and 10B (*caldarium* and *tepidarium*) is at an odd angle which might suggest that the bath-house was added on later. Details of masonry construction are similar, however, and it might be no more than a construction oddity.

85

Very little of the downhill (east) end of the building survived the heavy ploughing. The plan of the cold bath could just be seen as a pink mortar layer a few centimetres thick, and it was not possible to be sure that there had been a hot bath in the apse of the caldarium as at Chilgrove 1 and Upmarden, as the burial of a sheep within the apse in the last century had virtually destroyed it.

DETAILED DESCRIPTION OF ROOMS:
Room 10A (Caldarium)

Measured 8ft. (2.44 m.) square. The base floor was lined with tegulae with the flanges removed. All the pilae tiles had been robbed and the tegulae, which were butted up against one another, show no impressions where the pilae tiles should have been, so perhaps they were a later addition after the pilae had been robbed. The flue through which the caldarium was fired was 10ft. (3.05 m.) long and there was no trace of a support for a hot-water tank similar to that at Chilgrove 1, although the possibility is not excluded. Only a tiny amount of charcoal was found, nothing approaching the massive amounts found in the stokery at Upmarden (Fig. 35, Section A–A), and there was only a small circular depression at the south end of the flue, which may indicate that charcoal was the fuel instead of faggots. The full extent of the stoking area could not be traced due to the complete destruction of the walls by the plough, but it is likely that the wall at the south end returned northwards to the curtain wall.

Room 10B (Tepidarium)

The same dimensions as Room 10A and joined to it by an archway supported on tiled buttresses. No trace of the upper floor of the hypocaust remained, but the impressions of the large base tiles were found on the floor. The impressions were larger than the tegulae with which the caldarium had been later floored, being 14ins. (36 cms.) square (see below, Period 5).

Room 11 (Frigidarium)

Measured 9ft. 9ins by 11ft. 6ins. (2.97 m. by 3.50 m.), with an apsidal bath at the east end. Ploughing had destroyed everything except the last few foundation courses.

Rooms 12 and 13

The original dimensions of these two rooms were: Room 12, 19ft. 6ins by 15ft. (5.94 m. by 4.57 m.); and Room 13, 9ft. by 14ft. 6ins. (2.74 m. by 4.42 m.), but at some later date the wall between them was demolished, giving a large room 31ft. by 15ft. (9.45 m. by 4.57 m.). This was at some time after the mid-fourth century, as a coin of Magnentius (350–353 A.D.) was found on top of the demolished wall footing.

Few traces of the floors remained, but where they did, there were a number of late hearths built upon them (see Period 5 below). At some time, probably in Period 4, a doorway 5ft. 3ins. (1.60 m.) wide was inserted into the north-west corner of Room 13. It had a tiled sill. A coin of Constans (333–350 A.D.) was found in the east wall.

1. View of Heathbarn Down showing the course of the Roman road. The field banks on the left are post-medieval. North is to the right.

nilgrove 1, showing the field bank on three sides of the villa. North is to the right.

3. Chilgrove 1, the bath suite, looking east.

4. Chilgrove 1, Period 4, Phase A cold bath on right (north), with the Phase B cold bath on the south side.

5. Chilgrove 1, looking south, Room 15 in foreground.

6. Bignor (Sussex). From S. Lysons, *Reliquiae Britannico–Romanae III* (1817), Plates VII and IX.

7. Chilgrove 1, the Period 4 mosaic in Room 6.

8. Chilgrove 1, Room 15, showing mosaic collapsed into the hypocaust.

9. Chilgrove 1. Collapsed flue tiles in Room 7, looking south.

10. Chilgrove 1, Room 8, looking east, showing the base of the Period 5 iron-working furnace on the Period 4 tessellated floor.

11. Chilgrove 1; statuette of Fortuna. Scale in inches.

12. Chilgrove 1, Period 4, reconstruction by C. de la Nougerede.

14. Chilgrove 2, Building 2, Room 7, looking south.

15. Chilgrove 2, Building 1, the design on the floor of Room 1A. Scale in feet. North to the left.

16. Chilgrove 2, Building 2, Phase 3 hearths and ovens cut into the floor of the aisled barn.

17. Chilgrove 2, Building 2, showing the Phase 3 bread oven. North is to the left.

18.   Chilgrove 2, Building 3, bath house, looking east.

19. Chilgrove 2, Period 4, reconstruction by C. de la Nougerede.

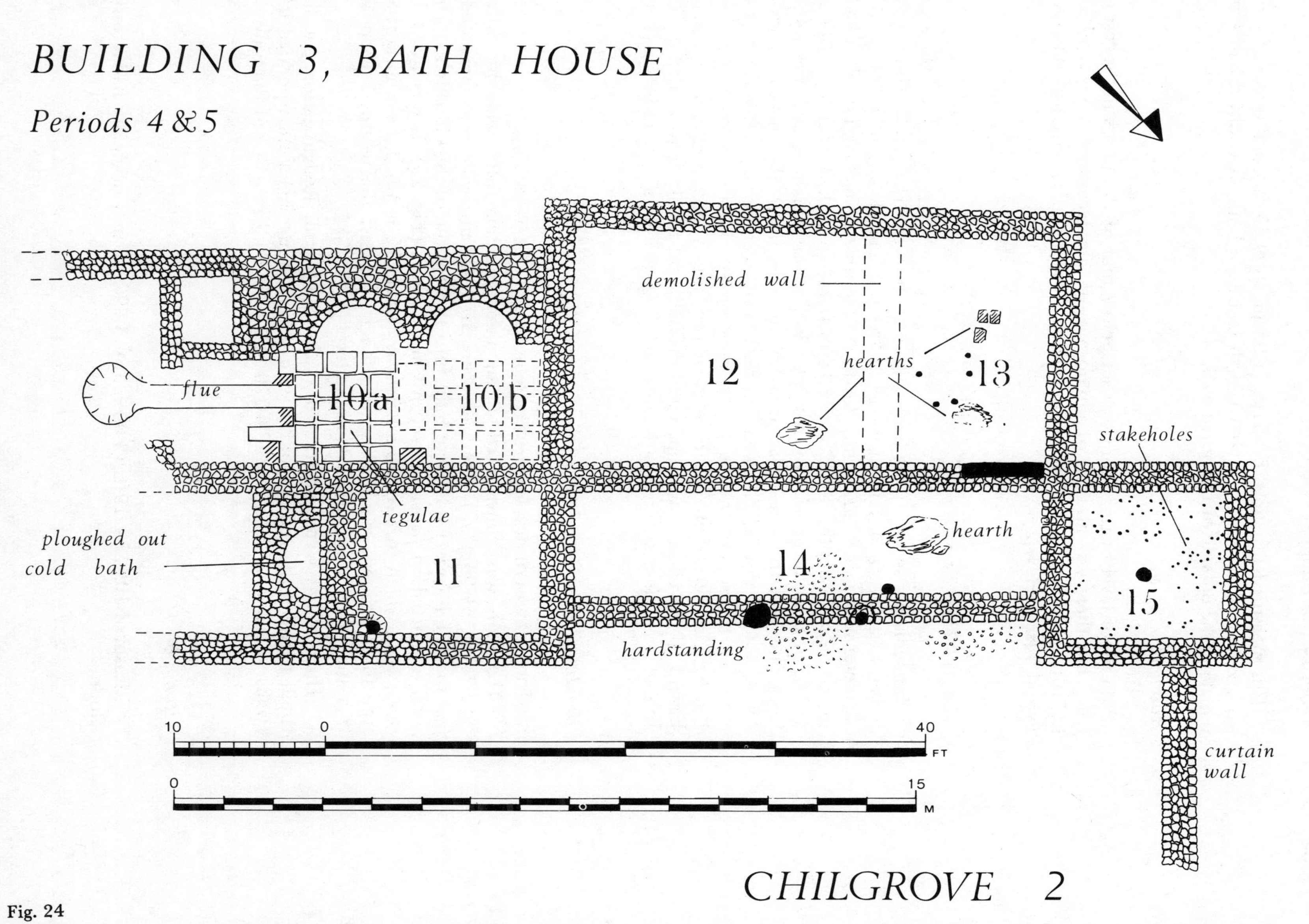

BUILDING 3, BATH HOUSE

Periods 4 & 5

demolished wall

hearths

12

10b

10a

tegulae

flue

11

ploughed out
cold bath

hearths

:13

hearth

14

hardstanding

stakeholes

15

curtain
wall

CHILGROVE 2

40 FT

10 0

15 M

Fig. 24

Room 14 (Corridor)

This measured 6ft. 6ins. by 31ft. (1.98 m. by 9.45 m.), and traces of a mortar floor remained on which a later hearth had been built. A cobbled hardstanding ran along the outside of the north wall.

Room 15

The floor level in this room was set below that of the floors in the rest of the wing, but there was no trace of a hypocaust or flue. Measurements were 9ft. 6ins. by 10ft. (2.89 m. by 3.05 m.). Considerable use had been made of this room in Period 5 (see below).

The Well (Fig. 22)

Immediately south of the bath suite was the well. The top was funnel shaped, being 14ft. (4.27 m.) in diameter at the top and closing in to 4ft. (1.22 m.) diameter about 11ft. (3.35 m.) down. At the time of writing (1978) it had been excavated to a depth of 122ft. (37.18 m.), and it is likely that it could be up to 160ft. or more in depth. No trace of a well-house remained, but there must have been one, and the water was probably brought up to the surface by means of ox or donkey power. The well was backfilled at some time after the bath-house went out of use, but there is no evidence of date for this. It could have been in the fifth century, but may have been very much later. Certainly it remained a hazard all the while it was open and disused, and finally it was filled in with the rubble from the destroyed bath-house and large amounts of food bones (Fig. 39).

Building 2—The Aisled Barn (Figs. 25 and 26)

Three phases of development were noted:

Phase 1

The barn was constructed as an aisled building 50ft. wide by 80ft. long (15.24 m. by 24.4 m.). The walls were 3ft (0.92 m.) wide, and the foundations on the uphill (west) side were built into the bottom of the old Ditch 1. The roof was supported on padstones set out in two rows (Fig. 25). It was noted that the west wall, which survived to a height of 4ft. (1.22 m.) had the pointing between the flints painted, presumably to protect it against the weather. There was an external offset at the original ground level (Fig. 32).

Phase 2

Three rooms were constructed at the south end. Rough masonry walls were built between the roof supports, with the padstones being incorporated into the walls. A coin of Victorinus (268–270 A.D.) was built into one of the walls.

Room 6

Measured 10ft. by 19ft. (3.05 m. by 5.79 m.), and originally had a tessellated floor.

88

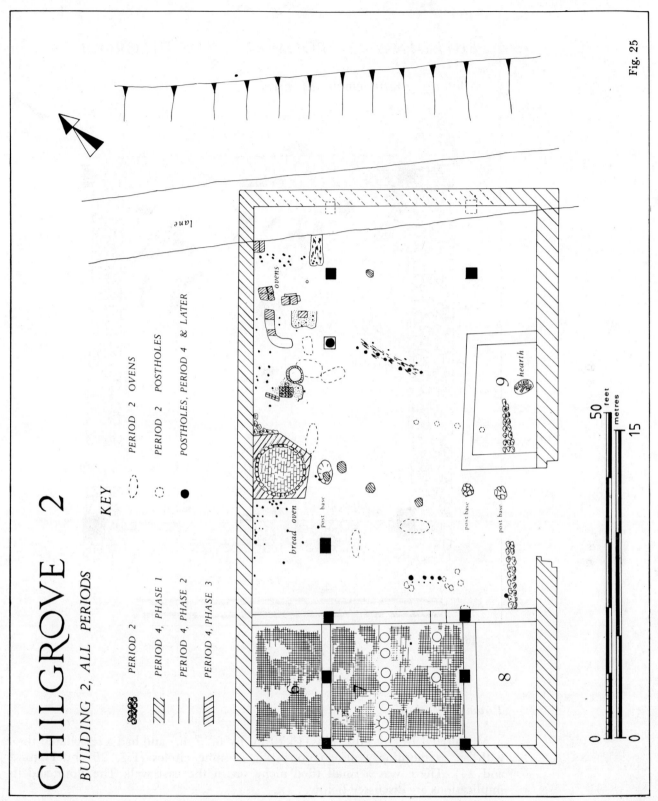

CHILGROVE 2

BUILDING 2, ALL PERIODS

KEY

⬡⬡⬡   PERIOD 2

▨▨   PERIOD 4, PHASE 1

▬▬   PERIOD 4, PHASE 2

▨▨   PERIOD 4, PHASE 3

⬭   PERIOD 2 OVENS

⬭   PERIOD 2 POSTHOLES

●   POSTHOLES, PERIOD 4 & LATER

lane

ovens

bread oven

post base

post base

post base

hearth

9

8

6

7

0   50 feet

0   15 metres

Fig. 25

89

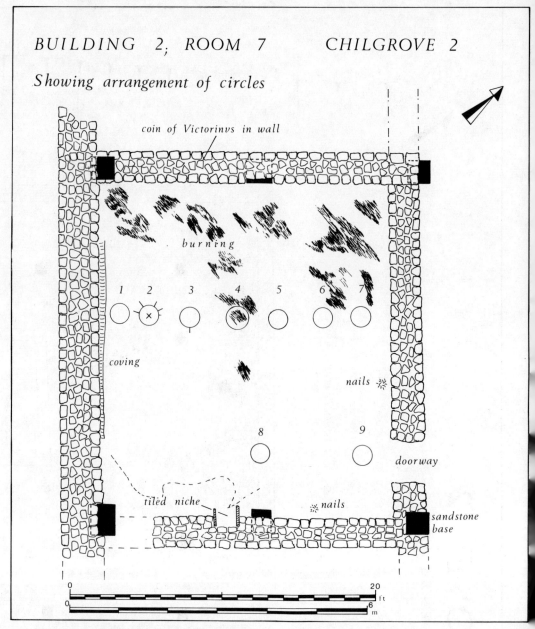

BUILDING 2; ROOM 7   CHILGROVE 2

Showing arrangement of circles

coin of Victorinvs in wall

burning

1 2 3 4 5 6 7

coving

nails

8 9

doorway

tiled niche   *nails*   sandstone base

0   20
                      ft
0   6
                      m

Fig. 26

Room 7

Measured 19ft. by 20ft. 6ins. (5.79 m. by 6.25 m.) and had a tessellated floor with an extraordinary design consisting of nine circles (Fig. 26 and Plates 2 and 14). There was a small tiled niche set in the east wall. The floor and its implications are discussed below.

Room 8

Had a mortar floor and measured 9ft. 6ins. by 19ft. (2.9 m. by 5.79 m.).

Room 9

Was possibly built at this time on the north side of the doorway. It was 9ft. by 16ft. 3ins. (2.74 m. by 4.95 m.), and no trace of a floor remained.

Phase 3

Room 6 went out of use; the floor was destroyed and the wall dividing it from the main part of the barn was demolished. This may have been due to subsidence caused by the presence of Ditch 1 which ran below the room. Probably also at this time a large bread oven was built against the west wall. The foundations were built on top of charcoal from ovens within the barn.

A number of tiled ovens were set into the chalk floor along the north end of the west side. They could not have all existed together and are best seen as a series of domestic ovens which were replaced from time to time by others. Some of the small oval ovens cut into the floor of the barn (Fig. 25) may pre-date the Period 4 barn and one was below the floor in Room 7.

The bread oven was constructed on a platform of flints. The floor of the oven was built from re-used tegulae and was 6ft. 9ins. (2.06 m.) in diameter on the inside. The superstructure was of clay and tile, and part of this was found collapsed across the oven when it was excavated.

Numbers of stakeholes were cut into the natural chalk which made up the barn floor. These could not be assigned to any particular phase, but most were probably hurdles, thrust into the ground to serve as temporary partitions or windbreaks around the ovens.

DISCUSSION

The phases of alteration to which the building was subjected are assessed below:

Phase 1

At this stage the barn was probably used for storing grain, with possibly some provision for the stalling of cattle in the winter.

Phase 2

Living quarters were built into the south end, with the remainder of the building still being used for storage and/or the stalling of beasts. The three rooms may have been either an enlargement of the living quarters for some of the family, perhaps the eldest son, or possibly for a farm manager or bailiff. The design on the floor of Room 7, which may have had some special significance for the occupants, makes one wonder what kind of people they were.

There remains a possibility that the floor design might be later than Phase 2. This would be possible if the original floor was of mortar and the tesserae added later, but it has not been possible to establish this point as the floor has not been raised, but remains on site, buried to a depth of four feet. As there are no known parallels for the design it is difficult to speculate about it, yet one is left with the strong impression that the design is not intended to be decorative; that the circles have some meaning, and that they were of special importance to the later inhabitants of the villa. It is clear that they owe nothing to classical Roman mosaic art, and like the funny stick horse and rider portrayed in Room 1A in Building 1 they may belong to a native tradition which was never completely overlaid by Romanisation. There are nine circles, all different, with a small niche set in the east wall which might perhaps have housed a statuette. These are the facts, and the temptation to indulge in uncontrolled incursions into the realms of fantasy must be firmly resisted. One can only say that the room was likely to have been of special significance and leave it at that.

Phase 3

Rooms 7 and 8 continued in use, while the north wall of Room 6 was demolished (probably due to instability), and the barn converted to domestic uses, e.g., baking and cooking, with possibly the centre part of the barn being open to the weather. It is noteworthy that the ovens are clustered within the western aisle and the collapsed roof tiles found by the excavators were very thick along the west, south and north sides, but sparse in the central areas, and this may indicate that in Phase 3 only the north, west and south sides were roofed.

BUILDING 4

This comprised a barn built into the north-east corner of the stockyard. It was divided into two rooms (Rooms 16 and 17), and another room (Room 18), abutted it on the west side and this might have been a later addition. Selective trial trenching into the hedge on the south side of the lane failed to produce evidence of other buildings within the stockyard wall and further work along the verge of the lane itself indicated that the return wall of the stockyard did not reach Building 2, but ended a few feet uphill from Room 18.

The south wall of Room 16 was a double one, or at least there was a double foundation, and it may be that some subsidence was feared because of the presence of Ditch 2 which ran below. Probably towards the end of the period a hardstanding of flints was built across Room 17 and there was evidence for demolition of part of the wall on the west side, with the metalling running across it. The flints in the hardstanding were set in puddled chalk and terminated just short of the line of the east wall, which was ploughed out at this point.

It is possible that in the later years of occupation, the entrance to the stockyard from the outside fields was through the barn (see reconstruction, Plate 19).

Two postholes, one filled with charcoal, the remains of a hearth, and a small gulley were found cut into the floor of Room 17 and sealed by the rubble from the walls. The gulley may well belong to an earlier phase, but it is likely that the postholes are contemporary with the building.

Building 4 measured 23ft. by 67ft. overall (7 m. by 20.43 m.); Room 18 was 7ft. by 16ft. 9ins. (2.14 m. by 5.10 m.) inside, while the dimensions of Room 16 were 8ft. 6ins. by 22ft. (2.44 m. by 6.71 m) inside.

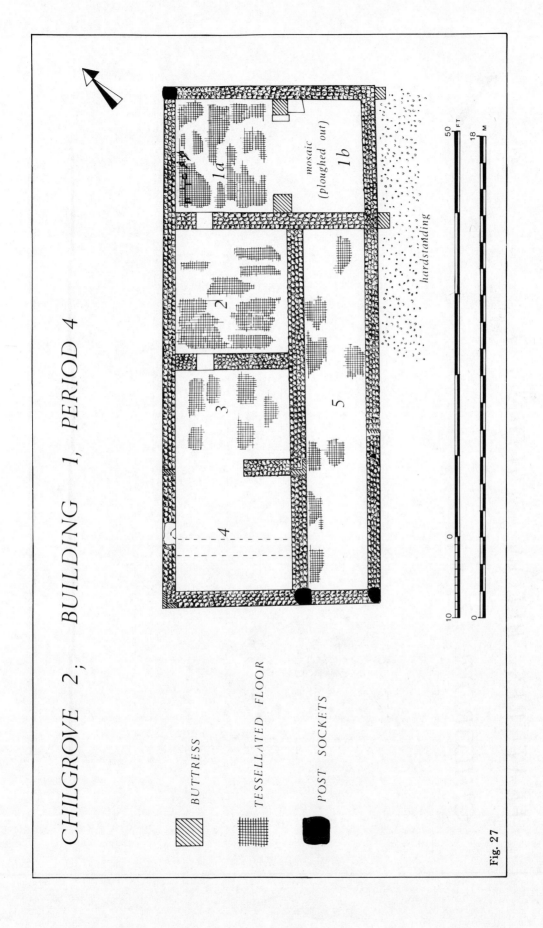

CHILGROVE 2; BUILDING 1, PERIOD 4

BUTTRESS

TESSELLATED FLOOR

POST SOCKETS

1a

1b
mosaic
(ploughed out)

2

3

4

5

hardstanding

Fig. 27

93

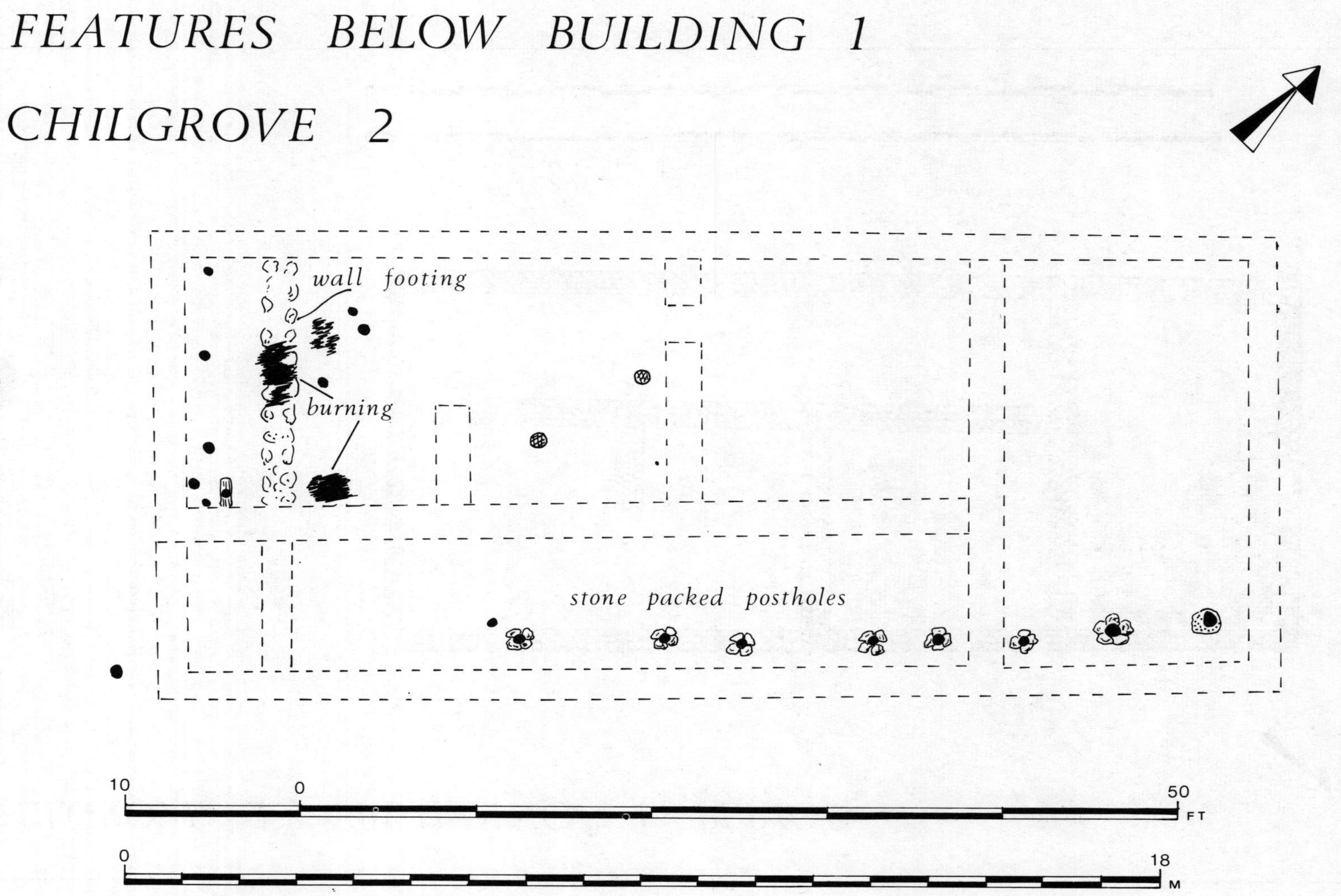

FEATURES BELOW BUILDING 1

CHILGROVE 2

wall footing

burning

stone packed postholes

FT
50

M
18

0

0

10

0

Fig. 28

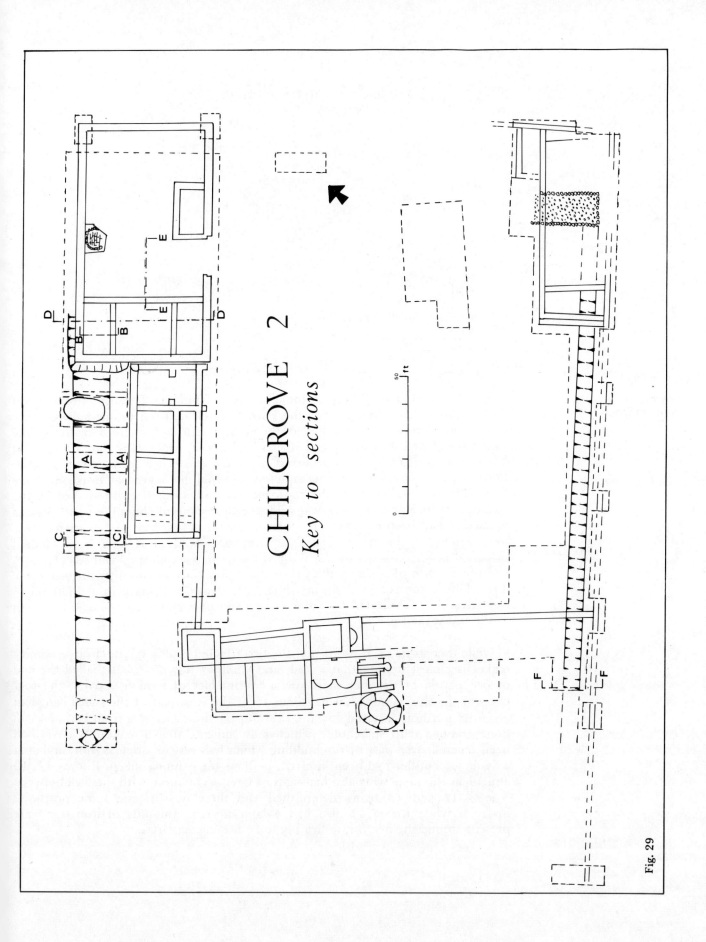

CHILGROVE 2
Key to sections

Fig. 29

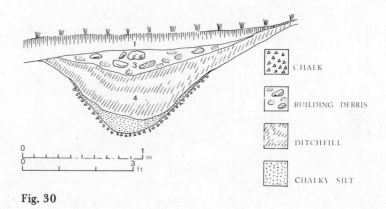

L3; Ditch 2, South section   F – F

CHALK

BUILDING DEBRIS

DITCHFILL

CHALKY SILT

Fig. 30

Period 5: The Villa in Decay

At some time after 375 A.D. the aisled barn (Building 2) caught fire and was burned down. The evidence for the burning is clear. Roof beams fell upon the floor of Room 7 and smouldered there, discolouring the floor badly at the western end and leaving layers of charcoal below which was found a coin of Valentinian 1 (375 A.D.). The bread oven and the other features cut into the floor on the west side were completely covered by layers of Horsham stone tiles which had fallen from the roof and lay undisturbed until removed by the excavators. In Room 7 there was evidence that some of the more usable beams remaining had been salvaged for other purposes, as two heaps of extracted nails were found on the floor (Fig. 26). The north wall of Rooms 7 and 8 had collapsed northwards across the floor of the barn, 'jack knifing' as it fell (Fig. 32) and the absence of roofing tiles below the rubble shows that either the wall came down before the roof fell in, in which case it can only have been built up to the eaves, or, as indicated by other factors (see above), the central part was open to the sky at the time.

While there is no clear proof that the fire affected Building 1, its close proximity makes it almost certain that it did, and whether this disaster signalled the end of occupation or whether there was a continuance of farming activity on other parts of the site, is not known. Room 15 at the west end of the south wing had a central posthole inserted and the thin mortar floor surviving from Period 4 was honeycombed with stakeholes, which may indicate that a makeshift cover had been erected over part of the building which had lost its original roof, and that a series of hurdles had been inserted, perhaps for penning sheep. Rooms 12, 13 and 14 in the same wing also had signs of later occupation, with the wall between Rooms 12 and 13 being demolished and three hearths and some postholes inserted, while Room 14 also had a later hearth. Amounts of iron slag were present around the hearths, indicating some forging activities.

CHILGROVE 2

Ditch 1, North sections   G1

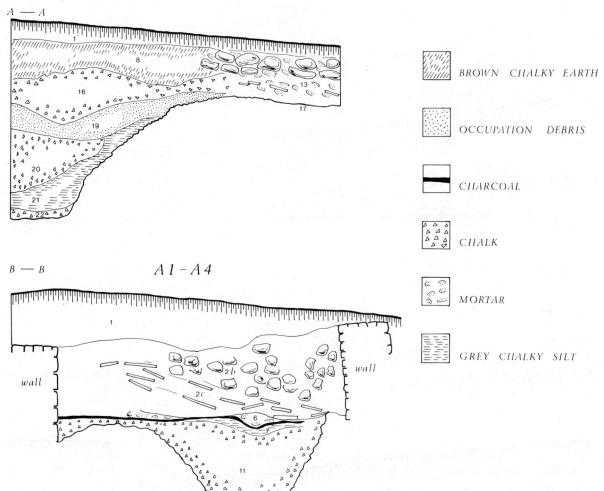

A — A

A1 - A4

B — B

wall   *wall*

C — C   K1

BROWN CHALKY EARTH

OCCUPATION DEBRIS

CHARCOAL

CHALK

MORTAR

GREY CHALKY SILT

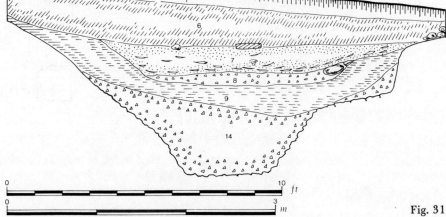

0   10 *ft*

0   3 *m*

Fig. 31

CHILGROVE 2

Ditch 1, North sections   G1

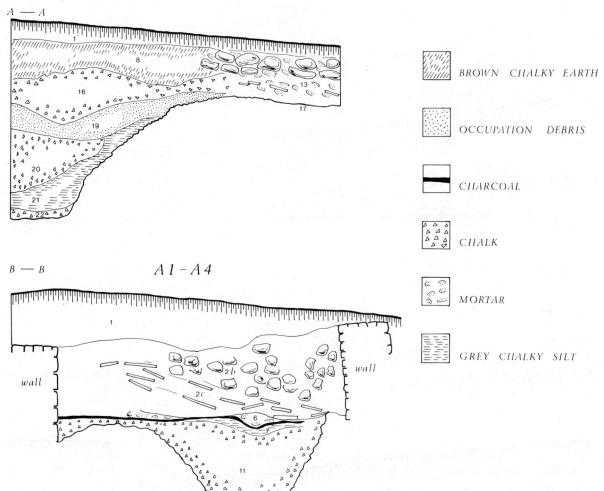

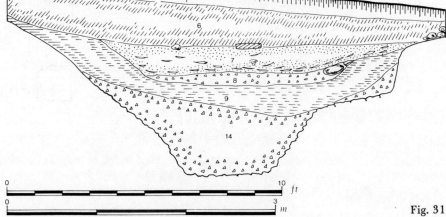

BROWN CHALKY EARTH

OCCUPATION DEBRIS

CHARCOAL

CHALK

MORTAR

GREY CHALKY SILT

Fig. 31

CHILGROVE 2

Building 2, Room 7; North section   D — D

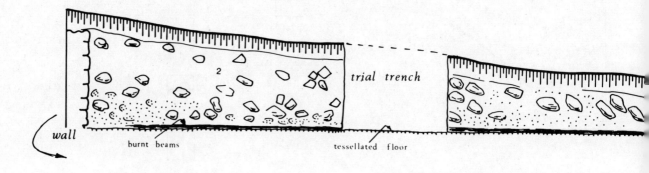

trial trench

wall

burnt beams

tessellated floor

A4, North face   Building 2, po

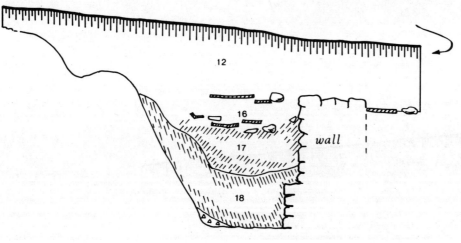

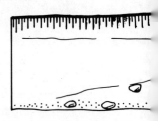

12

16

17

18

wall

MORTAR

CHALKY

Fig. 32

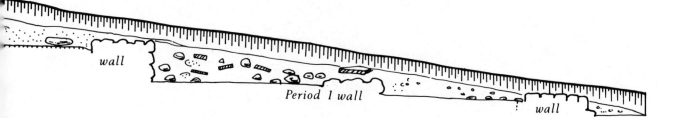

face   *E−E*

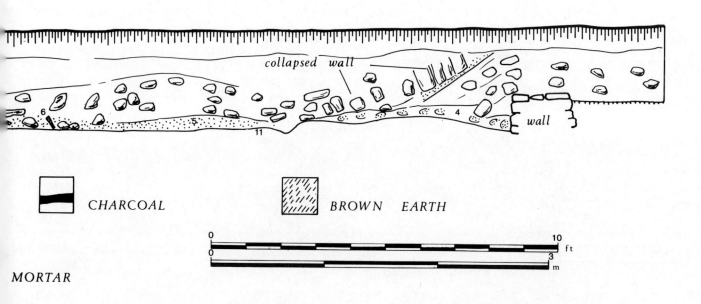

CHARCOAL   BROWN   EARTH

MORTAR

Two postholes had been set into the north wall of Building 3, 7ft. 9ins. (2.36 m.) apart. The wall between the posts had been demolished and an area of trodden chalk was present on both sides of the wall and across it, indicating that an entrance had been constructed at this point, wide enough to bring carts into the building from the north side.

In the former bath suite, the re-flooring of the base of the hypocaust in the caldarium (Room 10A) with re-used tegulae might be an indication that part of the bath-house was being used as a corn-drying oven, as it is possible to envisage the tiled floor as a suitable shovelling platform for the grain and the long flue being fired by charcoal. This is no more than a suggestion to account for what must otherwise be regarded as an odd modification, but there was no proof in the shape of carbonised grain to indicate that corn-drying had been carried out.

PITLANDS FARM, UPMARDEN

Due to the restricted nature of the excavations it is not possible to examine the origins of this villa, still less the eventual decay. Our investigations were necessarily circumscribed by the fact that we were digging in the home paddock and the kitchen garden of a working farm, and stripping large areas, as we did at the Chilgrove villas, was not practical. Five areas were investigated and of these four were trial trenched (see Fig. 33).

> *Areas 1 and 2*—Covered trial trenching in the kitchen garden close to the house and also in the adjoining paddock where the eastern end of the bath wing was located.
> *Area 3.*—This was not excavated, but walked after ploughing, and comprised the land above the paddock to the east. The ground rises steeply here and the field contained significant amounts of pottery, including samian.
> *Area. 4.*—North of, and uphill from, Areas 1 and 2. Part of a building with flint walls 2ft. (0.61 m.) wide was found. This was largely ploughed out.
> *Area 5.*—A small area dug by Philip Huxham, the farmer's son, in the old orchard north of Areas 1 and 2. Part of a small gulley running downhill (south), with fence posts on the west side was found. This need not have been Roman.

THE EXCAVATIONS—AREAS 1 AND 2:
Building 1—Bath Suite (Figs. 33–35)

This comprised a range of three rooms plus a frigidarium, tepidarium, caldarium and stokery aligned east-west. At the west end, the range was partly destroyed by the farmhouse, but it quite clearly did not extend any further than Room 1, which may mean that the bath suite was isolated from the rest of the villa, although the building might just turn south below the farmhouse. Along the north side of the range of rooms was a corridor, originally bounded by a wall, probably a dwarf wall on which the roof supports were mounted. This was later replaced by a series of wooden posts set on the inside of the wall footing and cutting through it.

On the east side of the bath suite was a sub-rectangular enclosure built on to the stokery wall, probably used for storing fuel for the furnace, and this was joined by a wall which ran northwards towards the slope at the back of the farm. It might well be part of the wall enclosing the stockyard and aligns with Building 2 in Area 4.

Building 1 underwent several phases of alteration during its life and these are discussed below.

Phase 1: (undated)

Due to the proximity of the bath wing to the farmhouse and to the need to preserve some at least of Mrs. Huxham's vegetable garden, the rooms at the west end could only be trial trenched. It was established that Room 2 had a clay floor and Room 3 a mortar one some 4ft. 3ins. (1.30 m.) from modern ground level, and although no impressions of hypocaust tiles were noted it is likely that both rooms were heated at an earlier stage.

Room 2 had been backfilled to a depth of 1ft. 9ins. (0.54 m.) with loose mortar and then given a floor of hard-packed chalk (Fig. 35, Section B–B, Layer 10), while Room 3 was similarly backfilled and a floor of chalk established at a higher level.

101

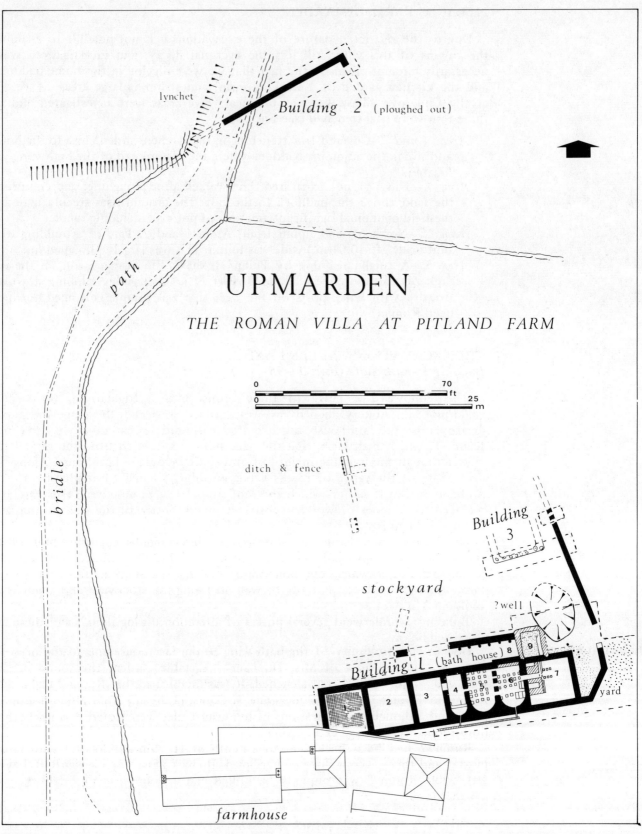

lynchet

Building 2 (ploughed out)

path

UPMARDEN

THE ROMAN VILLA AT PITLAND FARM

0   70 ft

0   25 m

bridle

ditch & fence

Building 3

stockyard

?well

Building 1 (bath house)   8   9

1   2   3   4   5   6   7

yard

farmhouse

Fig. 33

I. Chilgrove 1, the Period 4 mosaic in Room 6. Drawn by C. de la Nougerede.

Room 4 (later the frigidarium), had originally been heated and still had the box flues set in the walls. It was connected by a flue to Room 3 and another flue (later filled in), connected it to Room 5 on the east side. Impressions of hypocaust tiles were seen upon the original base floor of this room, which was of pink mortar, and there was evidence of considerable heat. It was backfilled with brown loam with some chalk, and the cross wall supporting the cold bath, which was placed in the apse on the south side, was laid upon the fill. Five sherds of New Forest ware were found in the fill. These have a wide date bracket of *c.* 280 to 400 A.D., but they serve to show that the modifications to the bath suite took place at some time after the last quarter of the third century.

It is possible that these three rooms which were all originally heated, may have been part of an earlier, shorter bath suite, with perhaps Room 4 being the caldarium and Room 3 the tepidarium. Such an arrangement might be fired from the east side where Room 5 was later constructed.

Alternatively, and more likely, in Phase 1 the wing was the main domestic range of rooms and three of these were heated.

Phase 2

At some time after the late third century, Rooms 2, 3 and 4 were converted to cold rooms, and Room 4 had a bath inserted into the south end. This was part of a complete reorganisation, with a *tepidarium* and *caldarium* being constructed at the east end. The alterations took place within the framework of the existing building as there are no signs of Rooms 4, 5 and 6 being butted on. The stokery appears to have had several phases of alteration, the earlier flue being east of the later one, which probably had a tank set over it to supply hot water to the bath. In the corridor (Room 8), along the north side of the range, an additional section of wall was built alongside the north wall of the caldarium. This may have been added in Phase 2 to reinforce the wall which had become unstable as a result of the intense heat. Precautions were taken to insulate the pilae and the tiled buttresses that supported the dividing walls between the caldarium and tepidarium by plastering them with Reading clay. This method appears to have been standard practice locally as it was noted during excavations of part of the Thermae in Chichester (*Chichester,* 3, p. 157).

Phase 3: (undated)

This involved modifications to the corridor. Room 9 was built at the east end, and the north wall of the corridor, which was probably no more than a dwarf wall carrying pilasters which supported the roof, was replaced by a series of posts which cut the mortar footings.

These posts are seen to be contemporary with or post-date the construction of Room 9 as they stop at the robbed-out foundations.

It is by no means certain that these alterations belong to Phase 3, they could equally have been executed in Phase 2.

DIMENSIONS OF ROOMS

Room 1
14ft. by 15ft. (4.27 m. by 4.58 m.). It had a tessellated floor of red tile and was partly cut away by the farmhouse wall. It was possible to establish the north-west corner of the room, and it could be seen that no other rooms lay to the west of it.

Room 2

14ft. 3ins. by 15ft. (4.34. m. by 4.58 m.). In Phase 2 it had a chalk floor above the earlier fill, and this floor was covered by a heavy deposit of charcoal and domestic rubbish.

Room 3

10ft. by 15ft. (3.05 m. by 4.58 m.). In Phase 2 it had a chalk floor.

Room 4

Measured 5ft. 6ins. by 14ft. (1.68 m. by 4.27 m.) including the apse. In Phase 2 it was the frigidarium, and had a floor of pilae tiles 7.5ins. (19 cm.) square. The bath in the apse at the south end end was connected by a lead pipe to a tiled drain which ran westwards from the direction of the caldarium.

Room 5

Measured 9ft. 3ins. by 14ft. (2.82 m. by 4.27 m.). In Phase 2 it was the tepidarium.

Room 6

This was the caldarium in Phase 2 and had a tiled hot bath in the apse at the south end. It measured 8ft. 6ins. by 14ft. (2.59 m. by 4.27 m.).

Room 7

The stokery: it measured 15ft. by 16ft. (4.57 m. by 4.88 m.), and in Phase 2 it is likely that the flue walls supported a large hot-water tank.

Room 8

The corridor: in Phase 3 it measured *c.* 74ft. by 6ft. (22.56 m. by 1.83 m.).

Room 9

Measured 7ft. by 8ft. (2.13 m. by 2.44 m.). It had a mortar floor and the walls had been robbed.

BUILDING 2

Most of this had been destroyed by the plough, but fortunately the north-east corner survived. The north wall ran westwards below the bridle path and the lynchet in the field on the west side of the path. The presence of tegulae in the plough soil demonstrated the existence of a building as opposed to a field wall, and Building 2 might well have been a barn, possibly at the north end of the stockyard (see below).

THE STOCKYARD WALL

The stockyard wall ran northwards from its junction with the bath wing, and there were signs of a cobbled hardstanding on the east side of it, across which the wall had collapsed. It is possible that the wall may have connected with Building 2 as it ran uphill on the same alignment, but it could not be traced beyond the point where the ground rises steeply. There was no evidence for it turning westwards along the bottom of the slope, and this suggests that it may indeed have originally continued up the hill.

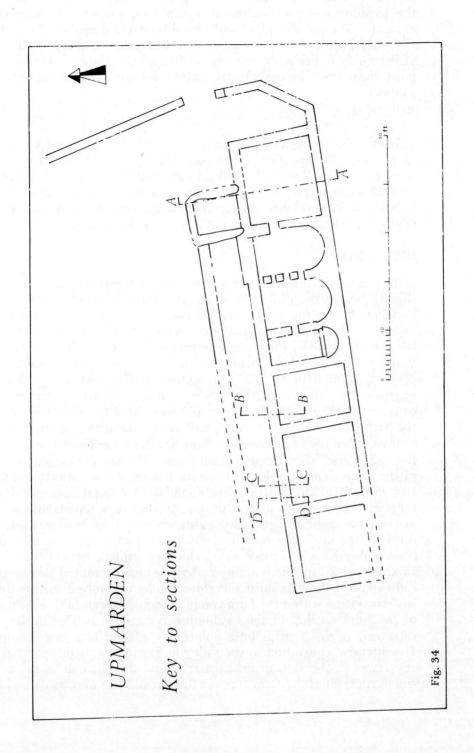

UPMARDEN

Key to sections

Fig. 34

There was a small opening 7ft. (2.14 m.) in the stockyard wall just east of the bath suite which must have been a gateway into the fields, and between it and the corridor was the outline of a very large pit which it was not possible to excavate. The pit was filled with flints from the demolished bath-house, and its size and shape are very similar to the waterhole at Chilgrove 1 and the well at Chilgrove 2. It probably was the well supplying water to the bath-house, but it must have been inconveniently placed for farm traffic entering through the gateway.

BUILDING 3

Within the stockyard, on the west side of the wall, were the robbed footings of a small structure 19ft. (5.79 m.) wide and of unknown length. The footings were cut into a layer of chalky loam and only a few flints remained of the original foundations, which might have carried a timber-framed structure. There is no definite evidence that this building was Roman, but it was built to conform to the stockyard wall and it is likely that it was.

DISCUSSION

The earliest samian on the site is Flavian, which suggests that the villa began slightly before the Chilgrove villas. The absence of any trace of earlier timber buildings below the only wing excavated is no proof that they did not exist. Indeed, if the same pattern of development was followed as at Chilgrove, then the earliest phase of the bath suite may well be no earlier than late third or early fourth century, with the final modifications taking place in the middle fourth century. If, as is likely, the wing excavated was originally part of the domestic quarters, then these must have been moved elsewhere when the bath suite was constructed. The domestic wing could well have been built on at right angles to the bath suite at the west end, which would mean that it was destroyed, in part at least, when the farmhouse was built. On the other hand, it may be remote from the bath-house, aligned north-south below the lawn and garden at the rear (north) of the house. The corridor in Building 1 is on the north side and normally these face inwards to the centre of the complex. A domestic wing with a corridor on the east side might well be a possibility, but it is remarkable that no building material has come to light, as the area which is now lawn and flower garden was formerly the kitchen garden and was landscaped at the same time as the previous lawn and garden was made into a kitchen garden, when deep digging by Mrs. Huxham turned up the building material which prompted this investigation. The full extent of the villa must therefore remain unresolved for the time being, but any excavation within the farm complex should be carefully watched. The quality of the workmanship in the bath-house is superior to that in the two Chilgrove villas and might perhaps be a pointer to a larger and more prosperous estate. The intensive cultivation in the valley in Saxon and medieval times has obscured any traces of the Roman field patterns, and the lynchets to be seen on the east and north sides of the farm are post-Roman and one overlies part of Building 2.

UPMARDEN, BATH HOUSE SECTIONS

N; East section, stokery, A – A

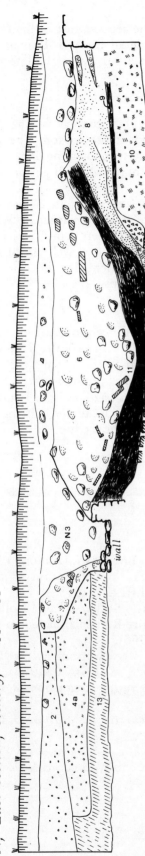

C; East section, B – B

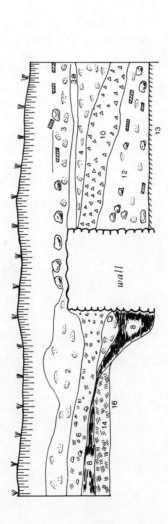

E; East section, C – C

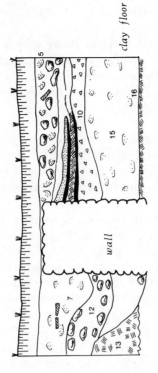

E; West section, D – D

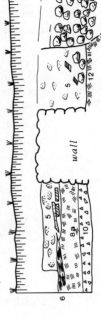

clay floor

wall

	GREY ASH		MORTAR AND RUBBLE
	CHALK		CHARCOAL
	BROWN EARTH AND FLINTS		CLAY
	CHALK FLOOR		CHALKY SOIL

Fig. 35

LATER PERIODS

The Origin of Villages study which will form the second part of the Chilgrove Valley Landscape Project will examine in more detail the post-Roman periods in the Mardens and other villages, and only a brief survey of the later periods discernable at Pitlands Farm will be given here:

Period 2: late Saxon— Saxo-Norman, c. early to late 11th century

Some evidence exists for occupation in the 11th century in the form of oxydised coarse gritty pottery found in pits and in the topsoil. The fabric is typical of the late Saxon wares found in Chichester, but the incised lattice decoration on one vessel is reminiscent of the Romano-British period (Fig. 73, No. 6).

The earliest documentary sources for Upmarden are in a late Saxon charter, which refers to Goda, a thegn, who gave four hides at Upmarden to Wichstan, his son-in-law, c. 900–905 A.D. No pottery has yet been found which would support a 10th-century date, but certainly occupation was well established on the site a century or so later. No structures could be identified, but these might well have occupied the same area as the present farmhouse.

Period 3: Medieval, c. 13th—14th century

Coarse and glazed wares of 13th-14th-century date were present in pits, and as residual material in the garden soil, and although no specifically 12th-century material could be identified, continuous occupation from the time the site was re-occupied in the 11th century throughout the medieval period is likely.

The earliest documentary record known dates from 1574 and the Tithe Award map of 1841 gives the farm a total size of 158 acres, just under half the size of Brick Kiln Farm at Chilgrove. Part of the present farmhouse probably dates from c. 17th century.

Note

1. Information from Mr. Henry Cleere, F.S.A., who kindly examined samples of the slag.

References

COLUMELLA — *On Agriculture,* Vol. 1. *Res Rustica,* I–IV. Trans. Harrison Boyd Ash, London (1941).

CUNLIFFE 1973 — 'Chalton, Hants.: the evolution of a landscape', *Ant. J.,* LIII (II), 1973.

CUNLIFFE 1966 — Cunliffe, B. W., 'Stoke Clump, Hollingbury and the Early pre-Roman Iron Age in Sussex'. *S.A.C.,* 104 (1966).

CURWEN 1929 — Curwen, E. C., 'Excavations at the Trundle, Goodwood, 1928', *S.A.C.,* 70 (1929).

CHICHESTER 2 — Down, A., *Chichester Excavations 2,* Chichester, 1974.

CHICHESTER 3 — Down, A., *Chichester Excavations 3,* Chichester, 1978.

DOWN (forthcoming) — Down, A., *Chichester Excavations 5.*

FRERE 1967 — Frere, S. S., *Britannia,* London 1967.

FULFORD, 1975

Fulford, M. G., 'New Forest Roman Pottery', *British Archaeological Report No. 17*, 1975.

HAWKES 1939

Hawkes, C. F. C., 'The Pottery from Castle Hill, Newhaven', *S.A.C.* 80 (1939).

LEEDS 1945

Leeds, E. T., 'The distribution of the Angles and Saxons archaeologically considered'. *Archaeologia,* 91 (1945).

WELCH 1978

Welch, M. G., 'Early Anglo-Saxon Sussex; from civitas to shire', in P. Brandon (ed.), *The South Saxons*. Chichester 1978.

The Mosaics of Chilgrove

by D. J. Smith

I am indebted to Mr. Alec Down, F.S.A., for the opportunity to report on the mosaics of the two sites at Chilgrove excavated under his direction, and to the Excavations Committee of the Chichester Civic Society as well as Mr. Down for the photographs, colour transparencies, and other data on which this report is based.

SITE 1

Remains of two mosaics were found on this site. One was in the central and evidently the principal room (Room 6) of the corridor house of Period 4, i.e., *c.* early fourth century (above, pp. 60–65). The other was in the large room with hypocaust (Room 15) which was added at the north-east end of the corridor in Period 4.

Room 6 (Plates I and 7)

The room measured 18ft. 6ins. by 20ft. (6.10 m. by 5.64 m.). The mosaic was 16ft. 4ins. (5 m.) square. It was surrounded by paving of irregular red (tile) tesserae averaging 2.7 cm.³ The tesserae of the mosaic averaged 1.2 cm.³ and comprised the following colours and materials: red (tile), white (chalk), yellow (baked chalk), grey-blue (lias limestone), and brown (a very soft shaley ironstone).

Nearly half of the mosaic had been destroyed (Plate 7), including the central motif, but sufficient remained to suggest that the design was symmetrical and so to enable it to be visualised and described as though intact (Plate I). In the centre was a medallion with a red outline, three tesserae wide, and a surrounding circle of three-strand guilloche. This was enclosed within two interlaced squares of simple guilloche set in an octagon of simple guilloche. Each angle of the squares touched a side of the octagon at its mid-point, and each alternate angle of the octagon touched a side of the containing linear square at its mid-point.

Between the interlaced squares and the octagon were eight lozenge-shaped interstitial spaces. Each of these was occupied by a simple motif in a linear lozenge of red, and diametrically opposite lozenges apparently contained identical motifs. These were: a short strip of simple guilloche, a knot with two buds or petals sprouting from opposite loops, two hearts contiguous at their lobes and two hearts similarly arranged but with the lobes rendered as involuted spirals. The points of the hearts and of the buds or petals were red and a small triangle of red protruded on either side of the hearts between the lobes.

In one angle of the containing square was a large bell-like flower, depicted in profile and opening towards the centre of the design. From the bifurcation at the top of this motif rose a stem bearing a very small bud, and from this a tendril sprang to either side, first falling to suspend a heart-shaped leaf, then curving to support a smaller and broader flower in profile, and then proceeding to terminate in another heart-shaped leaf. The diagonally opposite angle of the containing square was apparently embellished with the same pattern.

In one of the other two angles was depicted a fluted or gadrooned bowl with a chequered rim and a slightly domed lid. Above this was a small flower in profile. From either side of the bowl rose a tendril, first encircling a flower like the smaller flowers in the angle described above, then encircling a heart-shaped leaf, and then terminating in another heart-shaped leaf. The pattern in the diagonally opposite angle was evidently not identical, but presumably was essentially similar.

The upper half of all the flowers and the points of all the leaves were red. Then came a band of yellow. The rest was white. The white half of the large bell-like flower was divided horizontally by a strip of chequerwork. The pattern in each angle was enclosed by a grey-blue linear frame and the containing square was formed by a dark grey line.

As a freestanding design the basic geometry of this mosaic—a medallion enclosed by interlaced squares in an octagon contained in a square—is at present unparalleled in Britain. But only the set of the octagon relative to the containing square differentiates this design from that of Basildon (Berks),[1] or that of the panel portraying Winter at Bignor (Sussex),[2] to name two examples with motifs paralleled in the mosaic of Chilgrove. The motifs at Basildon included bell-like flowers and knots with opposed buds, and among those in the panel at Bignor are, as at Chilgrove, two short strips of simple guilloche.[3] Short strips of simple guilloche are also known in another mosaic of Bignor,[4] while in the angles of yet another mosaic[5] at Bignor (Plate 6) are remarkably close parallels for the patterns of bowls, flowers and leaves in the angles of the containing square at Chilgrove. Similar bowls, flowers and leaves again recur in other mosaics of Bignor[6] but it must be noted that the bowls of Bignor have a small triangular foot and are also more painstakingly designed than the surviving bowl at Chilgrove. In short, the mosaic of Chilgrove can clearly be attributed to the workshop which produced these particular mosaics of Bignor; and, although it appears possibly a little later, its dating affords for the first time an indication of the actual period of these mosaics.

The mosaic of Basildon and certain mosaics in Hampshire can also be attributed directly or indirectly to the same workshop. Among these, that of Sparsholt (Hants)[7] is especially noteworthy in the present context for the large bell-like flowers in two opposite angles. These have a small triangular foot and no transverse strip of chequerwork, but in form and colouring are almost identical with those of Chilgrove as well as also occupying opposite angles of the mosaic. These and the other inter-related mosaics can now be recognised as evidence for a fifth fourth-century school in Britain,[8] the period of which is at present indicated only by the dated mosaic of Chilgrove. But, although the most probable location for the workshop would be the *civitas* capital of Noviomagus Reg(i)norum,[9] six miles from Chilgrove and 10 from Bignor, more evidence is needed before one can speak plausibly of a 'Noviomagan school'.

110

Room 15 (Plate 8)

This room, 17ft. by 19ft. (5.18 m. by 5.79 m.), had also been paved with a mosaic, but of this there remained intact merely a fragment *c.* 2ft. 2ins. by 8ins. (67 cm. by 20 cm.), in which a heart-shaped leaf, similar to the leaves of the mosaic in Room 6, was the most conspicuous feature. No further observation is possible.

SITE 2

Building 1, Room 1A (Fig. 27 and Plate 15)

This building dates from Period 3 (above, p. 83), but the floor was probably laid in Period 4 (above, p. 85). Room 1A, 12ft. by 12ft. 9ins. (3.65 m. by 3.89 m.), was paved throughout with red (tile) tesserae, averaging 2.5 cm.[3], except at the foot of the west wall, where two features were executed in greensand tesserae. That to the left was a simple arrangement of straight lines suggesting a childish attempt to depict a horse with a rider, but the other seems an inexplicable jumble. Nothing comparable to either is recorded in Roman mosaic.

There had been another mosaic on this site, in Room 1B, of which only loose tesserae survived. These were similar in size and type to those from Room 6 of Site 1.

Building 2, Room 7 (Figs. 25 and 26, and Plate 2)

This building, an aisled barn, dated from Period 4 (above, pp. 88–92), Room 7, the largest and presumably the principal room, measured about 19ft. by 20ft. 6ins. (5.79 m. by 6.25 m.). It was paved throughout with red (tile) tesserae averaging 2.8 cm.[3], unrelieved except by nine circular motifs executed mainly in slightly smaller tesserae of white (chalk) and greensand. Some of the red tesserae within these circles had been laid so as to show the unoxidised blue core of the tile.

The circles varied from *c.* 29 cm. to *c.* 44 cm. in diameter. Seven (1–7 below) formed a row across the room from south to north at a distance of 8ft. (2.52 m.) from the west wall. The invervals between these varied between 9ins. to *c.* 1ft. 8ins. (23 cm. to 51 cm.). The other two (8, 9 below) were 5ft. 6ins. (1.72 m.) apart at a distance of 3ft. 6ins. (1.09 m.) from the east wall. One of these lay opposite the interval between the fourth and fifth from the left in the row of seven, and the other lay opposite the seventh. From left to right the circles can be described as follows:

(1) Four concentric white circles, the innermost formed of only four tesserae.
(2) A white saltire cross surrounded by two white concentric circles from the outer of which four short rays pointed to the west wall.
(3) A solid white circle surrounded by a white circle with dentils projecting all round except on the third of its circumference towards the east wall where a short white tail projected in the same direction.
(4) An irregular cluster of white tesserae surrounded by a double circle of white tesserae, those of the inner circle staggered in relation to those of the outer. Due to severe damage by burning, this circle is difficult to decipher.

(5)   A single white tessera central in a circle of white tesserae.

(6)   A circle of white tesserae.

(7)   Four white tesserae in a cruciform arrangement surrounded by two concentric white circles.

(8)   (second row) four white tesserae together in the centre of a white circle.

(9)   (second row) as (7), but slightly smaller and with only three tesserae in the centre.

Again there is nothing in Roman mosaic to compare with this most curious pavement,[10] and it seems futile even to attempt to comment further upon it.

Notes

1. The most convincing record is the pen and water-colour drawing by Wm. Church of Streatley (Berks.), probably made when the mosaic was discovered in October 1838, in the Haverfield Collection, Ashmolean Museum. In the same collection is another drawing, in pencil and water-colour, bearing the note: 'copied from a drawing by Mr. Harrow . . . made in 1839, H.E.S.' In the Department of Paintings, Prints and Drawings of the London Museum is another pen and water-colour drawing, anonymous, evidently not a copy of Church's. Hence, perhaps, the inferior coloured lithograph in C. R. Smith, *Collectanea Antiqua* I (1848), Plate XXIV.

2. S. Lysons, *Reliquiae Britannico-Romanae* III (1817), Plate XV. J. M. C. Toynbee, *Art in Roman Britain* (1962), Plate 218.

3. It is very interesting that, while strips of guilloche normally terminate with a loop at either end, one of those in this panel at Bignor is truncated at one end and the other at both ends, suggesting sections cut from a prefabricated length.

4. Lysons, *op. cit.*, Plate XVII.

5. *Ibid.*, Plate V.

6. *Ibid.*, Plates VII, VIII, IX, XII, XV, XVIII.

7. Plate 7, IVa, in J. Munby and M. Henig (eds.), *Roman Life and Art in Britain* (1977).

8. D. E. Johnston, 'The central southern group of Romano-British mosaics', pp. 195–215 in Munby and Henig (eds.), *op. cit.* There appears, however, little or no reason to derive the repertory of these mosaics from those attributable to the Corinian school; and apart from its border the fragmentary mosaic found on the site of Greig's shop, East Street, Chichester (1959), seems not to justify inclusion in the 'central southern group'. For a summary of the evidence for the other four fourth-century schools, see D. J. Smith in *The Roman Villa in Britain* (ed. A. L. F. Rivet (1969)), 95–113; *ibid., Ant. J.* XLIX (1969), 235–43; *ibid., Britannia* V (1974), 248–50.

9. For the form of the tribal name see *Britannia* I (1970), 50, 78–9.

10. Two circles reminiscent of circle (2) at Chilgrove flanked a lozenge in the crude late-second-century panel at the entrance of Temple 1 at Springhead (Kent): *Arch. Cant.* LXXII (1959), Plate 11, C; but otherwise this panel is hardly comparable with the Chilgrove mosaic.

Illustrations

Plate 7. Site 1, Room 6. (*Photo: G. Claridge.*)

Plate   I. Site 1, Room 6. (*Colour reconstruction by Cedric de la Nougerede.*)

Plate 6. Patterns in the angles of a mosaic at Bignor (Sussex). From Sl. Lysons, *Reliquiae Britannico-Romanae* III (1817), Plates V, VIII.

Plate 8. Site 1, Room 15. (*Photo: G. Claridge.*)

Plate 15. Site 2, Building 1, Room 1A. (*Photo: G. Claridge.*)

Plate 14. Site 2, Building 2, Room 7. (*Photo: G. Claridge.*)

Plate II. Site 2, Building 2, Room 7. (*Colour drawing by Cedric de la Nougerede.*)

The Animal Bones

by Alan Outen

CHILGROVE 1

The number of bones and fragments from the whole site totalled 681, including 167 fragments too small for positive identification.

The bones came from layers, pits, rooms, and the stockyard. In general, they were in good condition and could be handled firmly, but had a tendency to shatter if dropped or knocked sharply. The majority had suffered some damage in the soil, and this was particularly so in the case of limb bone epiphyses and scapula blades.

From 514 identified bones only 11 were complete and undamaged. Such measurements as were taken have been deposited with Chichester Excavations Committee.

BONE COUNTS

For the purpose of bone counts, those from the layers, pits, and rooms collectively called the Site were treated first, followed by the Stockyard. Ribs were not included in the counts.

The objective was to note any significant differences in the dispersal of the bones over the Site and the Stockyard. The approximate percentage result is as under:

	Ox	Sheep/Goat	Pig	Horse	Deer	Avion	Dog
	%	%	%	%	%	%	%
Site	56.6	19.6	3.3	3.6	0.3	3.6	13.0
Stockyard	57.6	22.3	4.3	12.5	2.7	1.0	—

With the exception of Dog which is absent from the Stockyard, the composition of the spread of bones over the two areas is similar. There is also a fairly close percentage agreement in respect of Ox, Sheep/Goat, and Pig.

It is with the Horse bones that the most marked difference occurs: 12.5 per cent. from the Stockyard as compared with 3.6 per cent. from the Site.

Following the above examination and for the purpose of obtaining an overall picture of the animal bones from the entire site, the bones were amalgamated and designated 'whole site'.

Table 1. Shows total bones and percentage for each species.

Table 2. As the total number of bones and fragments was not excessive, it was possible to examine the material for matching bones. This was carried out with each deposit and a minimum number of individuals for each species estimated'(*Chaplin* 1971, pp. 70–75.)

To illustrate more graphically the percentage of bones of each species from the whole site, a histogram (Fig. 36) was produced. From this it is clear that Ox and Sheep/Goat are the main animals represented.

A histogram (Fig. 36) shows the total numbers for each of the bones of Ox, Sheep/Goat and Pig from the whole site.

113

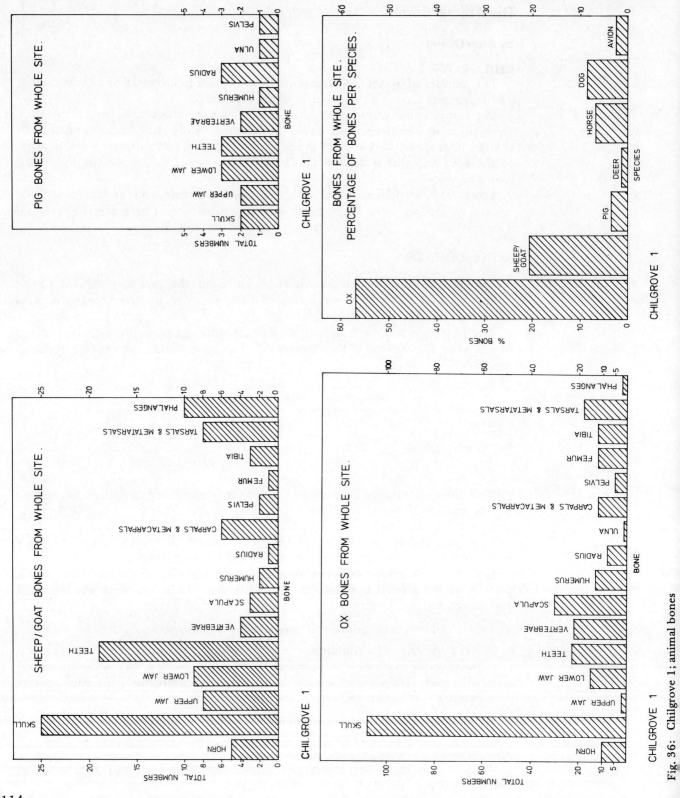

114

Fig. 36: Chilgrove 1; animal bones

AGE DETERMINATION

Age determination (*Silver* 1969), from bone fusion and teeth examination was carried out for Ox, Sheep/Goat, and Pig. With so few of the requisite bones available, it was realised that interpretations using the percentage figures given below can only be tentative, and should not be treated as firm conclusions.

Ox		
1–1½ years	2–3 years	3–4 years
20 per cent.	25 per cent.	55 per cent.

The above does not include one individual under one year.

Sheep/Goat		
0–10 months	1½–2½ years	2½–3½ years
25 per cent.	58.3 per cent.	16.7 per cent.

Pig

1 individual under 1 year.
1 individual 1–2 years.
2 individuals over 3 years.

1 individual about 2 years.
2 individuals 2–3 years.

Butchery

Bones and fragments displaying knife and chop markings totalled 35, and came mainly from Ox.

The appearance of some marks suggests that both a heavy and light type of knife were utilised.

Knife marks were numerous on the edges of Scapula blades. Of the limb bones, Humerus and Tibia exhibited the most.

On Skull fragments markings of knife were noticeable in the region of the Orbit, suggesting the removal of cheek flesh.

Chop markings were mainly on the epiphyses of limb bones, with Humerus showing the greatest number.

Three Ox Cervical Vertebrae from the Stockyard bones had been chopped right through, suggesting a division into joints.

In some instances the shafts of Ox Humerus and Tibia had been deliberately split, possibly for the extraction of marrow.

One example of the use of a saw was given by the right Radius of Horse, which had a cut on the distal epiphyses.

With fragments from Pit F3 it was possible to make a partial restoration of an Ox skull. When completed it exhibited a feature suggestive of the animal being struck a blow, possibly to stun it before slaughter. As the area concerned is thin-boned, the above is given with caution. The feature could have been caused after death by other means, e.g., soil pressure. The skull is now in Chichester City Museum.

It appears that some Horns were removed by chopping at the base, presumably to weaken it, then giving a heavy blow. Most of the Horn cores with chop marks at the base had fragments of skull attached.

Ox

Fig. 36 shows that the bones are a mixture of food and slaughter waste.

Of the food bones, Scapula is the most common, followed by Vertebrae (mainly from the Cervical and Thoracic regions). Humerus and Femur are nearly equal in numbers, but fall well below that for Scapula. One explanation for this contrast could be that some of the limb bones, in the form of joints, were dispersed elsewhere. It is also possible that these particular bones were favoured by the dogs, although none of the fragments displayed any indication of teeth marks.

Skull fragments form the highest peak of all, and came mainly from pits. As previously mentioned, it was possible to make a partial restoration with the fragments from Pit F3.

The low peak for Phalanges suggests that the hooves were removed from the site, possibly for further processing.

All the Horn core fragments indicate a shorthorn breed, but estimates as to size of the animals was not possible with the few available bones. It can only be said that the Metapodial lengths recorded are within the range of Bos longifrons.

For the same reason as above, sex determination was precluded. Mention should be made, however, of one fragment of Metacarpal with a distal epiphyses width exceeding those of others noted. This was probably from a male or castrate. The same fragment displayed an apparent arthritic condition and was the only visible form of abnormality found.

It will be seen under Age Determination for this animal, that the age ranges fall into three groups.

It is suggested that the oldest group (3–4+ years) represents the breeding herd which would have also supplied the individuals for draught work, as well as any dairy products. The bones in this group are probaly of animals culled from the herd at an age beyond which to keep them, would not be economical

If the above is correct, then it would seem that the middle group of bones (2–3 years) are from animals raised specifically for meat. They would be young animals, but grown.

The youngest group (1–1½ years) would consist of animals who had been kept through one winter at least. While some may have died from disease, injury, or other causes, the percentage figure does suggest some deliberate killing.

Sheep/Goat

In most cases it was not possible to distinguish between the two species, although Sheep was recognised. It is probable that Goat was represented also, but the absence of positive evidence does give a bias towards Sheep, and interpretations are made on this basis.

The only example of hornless sheep came in the form of a large fragment of skull from Pit F2. Two other skull fragments from the same pit were from horned individuals under one-and-a-half years.

Referring to Fig. 36, all the high peaks indicate slaughter waste which forms the bulk of the bones. Food bones as represented by Femur, Humerus, Scapula, and Vertebrae, have low peaks and as with Ox may suggest that some joints were dispersed elsewhere.

Under Age Determination three groups are indicated, and interpreted in the same way as for Ox.

The oldest group (2½–3½ years) probably represents the breeding flock, which would also supply the wool. For this reason, culling of the flock would no doubt be carried out sparingly, hence the low percentage figure.

It would appear that the middle group (1½–2½ years) consists of animals raised for their meat, and the high percentage figure suggests that this age range did produce the best quality.

The percentage figure for the youngest group (0–10 months) points to a fairly high mortality rate for the first year. This could be due in part to the killing of weak or sickly individuals, and some may have died from other causes. It is also possible that there was some demand for this young meat, but against this deliberate killing is the fact that the animals would not have gained a lot of weight in that period of time.

Pig

The bones are a fairly equal mixture of food and slaughter waste, and as Fig. 36 shows these animals were not kept on the same scale numerically as Ox and Sheep/Goat.

The low number of bones suggests that the animals were reared for consumption on the site where, as well as providing lard, their meat would have undoubtedly been a welcome alternative to beef and mutton. What is probably just as important is that they would have been available if meat from the other sources was in short supply.

In the instances where age determination was possible, it was found from examination of the teeth that the majority of the animals were two years or over at death.

Horse

At least eight individuals are represented, with the number of bones from the Stockyard being almost double those from the site. None of the animals had been found as burials, and the bones being mixed with those of other animals, suggests that after death the flesh was eaten.

Two right Metacarpals from the Stockyard bones were of interest due to differences in their measurements. Both were from adult animals, and indicate that one individual was small, possibly of pony size. Where estimates of age from teeth was possible, it was found that one individual was 5–7 years, and three were at least 13 years. No visible evidence of injury or disease was found.

Deer

The total evidence was six fragments, of which five came from the Stockyard bones. Red deer is indicated by two fragments of Antler beam; these were from naturally-shed Antlers which had probably been picked up and taken to the site. None of this material displayed any cut marks, or indications of being used as implements.

One fragment of Radius and one of Metatarsal formed the bone material, and both are suggestive of Red Deer. From the very slender evidence it would appear that Deer was of little importance as a source of meat.

Dog

All the fragments came from Pit F7 and represent two animals, one just under one year, the other over one-and-a-half years.

117

Avion

Only one fragment of bone came from the Stockyard bones, the remainder were from Pits F3 and F7. Altogether a minimum of five individuals is indicated.

Estimates as to body size suggests that the fragments from Pits F3 and F7 are from individuals with the body size of Pheasant. The single fragment from the Stockyard bones is possibly from an individual with the body size of Carrion Crow.

ANIMAL BONE MEASUREMENTS

OX

Bone			Length	Width mid-shaft	Width Prox. Epi.	Width Dist. Epi.	Side
Radius	..	..	—	44.5 mm.	82 mm.	—	left
Radius	..	..	—	—	81 mm.	—	—
Metacarpal	..	..	184 mm.	34 mm.	58 mm.	59 mm.	right
Metacarpal	..	..	—	—	47 mm.	—	—
Metacarpal	..	..	—	—	—	71 mm.	—
Metacarpal	..	..	188 mm.	34.5 mm.	55.5 mm.	58 mm.	right
Metacarpal	..	..	—	—	—	49 mm.	—
Metacarpal	..	..	—	28 mm.	49 mm.	—	—
Metacarpal	..	..	—	—	58 mm.	—	—
Femur	..	..	—	32 mm.	—	—	—
Tibia	..	..	—	31 mm.	—	—	—
Tibia	..	..	—	36 mm.	—	—	—
Tibia	..	..	—	37.5 mm.	—	—	—
Tibia	..	..	—	—	—	55 mm.	—
Tibia	..	..	—	—	—	51 mm.	—
Metatarsal	..	..	210 mm.	30 mm.	58 mm.	59 mm.	left
Metatarsal	..	..	—	—	—	46 mm.	—
Metatarsal	..	..	—	24 mm.	45 mm.	—	left
Metatarsal	..	..	—	—	—	53.5 mm.	—

PIG

Bone			Length	Width mid-shaft	Width Prox. Epi.	Width Dist. Epi.	Side
Humerus	..	..	—	12.5 mm.	—	28 mm.	immature
Radius	..	..	—	15 mm.	25 mm.	29 mm.	—

DOG

Bone			Length	Width mid-shaft	Width Prox. Epi.	Width Dist. Epi.	Side
Humerus	..	..	11 mm.	—	—	24 mm.	—

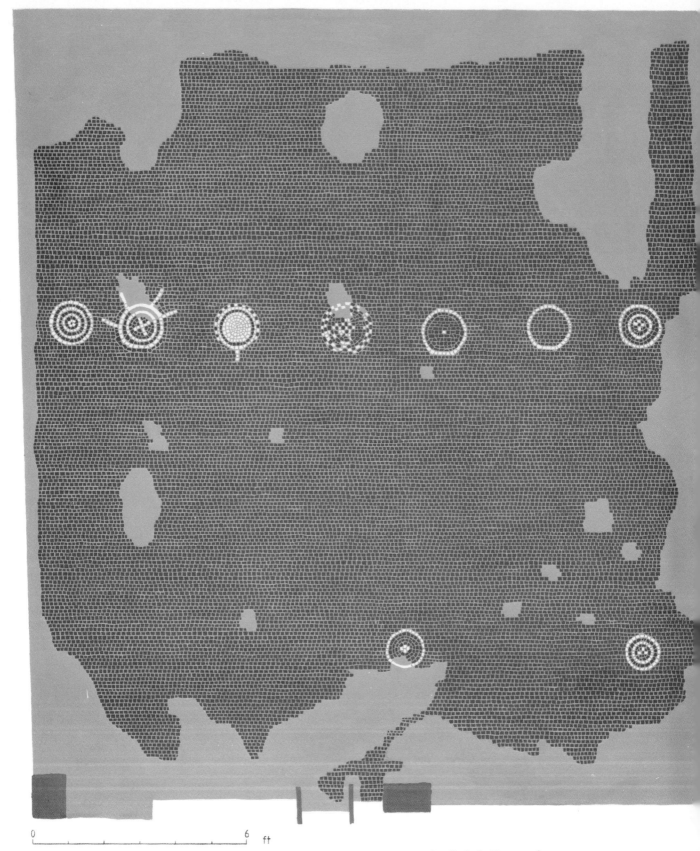

0   6 ft

II.   Chilgrove 2, Building 2, Room 7. Drawn by C. de la Nougerede.

SHEEP/GOAT

Bone	Length	Width mid-shaft	Width Prox. Epi.	Width Dist. Epi.	Side
Metacarpal	121 mm.	13 mm.	21 mm.	24 mm.	left
Metacarpal	121 mm.	13 mm.	21 mm.	24 mm.	right
Metacarpal	129 mm.	13 mm.	23 mm.	25 mm.	right
Metacarpal	—	—	23 mm.	25 mm.	—
Metacarpal	—	7.5 mm.	—	—	immature
Femur	—	—	—	36.5 mm.	—
Tibia	—	15 mm.	—	—	—
Metatarsal	131 mm.	11 mm.	20.5 mm.	23 mm.	left
Metatarsal	142 mm.	12 mm.	22 mm.	23 mm.	left
Metatarsal	—	12 mm.	21.5 mm.	—	—

HORSE

Bone	Length	Width mid-shaft	Width Prox. Epi.	Width Dist. Epi.	Side
Radius	—	36.5 mm.	74 mm.	—	right
Radius	308 mm.	37 mm.	75 mm.	68 mm.	left
Radius	—	35 mm.	76 mm.	—	left
Radius	—	36 mm.	—	—	left
Radius	—	39 mm.	—	—	—
Metacarpal	227 mm.	34 mm.	54.5 mm.	50 mm.	right
Metacarpal	205 mm.	30.5 mm.	44 mm.	43 mm.	right
Tibia	—	47.5 mm.	—	75 mm.	—
Tibia	—	36 mm.	—	—	—
Metatarsal	—	29 mm.	—	—	—

Animal Bones from Whole Site: TABLE 1

Bone	Ox	Sheep/ Goat	Pig	Horse	Deer	Avion	Dog
Horn/Antler	10	5	—	—	4	—	—
Skull	108	25	2	1	—	—	—
Upper jaw	2	8	2	—	—	—	1
Lower jaw	15	9	3	—	—	—	3
Teeth	23	19	3	8	—	—	—
Vertebrae	22	4	2	—	—	—	14
Scapula	30	3	—	3	—	—	1
Humerus	13	2	1	1	—	1	3
Radius	8	1	3	6	1	2	2
Ulna	1	—	1	1	—	6	2
Carpals and Metacarpals ..	12	6	—	3	—	1	2
Pelvis	5	2	1	6	—	—	—
Femur	12	1	—	1	—	—	1
Tibia	12	3	—	2	—	—	—
Tarsals and Metatarsals	18	8	—	2	1	3	2
Phalanges	2	10	—	1	—	—	12
Species total	293	106	18	35	6	13	43
Total bones..	514						
Percentage No. of Bones ..	% 57.0	% 20.6	% 3.5	% 6.8	% 1.2	% 2.5	% 8.3

Indeterminable fragments = 167.

Minimum Number of Animals: TABLE 2

Layer	Ox	Sheep/Goat	Pig	Horse	Deer	Avion	Dog	Total Bones
A4 (1)	2	1	1	—	—	—	—	6
L1 (1) Room 15 ..	1	—	—	—	—	—	—	6
H5 (1b)	—	1	—	—	—	—	—	10
F2 (1c)	—	—	—	—	—	—	—	1
A1 (2)	3	—	—	1	—	—	—	10
C2 (2)	2	—	—	—	—	—	—	13
D2 (2) Room 7 ..	1	1	—	—	—	—	—	7
E1 (2)	2	—	—	1	—	—	—	7
F1 (2) Pit F2	—	3	—	—	—	—	—	26
E6 (2)	1	—	—	1	—	—	—	7
E1 (2a) Room 6 ..	1	—	—	1	—	—	—	13
C2 (3)	2	1	1	1	—	—	—	19
K2 (4)	1	—	1	—	—	—	—	8
A1 (5)	1	—	—	—	—	—	—	3
F1 (10) Pit F7	1	—	2	—	—	2	2	86
F1 Pit F3	4	—	—	—	—	2	—	71
E2..	4	1	—	1	—	—	—	23
A2	1	1	—	—	—	—	—	14
Stockyard	10	3	2	2	1	1	—	184
Totals	37	12	7	8	1	5	2	514

Note.– The one bone from F2 (1c) is a fragment of naturally-shed Antler and has not been included in the minimum individuals represented.

Of the 86 bones from F1 (10) Pit F7, 63 are Ox skull fragments from one individual.

Molluscs (land)

In compiling this note the writer acknowledges the advice and assistance given by Mr. E. M. Venables, F.G.S. The samples noted above all came from below the ploughsoil in the rubble of the destroyed building.

Species	Numbers
Helix (cornu) aspera (*Müller*)	57
Hygromia (Trichia) striolata (*C. Pfeiffer*) ..	21
Arianta arbustorum (L)	1
Cepaea nemoralis (L)	19
Goniodiscus rotundatus (*Müller*)	8
Oxchychilus cellarius (*Müller*)	4
Cepaea hortensis (*Müller*)	3
Cochlicopa lubrica (*Müller*)	1
Hygromia (Trichia) hispida (L)	1

REMARKS

Climate—damp. A general picture suggests wasteland with rubble or rubbish and fairly sheltered. Woodland not far from the site.

Molluscs (marine)
Buccinum undatum.
Ostea edulis.
Cardium edulis.

THE INFANT BURIAL FROM ROOM 6

The bones, consisting of a crushed skull and a few fragments of limb bones, ribs and phalanges, came from a shallow grave approximately 61 cm. in length; and aligned north to south, with the skull fragments at the southern end. The bones had been subjected to considerable soil disturbance.

Only the skull fragments were available for examination. These were repaired, and the following identified:

Right and left Frontal bones (incompletely ossified).
Right and left Parietal bones (incompletely ossified).
One small fragment of Orbit.
One fragment of Temporal bone (petrous part).

The condition of the Frontal bones suggest the individual to have been under two years at death.

References

CHAPLIN 1971 — Chaplin, R. E., *The Study of Animal Bones from Archaeological Sites*, Seminar Press, London and New York, 1971.

SILVER 1969 — Silver, I. A., 'The Ageing of domestic animals', in *Science in Archaeology* (Brothwell and Higgs, eds.), Thames and Hudson, London, 1969.

CHILGROVE 2

The bone and teeth material from the whole site amounted to 5,000 items, including 1,257 fragments too small for identification or having no distinguishing features. Also examined and included in the total items were 378 unstratified fragments.

The material came from eight layers, two ditches, and a well. It should be mentioned that the well took up the largest part of the examination, and produced 2,205 determinable items.

The bones from the layers and ditches were similar in colour and condition to those from Site 1; most had suffered damage in the soil. Those from the well were of lighter colouration, and it was first thought that damage to individual bones would be minimal. However, this was not the case, the amount of damaged material appeared to be at least equal to that from the layers and ditches. Scapula blades, and Skulls in particular, were very fragmentary and gave the impression of having been crushed.

For the sake of uniformity the methods employed in the examination were the same as those used on Site 1, although due to the greater quantity of material, the time taken was considerably longer.

As with Site 1, measurements where possible were recorded and have been deposited with the Chichester Excavations Committee.

BONE COUNTS

Each of the layers was examined and recorded separately, although for the purpose of grouping (see below) the total number of fragments from all the layers is given. Each ditch and the well were also examined individually.

The figure of 5,000 items was considerably reduced by the exclusion of the following: 1,257 indeterminable fragments; 378 unstratified fragments; and 186 Rib fragments. This left a total of 3,179 items to be considered, and these have been grouped as under:

Layers	..	182
Ditch 1	..	639
Ditch 2	..	153
Well	..	2,205
Total	..	3,179

The percentage of bones per species for each of the groups is given in Figs. 37-40. These also show the individual bones of Ox, Sheep/Goat, and Pig; it should be noted, however, there is no Histogram for Pig from the layers.

During this part of the examination it became apparent that a fairly high proportion of the fragments was slaughter waste.

To determine the approximate percentage for each group, only the bones of Ox, sheep/Goat, Pig, Deer, and Horse were considered. The results are listed below.

Layers = 73.6 per cent. slaughter waste.
Ditch 1 = 68.8 per cent. slaughter waste.
Ditch 2 = 74.8 per cent. slaughter waste.
Well = 72.3 per cent. slaughter waste.

NUMBER OF INDIVIDUALS

At Site 1, estimates as to the number of individuals represented by the bones were obtained by finding the minimum possible number of animals for each species. It was therefore necessary to follow the same principles on the present site, even though a greater quantity of material was involved.

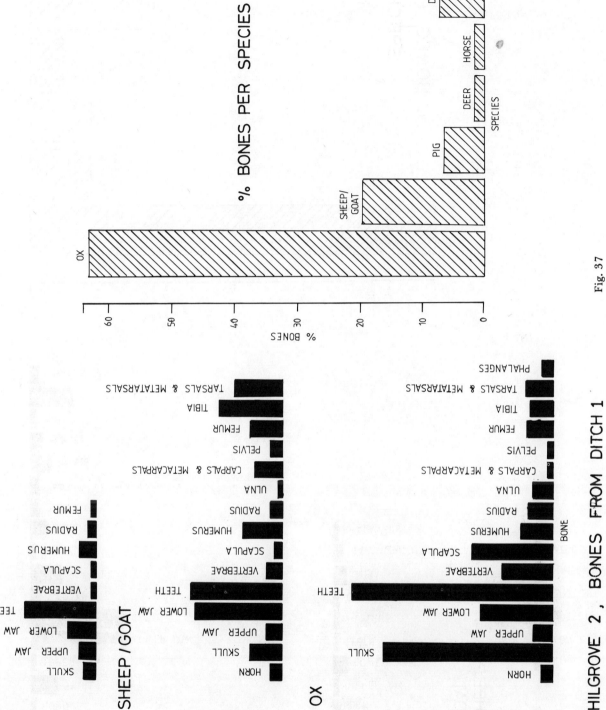

% BONES PER SPECIES

Fig. 37

CHILGROVE 2 , BONES FROM DITCH 1

123

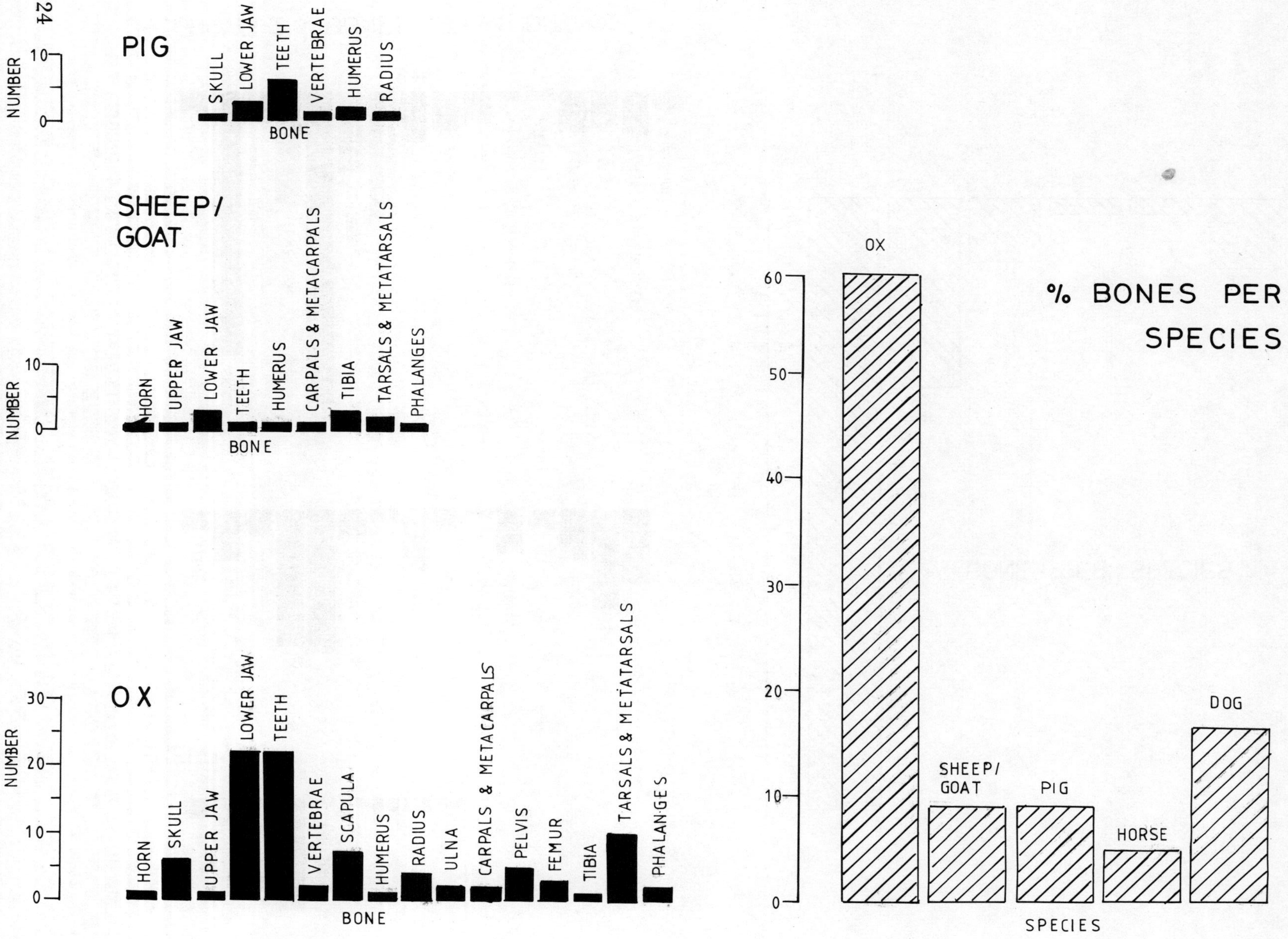

% BONES PER SPECIES

Fig. 38

124

CHILGROVE 2, BONES FROM DITCH 2

AGE DETERMINATION

With very few bones available from the Layers and Ditch 2, only the fragments from Ditch 1 and the Well were considered for the purpose of age determination. Both these groups contained the largest number of bones. It must also be mentioned that the percentage figures obtained for the well are the more reliable. Those for Ditch 1, due to the lower number of fragments, should be treated with caution.

Ox

				1–1½ years	2–3 years	3–4 + years
Ditch 1	..	..	..	33.3 per cent.	30.3 per cent.	36.3 per cent.
Well ..	..	..	..	26.9 per cent.	32.4 per cent.	40.5 per cent.

Sheep/Goat

				0–10 months	1½–2½ years	2½–3½ years
Ditch 1	..	..	..	44.4 per cent.	38.8 per cent.	16.6 per cent.
Well ..	..	..	..	23.1 per cent.	45.1 per cent.	31.7 per cent.

Pig

F1 (14) = 1 over 3 years.
F1 (19) = 1 over 3 years.
C1/C4 (14) = 1 under 2 years.
Ditch 1 = 2 under 2 years, 3 over 3 years.
Ditch 2 = 1 under 2 years, 1 between 2–3 years.
Well = 1 over 3 years.

Butchery

A total of 74 bones from the whole site displayed chop or knife markings, with almost half of these coming from Ditch 1. See p. 115 for comments on similar bones from Site 1.

Ox bones formed the bulk of this material, followed by Pig. Sheep/Goat fragments were rarely marked.

One fragment of naturally-shed Deer antler from Ditch 1 had indications of the use of saw, two tines having been severed by this means.

A large fragment of Sheep skull from the same ditch had both horns removed by this method.

Ox

The histograms make it clear that the bones of this animal were the most common, the percentage for each group ranging from 50.6 per cent. from the well to 70.8 per cent. from the layers.

Each group contained a mixture of slaughter and food waste and in Figs. 37–40 it will be seen that generally the highest peaks are obtained from slaughter waste. The best illustration of this is Fig. 39.

Scapula is the best representative of food waste and appears quite prominently in each group except the layers (Fig. 40). Femur and Humerus occupy fairly low peaks in each group; this was also the case at Site 1.

Although in most instances Horn cores were badly fragmented, it was possible to observe as at the previous site, that a shorthorn breed is indicated.

125

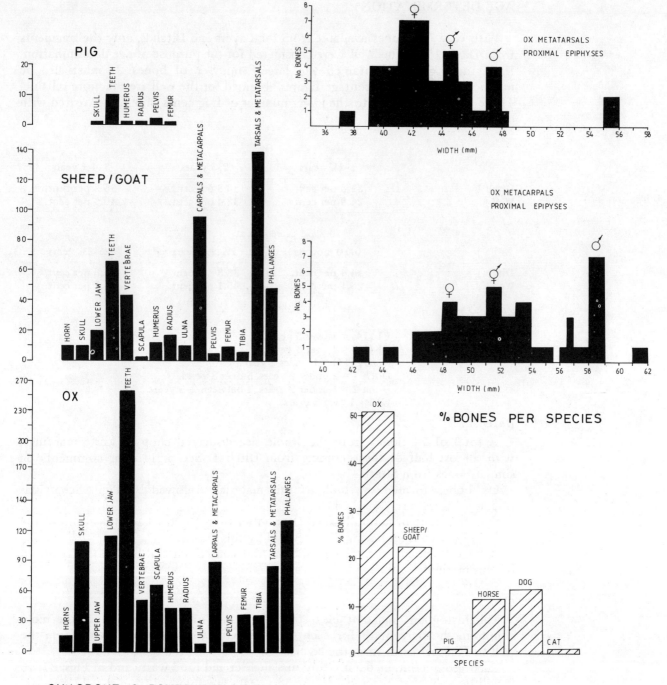

PIG

SHEEP/GOAT

OX

CHILGROVE 2, BONES FROM WELL

Fig. 39

OX METATARSALS PROXIMAL EPIPHYSES

OX METACARPALS PROXIMAL EPIPYSES

% BONES PER SPECIES

The majority of complete Metacarpals and Metatarsals came from the well; the bone lengths for these are listed as under:

Metacarpals

13 Bones = 173 mm. to 186 mm.
3 Bones = 191 mm. to 193 mm.

Metatarsals

13 Bones = 200 mm. to 219 mm.
1 Bone = 229 mm.

It will be seen from the above that most of the Metacarpals are in the range 173 mm. to 186 mm., while the bulk of the Metatarsals are from 200 mm. to 219 mm. Both these ranges are suggestive of *Bos longifrons*.

The three Metacarpals (191 mm.–193 mm.) and one Metatarsal (229 mm.) came from large individuals. Whether these were large individuals of the same breed, or animals imported perhaps to improve the stock, it is not possible to say. The evidence, however, does indicate that some larger individuals were present.

Layer A1 (6) and Ditch 1 each contained one complete Metatarsal; both were within the 200 mm.–219 mm. range. Ditch 2 also had one complete example of this bone, the length being 227 mm.

Sex determination was attempted with bones from the well, 43 measurements of Metacarpal proximal epiphyses being available together with 44 Metatarsal proximal epiphyses. For completeness, the Distal epihpyses measurements should also have been included. However, with fewer measurements to use, this was not possible.

Two histograms were constructed using only the proximal epiphyses measurements. In both figures the highest peaks have been given sex titles.

Sheep/Goat

The problem of distinguishing between the two species was the same on this site as at Chilgrove 1. However, it can be said that Goat was represented here in the form of a large fragment of Skull with sutures, and two fragments of Horn core; all came from Ditch 1. In cases where diagnosis was possible, Sheep were determined. In connection with this, it must be said that the condition of some of the material was such that species determination was impossible.

The evidence from Skull fragments and limb bones does suggest that the majority of bones came from Sheep, and as at the previous site, interpretations are made on this basis. As with Ox, the highest peaks in Figs. 37–40 are generally occupied by slaughter waste, Figs. 37 and 39 being the best examples. The bones from Ditch 2 are all slaughter waste, with the exception of Humerus.

In all the figures representing the bones of this animal, food waste is mainly confined to the lower peaks. At Site 1 it was suggested that the age group 1½–2½ years would have provided most of the meat of this animal. The same interpretation could apply here, even though, under Age Determination, the figure for Ditch 1 is exceeded by that for the 0–10 months. As previously stated, the figures for the well are the more reliable, and they indicate this group to be the largest.

127

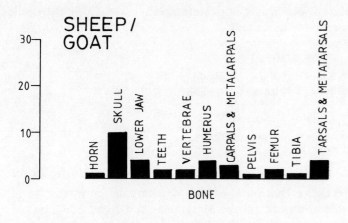

SHEEP/
GOAT

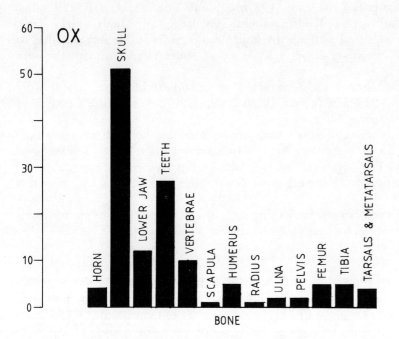

OX

CHILGROVE 2

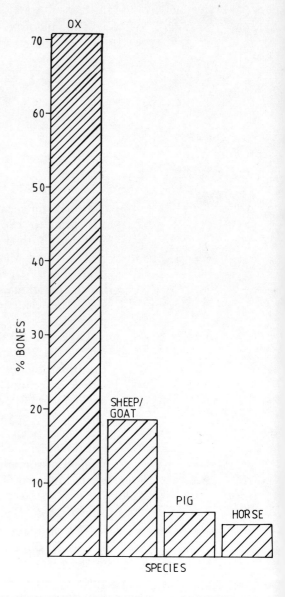

BONES FROM LAYERS
% OF BONES PER SPECIES

Fig. 40

The figure for the oldest age group (2½–3½ years) again suggests this to be the breeding flock. It is also probable that being the providers of wool, these animals would have had a longer life expectancy.

Regarding the youngest animals (0–10 months), the figure of 44.4 per cent. from Ditch 1 does appear high. Whether or not this is a true estimate, it does seem, as at Chilgrove 1, that the mortality rate during the first year was greater.

Pig

Most of the evidence for this animal came from Ditch 1, where 41 items represented a minimum of five individuals. Ditch 2 contained a minimum of two, and Layers F1 (14), C1/C4 (14), and F1 (19) each had one individual.

It has been stated above that no histogram was constructed from the layers for this animal; this was because only Lower jaw, teeth, and Vertebrae were available. In Figs. 37–39 it should be noted that although teeth are represented by high peaks, most of the bones are food waste.

The well, which yielded so many bone fragments, produced only enough of this species to represent one individual. It is possible that pig bones were deposited elsewhere, but, on the other hand, there may have been a decrease in the numbers maintained on the site. Another possibility is that Pig production had ceased, and animals were brought in from elsewhere, as and when required.

Age determination as given previously was arrived at by examination of the teeth and it will be seen that six individuals were over three years, one was between two and 3 years, and four were under two years.

Horse

The bones from the whole site represent a minimum of 12 individuals, none of which were found as burials. As at Chilgrove 1, the bones were mingled with those of other species, and it is presumed that the flesh was eaten. This view is supported by the finding of a chopped Tibia from Ditch 1, and a chopped Cervical vertebra from the well.

The well also contained most of the remains of this animal, the bones and teeth giving a total of 260 items, representing at least seven individuals.

Ditch 1 produced a minimum of two animals, Layers B1/4 (14), F1/ (19), and Ditch 2 each contained the bones of one individual.

With age ranges varying, it is thought best to present the information obtained under the appropriate desposit heading. It should be mentioned, however, that the animal from Layer B1/4 (14) was represented by Scapula fragments, and age determination was therefore not possible.

Layer F1/ (19)
One individual over 3½ years.

Ditch 1
Two individuals over 3½ years.

Ditch 2
One male or gelding of about 20 years.

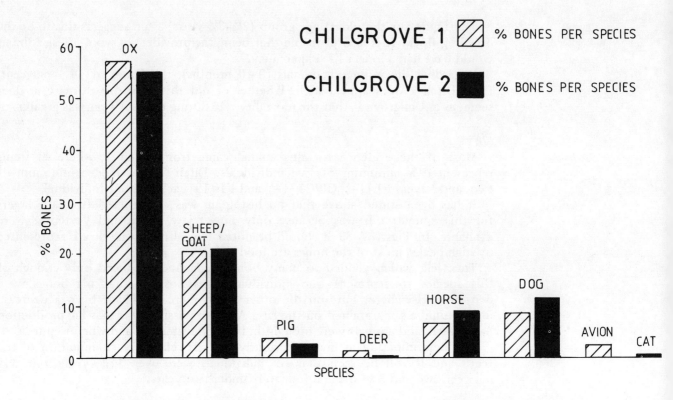

% BONES PER SPECIES — WHOLE SITE

WHOLE SITE	OX	SHEEP/ GOAT	PIG	DEER	HORSE	DOG	AVION	CAT
CHILGROVE 1	57%	20·6%	3·5%	1·2%	6·8%	8·3%	2·5%	——
CHILGROVE 2	54·7%	20·9%	2·5%	0·3%	9·0%	11·5%	——	0·7%

Fig. 41

Well

    Two individuals under 3 years.
    Two individuals over 3½ years.
    One individual of *c.* 5 years. A male or gelding.
    One individual 8–11 years.
    One individual 12–16 years.

Deer

    Ditch 1 was the only deposit containing evidence of Deer, in the form of four Antler tine fragments, together with seven bone fragments. The bone fragments were suggestive of Red Deer. A fragment of naturally-shed Antler also came from this deposit. Although the amount of material was numerically more than from Chilgrove 1, the interpretation is the same, viz., that this species was of little importance as a source of meat.

Dog

Bones of this animal came from Ditch 1 (two individuals); Ditch 2 (two individuals); and the well (12 individuals). It was interesting to observe that no Dog bones came from the layers. This was probably because the above features were ideal depositories for the bodies, which would otherwise rot on the surface and smell. None·of the animals were under nine months old, the majority being well over one-and-a-half years. There were no complete limb bones, so any estimations as to size can only be very tentative.

It is probable that the two individuals from Ditch 1 were of the same size; of the 12 individuals from the well, it is estimated that six at least were of differing sizes. Regarding the two animals from the ditch, lack of measurements ruled out any estimates.

Cat

The well was the only deposit with bones of this animal. Two individuals are represented by 25 bones, the only complete examples being, one Mandible, four Vertebrae, one Femur, and one Tibia.

Such measurements as could be taken were compared with those of an animal of later dating. It was found that generally there was a fairly close agreement with the well bones being slightly larger overall.

DISCUSSION

It is clear from the bone evidence from both Chilgrove sites that Ox was the main source of meat. It seems that slaughtering began when the animals attained an age of about one-and-a-half years, although the majority were killed when they were over three years old. Fig. 39 indicates that castrates were present and it may be that those not required for draught work were fattened up and killed at an age between two and three years.

Sheep as a source of meat appears to be of secondary importance, although it was probably a welcome alternative to beef. Animals between 1½–2½ years were the most favoured and some of these may have been castrates. It is possible, although no definite evidence was found, that Goat was present at Chilgrove 1. It was identified at Chilgrove 2, from Ditch 1, but no estimate can be made of numbers.

The Pig figures very low as a meat provider. This may suggest that few pigs were kept, but it might mean that what swine were raised were driven to the local market on the hoof.

Deer, which could be a useful source of meat is poorly represented, and the only birds came from Chilgrove 2. They were probably of a wild species, but their size makes them worthy of consideration as an item of diet.

The bones collected from both sites indicate that Ox and Sheep provided nearly all the needs of the inhabitants for animal protein, and the percentage figures for Ox, Sheep/Goat and Pig (Fig. 41) show remarkable similarity. While the total number of bones from Chilgrove 2 is greater than Chilgrove 1 it should be borne in mind that the boundary ditches and the well at Site 2 provided a convenient tip for refuse, whereas these features were not found or excavated at Site 1.

The Roman Coins from the Sites

compiled by Roger Lintott (Fig. 42)

LIST OF ABBREVIATIONS USED IN THE TABLES

RIC	*Roman Imperial Coinage.* Mattingley, Sydenham, Sutherland Carson.
LRBC	*Late Roman Bronze Coinage.* Carson, Hill and Kent.
Dup	Dupondius.
Ses	Sestertius.
Den	Denarius.
Æ	Copper, bronze or orichalcum.
Æ Ant	Antoninianus.
Æ 3	Coin diameter from 17 mm.
Æ Cent	Centenionalis.
Fol	Follis.
BR	Barbarous radiate.
AR	Silver.
1 std	One standard on Gloria Exercitus.
2 std	Two standards on Gloria Exercitus.
Px.	Reverse.

Location key for Chilgrove 1

P	Ploughsoil.
B1	Building 1.
B1 (BH)	Building 1, bath-house.
S	Stockyard.
SBH	Area south of bath-house.
US	Unstratified.

Location key for Chilgrove 2

B1	Building 1.
B2	Building 2.
B2 (F)	On floor of Building 2.
B3	Building 3.
B1 (BF)	Building 1, below floors.
D1	Ditch 1.
P	Ploughsoil.
W	Well.
B1 (AF)	Building 1, above floors.
US	Unstratified.

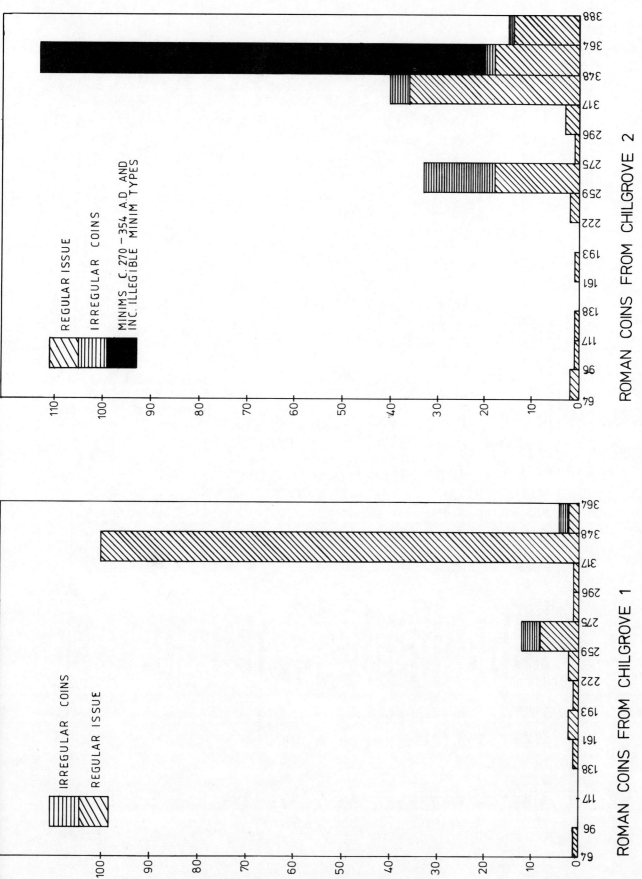

ROMAN COINS FROM CHILGROVE 1

ROMAN COINS FROM CHILGROVE 2

IRREGULAR COINS

REGULAR ISSUE

REGULAR ISSUE

IRREGULAR COINS

MINIMS C. 270 – 354 A.D AND
INC. ILLEGIBLE MINIM TYPES

Fig. 42:   Chilgrove 1 and 2; coin histogram

CHILGROVE 1

Find No.	Denom.	Emperor and Date	Reverse Type	Mint	Date of Coin	Ref. No.	Notes	Location (see key)
282	Dup	Vespasian 69–79	Victoria Navalis	Lyons	72–3	RIC 745	Worm	P
505	Ses	Faustina Junior	Venus	Rome	145–6	RIC 1388B	Struck under Ant Pius, 138–161 A.D.	S
2	Ses	Marcus Aurelius, 161–80			161–80		Very worn	B1
11	Ses	Marcus Aurelius, 161–80			161–80			B1
73	Den	Geta, 209–212	Nobilitas	Rome	200–202	RIC 3		B1 (BH)
434	Dup	Julia Mamaea	Vesta	Rome	222–35	RIC 709	Struck under Severus Alexander	S
426	As	Gordian III, 238–44	Requitas Aug	Rome	240	RIC 286B		S
191	Æ Ant	Gallienus, 253–68	Liberal Aug	Rome	260–8	RIC 227		B1
345	Æ Ant	Gallienus, 253–68	Salus Aug	Cologne	265–70	RIC 122		B1 (Room 14)
347	Æ Ant	Victorinus, 268–70						B1 (Room 14)
386	Æ Ant	Victorinus, 268–70						P
398	Æ Ant	Victorinus, 268–70					Reverse filed smooth	S
49	Æ Ant	Claudius II, 268–70	Pax Aug	Milan		RIC 157		P
288	Æ Ant	Claudius II, 268–70	Consecratio large altar					B1 (Room 5)
257	Æ Ant	Claudius II, 268–70	Consecratio large altar					B2
267B	Æ Ant	Claudius II, 268–70 BR						US
81	Æ Ant	Tetricus I, type BR						P
209	Æ Ant	BR						B1 (Room 14)
436	Æ Ant	BR						S
79	Fol	Carausius, 287–93						SBH (Pit F1)
178	Fol	Constantine I, 307–337	Soli invicto comiti	Arles	316	RIC 75		B1 (BH)
115	½ Fol	Maximinus II, 309–13;	Requies opt. mer	Trier	318	as RIC 205		P
292	Æ 3	Constantine I, 307–337	Beata Tranquillatis	Trier	320–4			B1 (BH)
131	Æ 3	Constantine I, 307–337	Gloria Exercitus 2 stds	Lyons	330–1	RIC 243		B1 (BH)
98	Æ 3	Constantine I, 307–337	Gloria Exercitus 2 stds.	Lyons	330–1	RIC 236		B1 (BH)
166	Æ Ant	Constantine I, 307–337	Gloria Exercitus 2 stds.	Trier	332–3	RIC 537		B1 (BH)
129	Æ 3	Constantine I, 307–337	Gloria Exercitus 2 stds	Lyons	333–4	RIC 262		B1 (BH)
108	Æ 3	Constantine I, 307–337	Gloria Exercitus 2 stds	Lyons	335–7		Not in LRBC with this mint mark	B1 (BH)

CHILGROVE 1 – continued

Find No.	Denom.	Emperor and Date	Reverse Type	Mint	Date of Coin	Ref. No.	Notes	Location (see key)
101	Æ 3	Constantine I, 307–337	Virtus Augusti 1 std	Rome	337	RIC 405		B1 (BH)
338	Æ 3	Constantine II, 317–340	Gloria Exercitus 2 stds	Lyons	332	RIC 254		S
121	Æ 3	Constantine II, 317–340	Gloria Exercitus 2 stds		330–5			B1 (BH)
447	Æ 3	Constantine II, 317–340	Gloria Exercitus 2 stds	Lyons	330–5			S
62	Æ 3	Constantine II, 317–340	Gloria Exercitus 2 stds	Trier	330–5			P
150	Æ 3	Constantine II, 317–340	Gloria Exercitus 2 stds		330–5			B1 (BH)
141	Æ 3	Constantine II, 317–340	Gloria Exercitus 1 std	Lyons	336–7	LRBC 232		B1 (BH)
134	Æ 3	Constantine II, 317–340	Gloria Exercitus 1 std		336–341			B1 (BH)
469	Æ 3	Constantine II, 317–340	Gloria Exercitus 1 std		336–341			S
164	Æ 3	Constans, 333–350	Gloria Exercitus 1 std		336–341			B1 (BH)
475	Æ 3	Constans, 333–350	Gloria Exercitus 1 std		336–341			S
203	Æ 3	Constans, 333–350	2 victories	Trier	341	LRBC 139		B1
27	Æ 3	Constans, 333–350	2 victories	Trier	343	LRBC 148–150	Little wear	B1 (BH)
50	Æ 3	Constans, 333–350	2 victories	Trier	343	LRBC 148–150	Little wear	P
106	Æ 3	Constans, 333–350	2 victories	Trier	343	LRBC 149	Little wear	B1 (BH)
189	Æ 3	Constans, 333–350	2 victories	Trier	343	LRBC 148–150	Little wear	B1 (BH)
249	Æ 3	Constans, 333–350	2 victories	Trier	343	LRBC 148–150	Little wear	P
112	Æ 3	Constans, 333–350	2 victories	Trier	343	LRBC 148–150	Little wear	B1 (BH)
55	Æ 3	Constans, 333–350	2 victories	Arles	344	LRBC 456–7	Little wear	B1 (BH)
176	Æ 3	Constans, 333–350	2 victories	Lyons	346	LRBC 274–274A	Little wear	SHB

CHILGROVE 1—continued

Find No.	Denom.	Emperor and Date	Reverse Type	Mint	Date of Coin	Ref. No.	Notes	Location (see key)
470	Æ 3	Constans, 333–350	2 victories	Arles	346	LRBC 462	Little wear	S
94	Æ 3	Constans, 333–350	2 victories	Trier	343	LRBC 148–50	Little wear	P
285	Æ 3	Constans, 333–350	2 victories	Arles	345		Little wear	B1 (5)
51	Æ 3	Constans, 333–350	2 victories		346		Little wear	B1 (BH)
277	Æ 3	Constans, 333–350	2 victories	Trier	341–6		Little wear	B1
95	Æ 3	Constans, 333–350	2 victories		341–6		Little wear	P
221	Æ 3	Constans, 333–350	2 victories		341–6			SBH (Pit F 6)
28	Æ 3	Constans, 333–350	2 victories		341–6			B1 (BH)
325	Æ Cent.	Constans, 333–350	Emp. on Galley	Trier	349	LRBC 45		B1
204	Æ 3	Constantius II, 324–361	Gloria Exercitus 2 stds	Arles	332–3	RIC 367	EF	B1
29	Æ 3	Constantius II, 324–361	Gloria Exercitus 2 stds		330–5			B1 (BH)
116	Æ 3	Constantius II, 324–361	Gloria Exercitus 2 stds		330–5			B1 (BH)
122	Æ 3	Constantius II, 324–361	Gloria Exercitus 2 stds		330–5			B1 (BH)
100	Æ 3	Constantius II, 324–361	Gloria Exercitus 2 stds		330–5			B1 (BH)
119	Æ 3	Constantius II, 324–361	Gloria Exercitus 2 stds		330–5			B1 (BH)
124	Æ 3	Constantius II, 324–361	Gloria Exercitus 2 stds		330–5			B1 (BH)
125	Æ 3	Constantius II, 324–361	Gloria Exercitus 2 stds		330–5			B1 (BH)
272	Æ 3	Constantius II, 324–361	Gloria Exercitus 2 stds		330–5			B1 (BH)
93	Æ 3	Constantius II, 324–361	Gloria Exercitus 1 std	Lyons	337	LRBC 242		P
139	Æ 3	Constantius II, 324–361	Gloria Exercitus 1 std	Trier	337	LRBC 108A		B1 (BH)
154	Æ 3	Constantius II, 324–361	Gloria Exercitus 1 std	Trier	337	LRBC 108A		B1 (BH)
210	Æ 3	Constantius II, 324–361	Gloria Exercitus 1 std.	Trier	339	LRBC 126		B1
132	Æ 3	Constantius II, 324–361	Gloria Exercitus 1 std.	Trier	339	LRBC 126		B1 (BH)

CHILGROVE 1 –continued

Find No.	Denom.	Emperor and Date	Reverse Type	Mint	Date of Coin	Ref. No.	Notes	Location (see key)
56	Æ 3	Constantius II, 324–361	Gloria Exercitus 1 std	Arles	341	LRBC 441		B1 (BH)
97	Æ 3	Constantius II, 324–361	Gloria Exercitus 1 std		336–41			B1 (BH)
102	Æ 3	Constantius II, 324–361	Gloria Exercitus 1 std		336–41			B1 (BH)
148	Æ 3	Constantius II, 324–361	Gloria Exercitus 1-std		336–41			B1 (BH)
69	Æ 3	Constantius II, 324–361	2 victories	Lyons	343	LRBC 264	Little wear	P
26	Æ 3	Constantius II, 324–361	2 victories	Arles	343	LRBC 455	Unworn	B1 (BH)
295	Æ 3	Constantius II, 324–361	2 victories	Arles	343	LRBC 455	Little wear	B1 (Room 14)
10	Æ 3	Constantius II or Constans	Gloria Exercitus 1 std	Trier	340	LRBC 132 or 133		B1.
135	Æ 3	Constantius II or Constans	Gloria Exercitus 1 std	Trier	336–7	LRBC 107, 108 or 108A		B1 (BH)
165	Æ 3	Constantius II or Constans	Gloria Exercitus 1 std	Trier	336–41			B1 (BH)
41	Æ 3	Constantius II or Constans	Gloria Exercitus 1 std	Trier	336–41			B1 (BH)
432	Æ 3	Constantius II or Constans	2 victories	Trier	343	LRBC 145–50	Little wear	S
61	Æ 3	Constantius II or Constans	2 victories	Trier	346	LRBC 158–160	Little wear	B1 (BH)
42	Æ 3	Constantius II or Constans	2 victories	Trier	346		Unworn	B1
140	Æ 3	Constantius II or Constans	2 victories	Trier	341–6			B1 (BH)
484	Æ 3	Constantius II or Constans	2 victories		341–6			S
450	Æ 3	Constantius II or Constans	2 victories		341–6			S
52	Æ 3	House of Constantine	Gloria Exercitus 1 std		336–341			B1 (BH)
136	Æ 3	House of Cor-stantine	Gloria Exercitus 1 std		336–341			B1 (BH)

137

CHILGROVE 1—continued

Find No.	Denom.	Emperor and Date	Reverse Type	Mint	Date of Coin	Ref. No.	Notes	Location (see key)
46	Æ 3	House of Constantine	Gloria Exercitus 1 std		336–341			B1 (BH)
153	Æ 3	House of Constantine	Gloria Exercitus 1 std		336–341			B1 (BH)
392	Æ 3	House of Constantine	Gloria Exercitus 1 std		336–341			S
452	Æ 3	House of Constantine	Gloria Exercitus 1 std		336–341			S
464	Æ 3	House of Constantine	Gloria Exercitus 1 std		336–341			S
53	Æ 3	House of Constantine	Gloria Exercitus 1 std		336–341			B1 (BH)
476	Æ 3	House of Constantine	Gloria Exercitus 1 std		336–341			S
30	Æ 3	Urbs Roma	Wolf and twins	Lyons	330	LRBC 190		B1 (BH)
161	Æ 3	Urbs Roma	Wolf and twins	Arles	330–5			B1 (BH)
7	Æ 3	Urbs Roma	Wolf and twins	Arles	330–5			P
107	Æ 3	Urbs Roma	Wolf and twins		330–5			B1 (BH)
155	Æ 3	Urbs Roma	Wolf and twins		330–5			B1 (BH)
299	Æ 3	Constantinopolis	Victory on prow	Arles	331	RIC 357		S
151	Æ 3	Constantinopolis	Victory on prow	Trier	330–331	RIC 523		B1 (BH)
163	Æ 3	Constantinopolis	Victory on prow	Trier	330–331	RIC 523		B1 (BH)
103	Æ 3	Constantinopolis	Victory on prow	Lyons	331–332	RIC 251		B1 (BH)
35	Æ 3	Constantinopolis	Victory on prow		330–5			B1 (BH)
12	Æ 3	Constantinopolis	Victory on prow		330–5			B1
63	Æ 3	Constantinopolis	Victory on prow		330–5			B1 (BH)
152	Æ 3	Constantinopolis	Victory on prow		330–5			B1 (BH)
162	Æ 3	Constantinopolis	Victory on prow		330–5			B1 (BH)
219	Æ 3	Constantinopolis	Victory on prow		330–5			SBH
342	Æ 3	Constantinopolis	Victory on prow		330–5			B1 (Room 14)
442	Æ 3	Constantinopolis	Victory on prow		330–5			S
70	Æ 3	Helena, w. of Constantius	Helena	Trier	337–41			US
109	Æ 3	Helena, w. of Constantius	Helena		337–41			B1 (BH)
268	Æ 3	Theodora	Pietas	Trier	337	LRBC 113		B1
110	Æ 3	Theodora	Pietas	Trier	338	LRBC 120		B1 (BH)
43	Æ 3	Theodora	Pietas	Trier	339	LRBC 129		B1
123	Æ 3	Theodora	Pietas	Trier	339	LRBC 129		B1

CHILGROVE 1—continued

Find No.	Denom.	Emperor and Date	Reverse Type	Mint	Date of Coin	Ref. No.	Notes	Location (see key)
123	Æ 3	Theodora	Pietas	Trier	339	LRBC 129		B1 (BH)
202	Æ 3	Theodora	Pietas		337–41			B1
99	Æ C	Magnentius, 350–353	Emp. on galley	Trier	350	LRBC 48	Unworn	B1 (BH)
82	Æ 3	Magnentius, 340–353 (barb)	Fallen horseman		c. 350–355		Little wear	B1 (Room 7)
446	Æ 3	Magnentius, 350–353 (barb)	Fallen horseman		c. 350–353		Unworn	S

CHILGROVE 2——

Find No.	Denom.	Emperor and Date	Reverse Type	Mint	Date of Coin	Ref. No.	Notes	Location (see key)
291	AR Den	Vespasian, 69–79	Annona Aug		78–9	RIC 131B	F	P
606	AE Ses	Vespasian, 69–79					Worn smooth	P
548	Æ As	Trajan, 98–117					Worn smooth	P
609	Æ Ses	Hadrian, 117–138					Worn smooth	P
509	Æ As	Commodus, 177–192					Worn smooth	B3
53	AR Den	Severus Alexander, 222–235	Liberalitas Aug.		222–8	RIC 153	Worn smooth	B1
146	AR Den (plated)	Julia Maesa obv. Sevalex Rev.	P.M.TR.P.V. Cos II. P.P.		226	as RIC 55	cf. Sev. Alex., but Emp. holding globe	D1
574	Æ Ant	Gallienus, 253–268						W
580	Æ Ant	Gallienus, 253–268						W
474	AR Ant	Postumus, 259–268	Hercules ?			RIC 64		B3
83	Æ Ant	Victorinus, 268–70	Salus Aug.			RIC 71 ?		B2 {wall}
231	Æ Ant	Victorinus, 268–70						B2 (F)
313	Æ Ant	Victorinus, 268–70						B2 (F)
245	Æ Ant	Claudius II, 268–70	Virtus Aug			RIC 111 ?		B2
102	Æ Ant	Claudius II, 268–70	Salus Aug					B1 (BF)
243	Æ Ant	Claudius II, 268–70	Consecratio type with altar		after 270			B2, Per 3 posthole
519	Æ Ant BR	Claudius II, 268–70	Large altar type					B3, below Per 4 floor
475	Æ Ant	Tetricus 1, 270–3	Hilaritus Augg			RIC 80		B2 (F)

CHILGROVE 2 –continued

Find No.	Denom.	Emperor and Date	Reverse Type	Mint	Date of Coin	Ref. No.	Notes	Location (see key)
64	Æ Ant	Tetricus 1, 270–3	Pax Aug					B2 (wall)
413	Æ Ant	Tetricus 1, 270–3	Pax Aug					B2 (F)
362	Æ Ant	Tetricus 1, 270–3	Pax Aux					B2 (F)
180	Æ Ant	Tetricus 1, 170–3	Salus Augg			RIC 127		B2 (F)
439	Æ Ant	Tetricus 1, 270–3	Spes publica			RIC 135 or 136		B1 (BF)
13	Æ Ant	Tetricus 1, 270–3	Victoria Aug			RIC 141		B1
11	Æ Ant	Tetricus 1, 270–3	Virtus Aug			RIC 145 or 146		B2 (F)
491	Æ Ant BR	Tetricus 1, 270–3	Salus Aug type			as RIC 123–4		B1
247	Æ Ant	Carausius, 287–293	Pax Aug	London ?	287–8	RIC 11		B2 (F)
258	Æ follis	Constantine 1, 307–337	Soli invicto	London	313–4			P
395	Æ follis	Constantine 1, 307–337	Soli invicto	London	313–4	RIC 10		B2 (F)
399	Æ 3	Constantine 1, 307–337	Victoriae Laetae princ. perp.	Trier ?	318–9			P
425	Æ 3	Constantine 1, 307–337	Gloria Exercitus 2 std		330–5			B2 (F)
268	Æ 3	Licinius, 308–324	Soli invicto	London	316–7	RIC 98		P
386	Æ 3	Constantine II, 317–340	Victoriae Laetae princ. perp.	Trier	319	RIC 219	No star in field	B3 (Pit K4)
424	Æ 20 mm	Constantine II, 317–340	Gloria Exercitus 2 std	Trier	330–1	RIC 527		B2 (F)
457	Æ 3	Constantine II, 317–340	Gloria Exercitus 1 std	Trier	335–41			B3
414	Æ 3	Constans, 333–350	Gloria Exercitus 2 std	Trier	333–4	RIC 560		B2 (F)
91	Æ 3	Constans, 333–350	Gloria Exercitus 1 std		335–41			B2
160	Æ 3	Constans, 333–350	Victoriae DD. Augg. Q.NN	Trier	341–6	LRBC 163		B1 (AF)
106	Æ 3	Constans, 333–350	Victoriae DD. Augg Q.NN	Trier	341–6	LRBC 158		B2 (F)
347	Æ 3	Constans, 333–350	Victoriae DD. Augg Q.NN	Trier	341–6	LRBC 159		P
351	Æ 3	Constans, 333–350	Victoriae DD. Augg Q.NN		341–6			B2 (F)

CHILGROVE—continued

Find No.	Denom.	Emperor and Date	Reverse Type	Mint	Date of Coin	Ref. No.	Notes	Location (see key)
423	Æ 3	Constans, 333–350	Victoriae DD. Augg Q.NN		3416			B2 (F)
372	Æ 3	Constans, 333–350	Victoriae DD. Augg. Q.NN		341–6			B2 (F)
412	Æ 3	Constans, 333–350	Fel temp reparatio (Phoenix on pyre type)	Trier	340–50	LRBC 36		B3 (wall)
248	Æ cent	Constans, 333–350	Fel temp reparatio (hut type)	Aquilea	348–50	LRBC 888	Mint condition	B2 (F)
360	Æ cent	Constans, 333–350	Fel temp reparatio (hut type)	Aquilae	348–50	LRBC 888		B2 (F)
251	Æ cent	Constans, 333–350	Fel temp reparatio (hut type)	Rome	348–50	LRBC 604		B2 (F)
385	Æ 3	Constantius II, 324–361	Gloria Exercitus, 2 stds		332–3	RIC 540		B3, Pit K5
300	Æ 3	Constantius II, 324–361	Gloria Exercitus, 2 stds		330–5			B3
540	Æ 3	Constantius II, 324–361	Gloria Exercitus 1 std		335–41			Well
246	Æ cent	Constantius II, 324–361	Fel temp reparatio (hut type)	Trier	348–50	LRBC 30		B2 (F)
318	Æ cent	Constantius II, 324–361	Fel temp reparatio (galley type)	Trier	348–50	LRBC 42		B2 (F)
234	Æ cent	Constantius II, 324–361	Fel temp reparatio (falling horseman type)	Lyons	348–54	LRBC 253 to 259		B2 (F)
317	Æ cent	Constantius II, 324–361	Fel temp reparatio (falling horseman type)		348–54			B2 (F)
340	Æ cent	Constantius II, 324–361	Fel temp raparatio (falling horseman type)		348–54			B2
99	Æ cent	Constantius II, 324–361	Fel temp repartio (falling horseman type)		348–54			B2
333	Æ cent	Illegible	Fel temp reparatio (falling horseman type)				Barb	B2 (F)

CHILGROVE—continued

Find No.	Denom.	Emperor and Date	Reverse Type	Mint	Date of coin	Ref. No.	Notes	Location (see key)
390	Æ cent.	Illegible	Fel temp reparatio (falling horseman type)		348-54			B2 (F)
428	Æ 3	Constans or Constantius II	Victoriae DD Augg Q.NN	Trier	341-6			B2 (F)
183	Æ 3	Constans or Constantius II	Victoriae DD Augg Q.NN	Trier	341-6			B2 (F)
451	Æ 3	Constans or Constantius II	Victoriae DD Augg Q.NN	Trier	341-6			P
76	Æ 3	Constans or Constantius II	Victoriae DD Augg Q.NN		341-6			P
637	Æ 3	Constans or Constantius II	Victoriae DD Augg Q.NN		341-6			Well
339	Æ 3	Constans or Constantius II	Fel temp reparatio (globe type)		348-50	LRBC 888		B2
365	Æ 3	Constans or Constantius II	Fel temp reparatio (globe type)		348-50			B2 (F)
406	Æ 3	Constans or Constantius II	Fel temp reparatio (globe type)		348-50			P
370	Æ 3	Constans or Constantius II	Fel temp reparatio (globe type)		·348-50			B2 (F)
238	Æ 3	Constans or Constantius II	2 std type		330-5			B2 (F)
624	Æ 3	Constans or Constantius II	2 std type		330-5			US
363	Æ 3	Constans or Constantius II	1 std type		330-5			B2 (F)
364	Æ 3	Constans or Constantius II	1 std type		330-5			B2 (F)
382	Æ 3	Constans or Constantius II	1 std type		330-5			B2 (F)
402	Æ 3	Urbs Roma	Wolf and twins	Trier	332-3	RIC 547		B1
276	Æ 3	Urbs Roma	Wolf and twins	Trier	333-4	RIC 553		P
429	Æ 3	Urbs Roma	Wolf and twins	Trier	333-4	RIC 553		B2 (F)
30	AE barb	Urbs Roma	Wolf and twins					P
501	AE barb	Urbs Roma	Wolf and twins					B3
342	AE barb	Urbs Roma	Wolf and twins					B2 (F)
253	AE barb	Urbs Roma	Wolf and twins					B2 (F)

Find No.	Denom.	Emperor and Date	Reverse Type	Mint	Date of Coin	Ref. No.	Notes	Location (see key)
3	Æ 3	Constantinopolis	Victory on prow	Trier	333–4	RIC 554		P
361	Æ 3	Constantinopolis	Victory on prow	Cyzicus	330–5	LRBC 1234		B2 (F)
413	Æ 3	Constantinopolis	Victory on prow	Trier	330–41			B2 (F)
456	Æ 3	Theodora	Pietas	Trier	337–41	LRBC 120		B3
582	Æ Cent	Magnentius 350–3	2 victories	Trier	350–3	as LRBC 56		B3 (wall)
249	Æ Cent	Decentius 351–3	Large P	Trier	351–3	LRBC 63		B2 (F)
319	Æ Cent	Decentius, 351–3	2 victories	Amiens	351–3	LRBC 14		B2 (F)
398	Æ Cent	Magnentius or Decentius	2 victories		350–3			B2
132	Æ Cent	Magnentius or Decentius	2 victories		350–3		barb	B2 (F)
250	Æ Cent	Constantius Gallus, 351–4	Falling horseman	Rome	352–4	LRBC 663	B on obv.	B2 (F)
17	Æ 3	Valentinian 1, 364–375	SR	Arles	375	LRBC 527	RIC 19c ?	B2 (F)
57	Æ 3	Valentinian 1,	SR	Lugdunum	365–75	RIC 20A		B2 (F)
21	Æ 3	Valentinian 1,	GR	Lugdunum	367–75			B1
111	Æ 3	Valens, 364–78	SR	Lugdunum	367–75	LRBC 305, 309, or 315		B2 (F)
101	Æ 3	Valens, 364–78	SR		364–78			B2
134	Æ 3	Valens, 364–78	GR		364–78			B2
169	Æ 3	Valens, 364–78	GR		364–78			B1
178	Æ 3	Valens, 364–78	GR		364–78			B2 (F)
196	Æ 3	House of Valentinian	GR		364–78			P
90	Æ 4	House of Valentinian	GR		364–78			P
84	Æ 3	House of Valentinian	GR		364–78			P
377	Æ 3	House of Valentinian	GR		364–78			B2 (F)
92	Æ 3	House of Valentinian	SR					B2
128	Æ 3	House of Valentinian	SR					B2 (F)
27	Æ 3	House of Valentinian	SR					B1

Minims under 10 mm.

A total of 78 minims were found on the floor of Building 2. Of these, the following could be identified:

Large altar type of Claudius II	..	5
Fallen horseman type ..	..	6
House of Valentinian type	..	1
Tetricus II type	..	2
Magnentius type	..	1
Constantius Gallus type ..	..	1

UPMARDEN

Find No.	Denom.	Emperor and Date	Reverse Type	Mint	Date of Coin	Ref. No.	Notes	Location (see key)
26	Æ Ant	Gallienus, 253–268						Stockyard
15	Æ Ant	Posthumus, 259–268	Pax Aux	Lugdunum		RIC 78		Above Room 1
1	Æ Ant	Victorinus, 268–270	Invictus	Cologne		RIC 114		Garden soil
24	Æ Ant	Carausius, 287–293	Apollinicor	Camulo-dunum		RIC 193	Rare	On floor of Room 1
20	Æ Ant	Valens ?, 364–78						Pit N1 (Well)

The Brooches

by D. F. Mackreth (Fig. 43) *

Chilgrove 1

Nauheim Derivatives

1. (350) L1.4. The bow has a broad top and tapers markedly to a narrow foot. The upper two-thirds has a series of nicks down each side lying in a narrow zone defined by a groove. The lower third has a double cross-cut at the top and two more beneath it which leave broad areas with chamfers on each side. The catch-plate is a thin strip of metal running at right angles to the bow and ending in a small return. The spring has three coils and an internal chord.

The marked characteristic of the brooch is the manner in which the catch-plate is formed. There are three parallels from Winchester (unpublished) for the general shape, although only one has similar decoration, and another from Newport, Isle of Wight (*Ant. J.*, IX, 1029, p. 148, Fig. 2). None is dated, and a general date range of the second half of the first century may be suggested, especially as the type appears to be local to Sussex and Hampshire and the Nauheim Derivative may well have lasted longer here as a replacement for the Colchester Derivative, which is by no means common in this region.

2. (331) P2, 1. The form of this brooch is as the last. The head of the bow has, between one cross-groove above and three below, a narrow lozenge which was formed by filing the edges of the bow. Below the lower grooves the bow is divided into two main panels by a series of diagonal cuts. The face of the upper panel is shaped to an oval, while the lower has a wide chamfer down each side. The bottom of the bow is filed to leave in relief a crude saltire with a downward-pointing lobe. The catch-plate has further ornamental filing along its lower edge.

3. (463) O8, 4. A badly corroded brooch with a three-coil spring and an internal chord. The catch-plate is missing. There is little that can be said about this specimen, and a date range largely the same as the last is suggested.

Rosette

4. (21) The corrosion on this brooch obscures many of the details. The spring is housed in a case made up of two flanges which were closed round the spring leaving only a slot for the pin. The front of the case has signs of a series of radial lines springing from the short bow which has a shallow curve and three main ridges; these may be reeded, which are stopped to top and bottom by cross-grooves. The lower end of the bow is attached to the top of a raised circular plate centred on the upper part of the rosette foot-plate. The lower part of the boss has three triangular stamps each of which has a series of horizontal ridges. Round the edge of the boss is a series of short, straight-sided punch-marked ridges like the triangular ones. These stamps were also used to mark the gaps in an applied raised plate which is now entirely missing except for the 'roots' at the inner end. The outer edge of the applied plate was almost certainly near the edge of the main plate which has lost most of its own border. The fantail foot is small and was reeded, but the corrosion makes the details a little obscure. The damaged catch-place has the remains of a trapezoidal piercing. There is a similarity between this brooch and one from Chichester (*Down* 1978, 285, Fig. 10.28, 48) as far as form is concerned. However, it is possible that the Chilgrove brooch displays signs of having come from a mass-production workshop. This may not reflect upon the date, which is probably in the two or three decades before the Conquest, the multi-piece Rosette brooches belonging to Augusto-Tiberian times.

Knee

5. (307) F1. The spring, now missing, was held in a case by means of an axis bar passing through the coils and through pierced plates at the ends of the case. The bow, in profile, consists of two conjoined but opposed 'Cs' with a step at the top of the bow and to the front and rear of the junction. The foot splays out and the catch-plate is in the same plane as the bottom surface. The return is damaged.

The Knee is not a very common brooch in Britain and the present type belongs to a distinct variety of the type. Unfortunately, as a type, it is not dated to any particular period, and all that can be offered is the general floruit of the type in this country; late second-century into the third (*Neal* 1974, p. 127, Fig. 55, 25; *Cunliffe* 1971, p. 104, Fig. 38, 38); *Kenyon* 1948, p. 251, Fig. 81, 3; *Bush-Fox* 1949, p. 118, Plate XXIX, 52).

*With the exception of No. 7, all are of copper alloy.

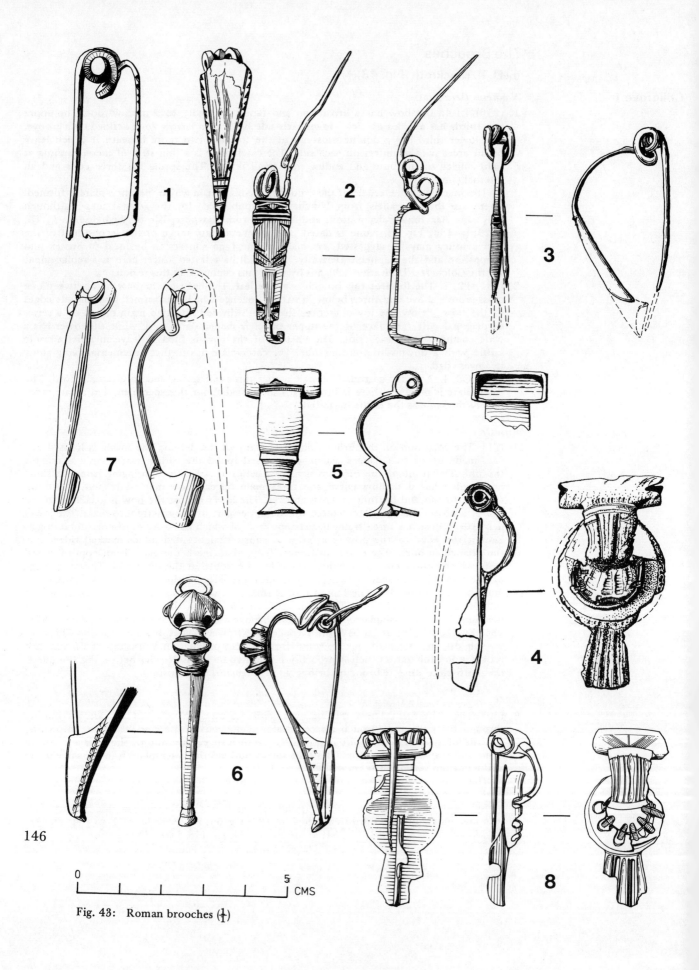

146

0   5 CMS

Fig. 43: Roman brooches (⅟₁)

Trumpet

6. (56) K1.8. Complete and undamaged except for the collar around the loop, this brooch has its spring held to the single pierced lug behind the head by a tube of sheet bronze running through the coils. The tube itself is secured by the end of the wire forming the loop. The head of the brooch has been trimmed so that the loop wire can sit properly and not fall forward over the head of the brooch. The upper and lower part of the bow are plain except for a median arris. The head itself is not of a complete trumpet shape as the top is a triangle with a 'wing' on each side rounding off the head when viewed from the front. The ornament on the crest of the bow consists of a pair of mouldings to top and bottom, separated by wide flutes from the central element of three mouldings, the central one of which is very prominent. The outermost mouldings of the ensemble show a tendency to dip towards the centre in the middle. On the central moulding there are two grooves which also dip in the middle. The foot knob is made up of a double moulding; the lower projects more than the other and is finished off in a curve.

Down each side of the junction of the catch-plate with the bow there is a line of rocker-arm ornament. The whole brooch is carefully finished. This is a representative of a fairly common Trumpet type which is to be found generally in the Marches, with outliers in South Wales and in the English counties to the east and south. None is particularly well dated. One from Wroxeter belongs to the second half of the second century (*Bushe-Fox* 1914, p. 13, Fig. 4, 5), although this may be beyond its period of manufacture, as it is clear that the Trumpet had been fully developed by *c.* 75 A.D. (*T.P.B.A.S.* 83, p. 110, Fig. 19.9; *T.B.W.A.S.* 85, p. 66, Fig. 19.8.)

Nauheim Derivative

7. (12) Area 3, Y1. Iron; a corroded Nauheim Derivative with a roughly rectangular sectioned bow curved at the top. Of the spring, only the start, part of the coil leading to the pin, and part of the internal chord survive. The catch-plate was simply made by hammering out the lower part of the bow and bending the end to form the return.

In general, iron brooches are to be found in the period before the Roman Conquest and for a few years after that event. However, it is normally difficult to distinguish which are pre-Conquest ones from the rest. The only major characteristic to be expected more often before the Conquest than after is that the earlier specimens are large (*cf. Pitt-Rivers* 1888, 126, Plate C1, 6; *Bushe-Fox* 1925, 40, Plate XII, 1.) It is hard to establish a date by which production ceased owing to the paucity of published dated examples, but it may be as early as A.D 50–60, even though copper-alloy specimens appear to continue until near to the end of the first century (*Down* 1978, 280–2).

Rosette

8. (25) P4, Pit P1. Although small in size, this brooch has all the main attributes of its bigger and more elaborate kin. The spring is enclosed in flaps creating a cylinder from which the bow springs. The front of the cylinder bears traces of ornament consisting of lines forming a panel bisected in the centre by a single line. In each half of the panel are a series of parallel diagonal lines which splay out from the top of the bow. The bow itself is short and has a shallow curved profile. The front has three flutes with a buried ridge between each one. These elements are stopped to top and bottom by an incised line across the width of the bow. There is no evidence for a bolt behind the bow and there does not seem to have been room for one. The lower end of the bow joins a roughly circular disc just above the centre. There are traces of a series of incisions around the periphery of the disc, the centre of which is slightly raised. Depending from the bottom of the bow is a curved groove, probably cut by a chisel and there is another near the outer edge along the lower part of the disc. Into the two grooves is fitted a curved copper alloy sheet which is curved in section. There are cut-outs in the upper surface of the sheet and a punch with close-set ridges has been used to form ridged depressions running from each cut-out into the central area. The punch appears to have been applied after the curved sheet had been fitted. Running down from the disc is a fantail foot which is damaged along the bottom and partly up the left-hand side. The fantail has three wide flutes with a narrower one lying between each. The catch-plate is damaged but has a rectangular piercing. It is highly

likely that the brooch was made in two parts and that the bow was fitted to the disc to form the whole. There is no sign of a rivet or of a joint between the raised central element of the disc and the back. It is possible that corrosion or the finishing of the product has removed signs of a join; the back of the lower part of the brooch, especially on either side of the catch-plate, shows signs of filing. There is a slight trace of tinning or silvering on the front of the bow.

The rosette was evolving during Augustian times and the early specimens are clearly made in two parts. It is not possible to be sure that the present specimen was so made, nevertheless its relationships are with those of the same kind of design which are, and it may be suggested that its date range is the 20 or 30 years before the Conquest. The use of ridged punches is distinctive and parallels may be quoted from Holbrooks, Old Harlow (unpublished), as well as No. 4 above. It is possible that the three brooches came from the same workshop.

References

DOWN 1978 — Down, A., *Chichester Excavations 3*, 1978.

NEAL 1974 — Neal, David S., *The Excavations of the Roman Villa in Gadebridge Park, Hemel Hempstead, 1963–8.* Society of Antiquaries Research Report No. XXXI, London, 1974.

CUNLIFFE 1971 — Cunliffe, B. W., *Excavations at Fishbourne 1961–69,* Vol. II: The Finds. Society of Antiquaries Research Report No. XXVII, Leeds, 1971.

KENYON 1948 — Kenyon, Kathleen M., *Excavations at the Jewry Wall Site, Leicester.* Society of Antiquaries Research Report No. XV, Oxford, 1948.

BUSHE-FOX 1949 — Bushe-Fox, J. P., *Fourth Report on the Excavations of the Roman Fort at Richborough, Kent.* Society of Antiquaries Research Report No. XVI, Oxford, 1949.

BUSHE-FOX 1914 — Bushe-Fox, J. P., *Second Report on the Excavations on the site of the Roman Town at Wroxeter, Shropshire, 1913.* Society of Antiquaries Research Report No. II, Oxford, 1914.

BUSHE-FOX 1925 — Bushe-Fox, J. P., *Excavations of the Late-Celtic Urn-Field at Swarling, Kent.* Society of Antiquaries Research Report No. V, Oxford, 1925.

PITT-RIVERS 1888 — Pitt-Rivers, A. H. L. F., *Excavations in Cranborne Chase*, 1888.

Abbreviations

Ant. J. — *Antiquaries Journal.*

T.P.B.A.S. — *Transactions and Proceedings of the Birmingham Archaeological Society.*

T.B.W A.S. — *Transactions of the Birmingham and Warwickshire Archaeological Society.*

The Finds

The two Chilgrove villas produced a large amount of loose finds, many in a good state of preservation, due to the calcareous soil. The ironwork in particular is very prolific, partly because Chilgrove 1 had a large iron-working forge operating in the late fourth century.

It has been found convenient to publish the finds from the three sites in groups, with reference to their site locations. In this way it is hoped that students will find it easier to view (for example) all the carpenters' tools or ploughshares on one or more adjacent pages rather than to look at three separate finds reports from the three sites.

Only a representative selection is illustrated, but numbers and locations of similar finds from the sites are given in the schedule lodged in the Museum. Small finds numbers are placed in brackets beside the publication number. The pottery is dealt with on a site-to-site basis, with only key groups of coarse wares being illustrated. The reasons for this are partly because of the very high cost of publishing line drawings and partly because a large amount of Roman coarse wares of the Chichester region has been published in the Chichester and Fishbourne volumes, and there seems little point in repeating the exercise for sites which are so close to the cantonal capital as to make it certain that the same pottery production sources were used.

All the finds have been deposited in the Chichester District Museum.

Bronze and Silver

JEWELLERY (Fig. 44)

(i) *Rings and bangles*

Chilgrove 1

1. (378) Part of bronze signet ring. M1, layer 2 (Stockyard).
2. (196) Complete bracelet with chip-carved decoration. A1, layer 2.
3. (281) Part of a cast bronze bangle. E4, layer 3a.

Chilgrove 2

4. (546) Silvered bronze finger ring. L3, Pit L2.
5. (379) Child's bronze bangle with punched decoration. H6, layer 7.
6. (185) Fragment of a three-start twisted bronze bangle. H4, layer 34 (Building 2).
7. (324) Fragment of a two-start twisted bronze bangle. H4, layer 34 (Building 2).
8. (167) Silver bangle. J1, layer 8.
9. (94) Bronze bangle. The ends were soldered on a diagonal overlap joint. H4, layer 13 (Building 2).

Upmarden

10. (16) Bronze signet ring. E2, layer 8. Dr. Martin Henig writes: 'The ring, which is of copper alloy, has pronounced shoulders and a raised octagonal bezel. Marshall dates the type to the third century and a number of examples may be noted from British sites.[1]

    Dimensions.—External diameter of hoop, 21 mm.; internal diameter, 18 mm.; length of bezel, 9 mm.; width of bezel 9 mm.; height of bezel, 3 mm. Within the bezel is a setting of black glass containing three depressions, which allow the ring to be used as a signet. The 'intaglio' device is, of course, exceedingly crude, but it may be a debased rendering of a standing figure; imitation gems of this type appear to be a Romano-British speciality and amongst other examples we may note one from Highdown and another from Chichester.[2] It may be suspected that they represent the spread of signet-ring use amongst the lower orders of society (at the very time, incidentally, that the workshops producing more regular pastes and even engraved gems appear to have ceased production).[3]

    Dimensions of paste.—Length, 7 mm.; width, 5.5 mm.; height above bezel, 1 mm.'.

References

1. F. H. Marshall, *Catalogue of the Finger Ring Greeks, Etruscan and Roman in the Department of Antiquities*, British Museum, London, 1907, xlviii, Type Exxx. British Museum, *Guide to the Antiquities of Roman Britain*, third edition, 1964, 25f, Fig. 13, No. 3 (near Wittering, Northants.); Martin Henig, *A Corpus*

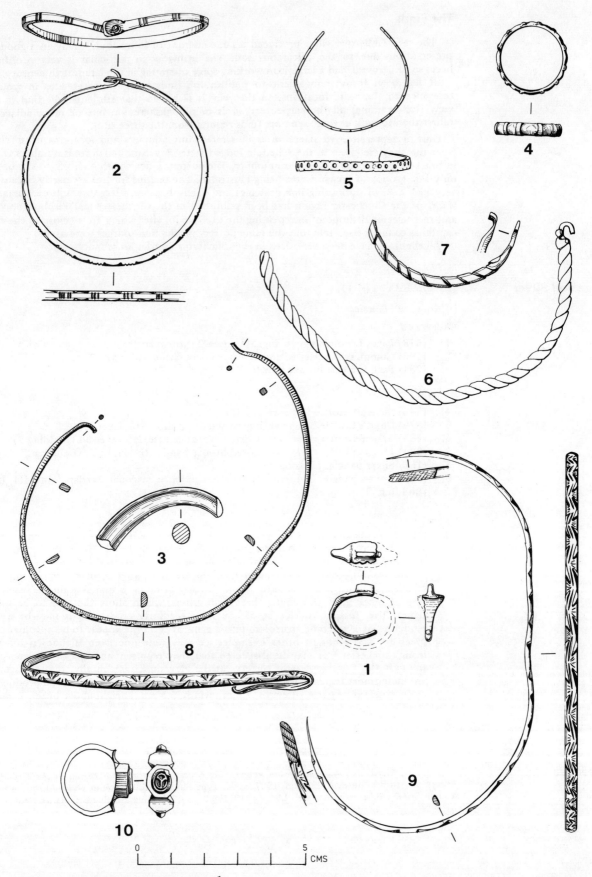

Fig. 44: Jewellery: rings and bangles ($\frac{1}{1}$)

of Roman Engraved Gemstones from British Sites, BAR 8, 1974, part 2, 78, No. 562 (ring not illustrated) (Frocester, Gloucestershire contains an intaglio similar to the Upmarden ring. From a context dated *c.* A.D. 275).

2. *Ibid.,* 77–80 and Plate XVII f. Note 78, No. 555 from Highdown. For the Chichester ring, A. Down, *Chichester Excavations* 2, Chichester 1974, 141, and Figs. 8, 16. No. 35. 'Bronze signet ring with intaglio of green glass'.

3. Henig, *op. cit.,* part 1, 164 f, and Fig. 3.

MISCELLANEOUS (Fig. 45)

Chilgrove 1

11. (473) Belt buckle with punched decoration. O8, layer 4 (Stockyard).
12. (39) Small handle. B1, layer 1.
13. (22) Bronze fitting with letters AQV. A1, layer 2 (Bath-house).
14. (309) Bronze implement, use uncertain. B2, layer 8.

Chilgrove 2

15. (556) Hair pin. L3. The grooves below the head may be a key for a glass knob which has broken off. L3, Ditch 2 layer 4.
16. (148) Silver tang, possibly from a hand mirror. K1, layer 6.
17. (350) Bronze tweezers. H4, layer 51 (Building 2).
18. (254) Bronze plate, slightly convex with stitching holes for attachment to cloth or leather. H4, layer 3 (Building 2).
19. (504) Part of bronze sewing needle. K6, layer 19.
20. (61) Hollow bronze tube, possibly a catheter. D2, layer 5.
21. (403) Zoomorphic belt stiffener in the form of two opposed dolphins and shells. K5, layer 6.
22. (480) Cast bronze handle fitting. K6, layer 25 (*cf.Chichester* 3, p. 296, and Fig. 10.34, 58).
23. (349) Cast bronze decorative piece. H4, layer 51 (Building 2).
24. (26) Cast bronze handle. C1, layer 17.

Upmarden

25. (32) Bronze handle. N6, layer 2.

The Iron (Figs. 46—53)   (i) *Carpenters' tools*

Chilgrove 1

1. (251) Small square-sectioned punch. Trial trench 2, layer 3.
2. (8) Carpenter's bit. Trial trench 2, layer 2.
3. (326) Small chisel. P2, layer 1 (Stockyard).

Chilgrove 2

4. (455) Part of small chisel or punch. K6, layer 16 (Building 3).
5. (628) Carpenter's bit. L2, layer 1 ('Building 4).
6. (544) Carpenter's bit. K5, layer 6 (Building 3).
7. (633) Chisel. L2, layer 44 (Building 4, below floor).
8. (156) Hand gouge. C1, layer 6 (from wall of Building 1).
9. (516) Probably a chisel. C4, layer 22 (destruction debris outside Building 1).
10. (531) Mortice chisel. This was probably fitted with a wooden handle and would have been used in conjunction with a mallet, but the latest user evidently did not bother to renew the handle when it split, and used an iron hammer on it, as the burring indicates. C3, Pit C1.
11. (421) Part of a bow saw blade (Ditch 1).

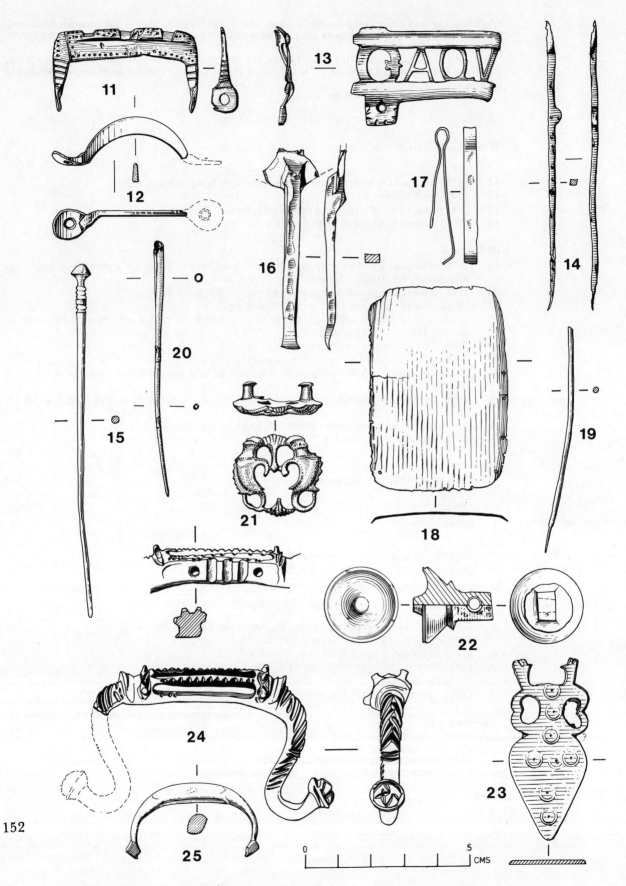

152

Fig. 45: Objects of bronze (⅓)

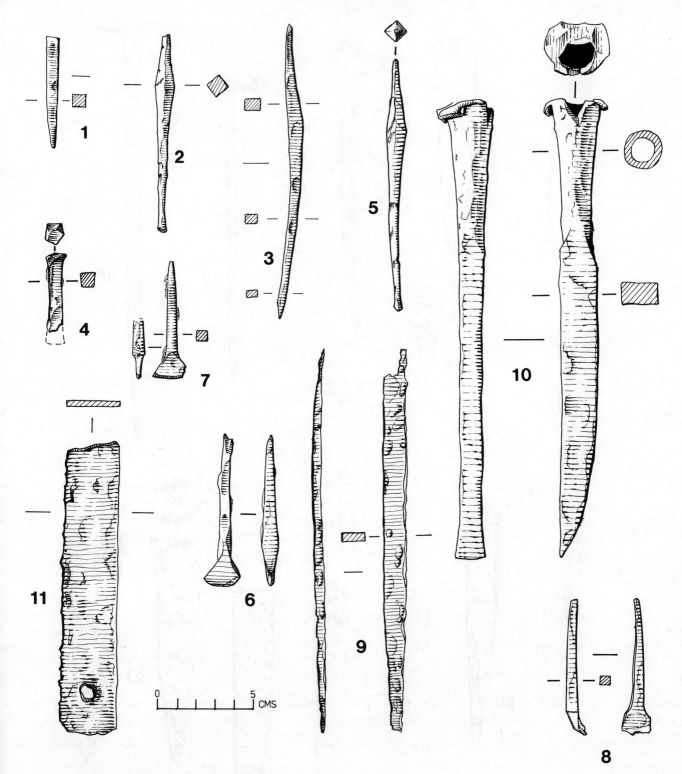

Fig. 46: Objects of iron; carpenters' tools ($\frac{1}{2}$)

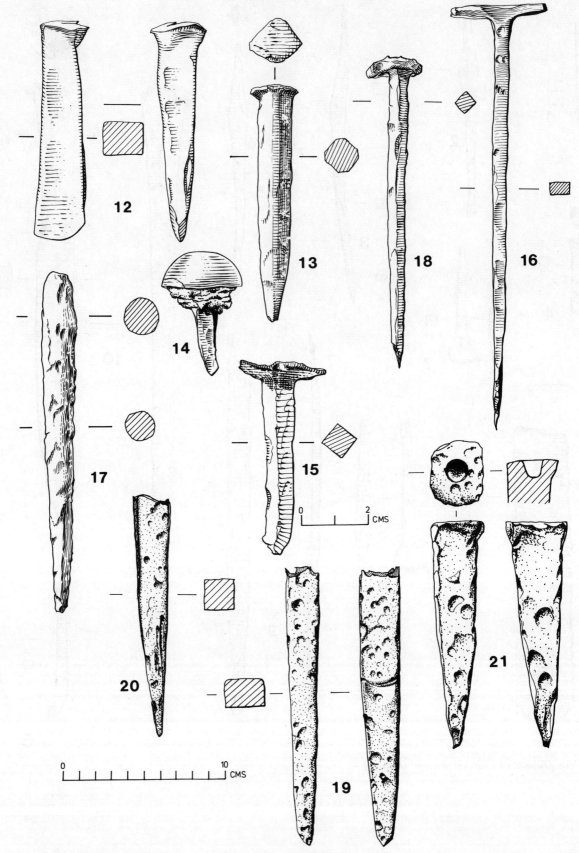

154

Fig. 47: Objects of iron; Nos. 12, 14 and 15 (⅟₁), remainder (½)

(ii) *Chisel, spikes, nails, punches, and pivots*

Chilgrove 1

12. (390) Small iron chisel, probably for metal working rather than carpentry. O1, layer 2, (Stockyard).
13. (117) Mason's or blacksmith's punch. C3, layer 2 (chalky hillwash south of Bath-house).
14. (382) Spike with bronze head. M1, layer 5; found in the road just inside the Stockyard gate, and may have been from the gate itself.
15. (482) Heavy spike. O8, layer 4 (Stockyard).
16. (48) Holdfast or spike, (*cf. Money* 1977, p. 347, Fig. 6). A2, layer 3 Room 1A (caldarium).

Chilgrove 2

17. (396) Hand spike, similar to a marlin spike, with rounded end. H4, layer 55 (Building 2, aisled barn).
18. (438) Large nail. K5, layer 8.
19. (130)
20. (107) Heavy spikes, possibly door pivots. J2, layer 2, and B2, layer 2 (Building 1).
21. (237) Door pivot. H4, layer 41 (Building 2).

(iii) *Knives, shears and pruning hooks*

Chilgrove 1

22. (314) Knife blade. L1, layer 16, Room 14 (rakeback from forge).
23. (341) Knife blade. L1, layer 5, Room 14 (rakeback from forge).
24. (323) Knife blade. H4, Pit H1, below Building 2.
25. (474) Knife blade. O8, layer 4 (Stockyard).
26. (170) Table knife. F1, layer 1 (ploughsoil).

Chilgrove 2

27. (345) Knife. H4, layer 5 (Building 2).
28. (320) Knife. H4, layer 34 (Building 2).
29. (299) Iron knife handle with rivet. H4, layer 47 (Building 2).
30. (12) Broad-bladed knife with wooden handle. C2 (Below ploughsoil in destruction debris).
31. (73) Shears. A2, layer 2 (Building 2, above floor in Room 7).
32. (325) Socketted pruning hook. H4, layer 34 (Building 2).

(iv) *Keys and latches*

Chilgrove 1

33. (4) Key. Trial trench 2 (ploughsoil).
34. (263) Part of key. K2 (south of Building 2).
35. (278) Key. D1, layer 1A (Room 5).

Chilgrove 2

36. (15) Key. B3, layer 3 (Building 2, above floor of Room 9).
37. (286) Key. F1, layer 14.
38. (422) Three-bladed key (unstratified).
39. (—) Four-bladed key (unstratified).

Upmarden

40. (33) Key. M4, layer 2. .

Chilgrove 1

41. (231) Latch. H5, layer 1B (south of Building 2).

Chilgrove 2

42. (283) Latch with two fixing holes in the handle, possibly for some kind of decoration. K9, layer 4 (Ditch 1).

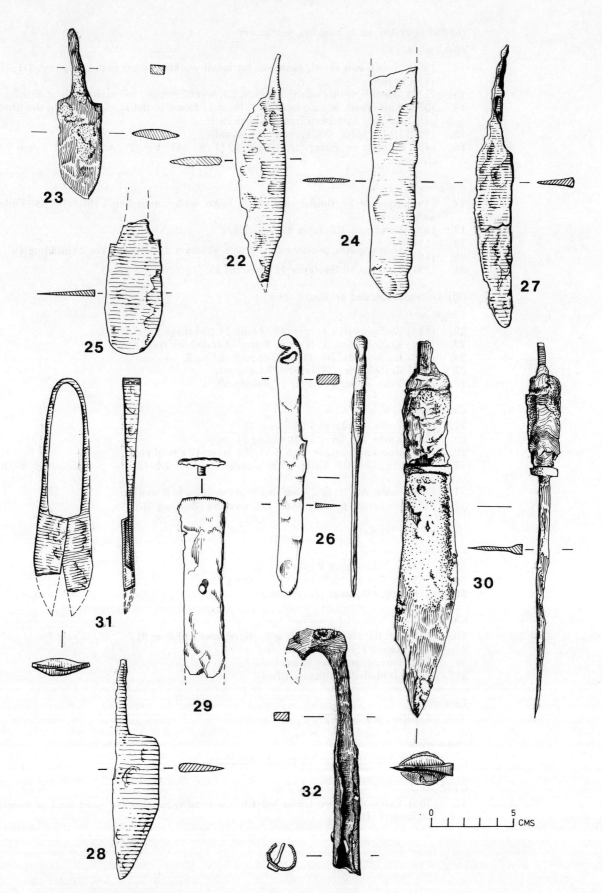

Fig. 48: Objects of iron; knives, shears and pruning hooks ($\frac{1}{2}$)

156

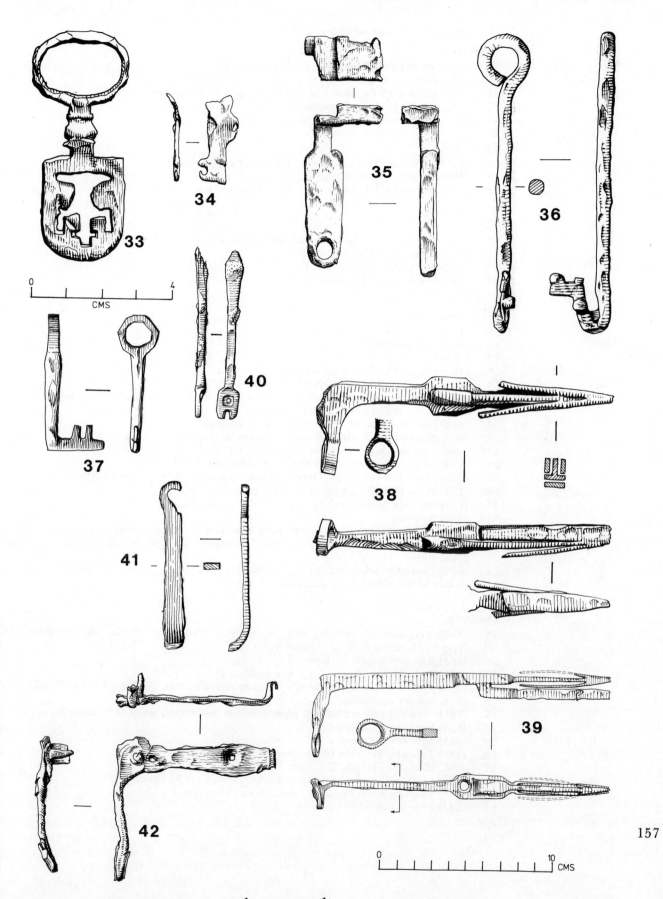

Fig. 49:   Iron keys and latches; No. 33 ($\frac{1}{1}$), remainder ($\frac{1}{2}$)

157

(v) *Hinges, staples and ploughshares*

Chilgrove 1

43.   (86) Part of a strap hinge. D2, layer 2 (Room 2).
44.   (286) Part of a hinge. E4, layer 4 (Room 13).
45.   (388) Hinge with two punched holes. M4, layer 2 (Stockyard).
46.   (275) Staple. J1, layer 2 (roadway).
47.   (208) Ring staple. C1, layer 7 (Bath-house fill).

Chilgrove 1

52.   (14) Ploughshare tip (*Manning* 1964). Trial trench 5, layer 3c.
53.   (409) Ploughshare tip. O3, layer 3 (Stockyard).
54.   (280) Pole spike. C1, layer 10 (south of Bath-house).

Chilgrove 2

48.   (86) Strap hinge. E2, layer 2 (Building 1, Room 1).
49.   (285) Hinge. K5, layer 3 (Building 1).
50.   (312) Staple. F1, layer 19 (Pit F1).
51.   (282) Staple. K9, layer 4 (Ditch 1).

(vi) *Miscellaneous*

55.   (186)
56.   (302) Iron needles.
57.   (252)
58.   (502) Stylus. P5, layer 1 (Stockyard).
59.   (9) Stylus. Trial trench 2, layer 2.
60.   (47) Iron hoop for joining wooden water pipes, 8 cms. in diameter. Trial trench 5 (one of a number found south of the Bath-house).
61.   (114) Iron hoop, as No. 61, but 14 cms. in diameter.
62.   (420) Flat iron strap with square punched hole. O7, layer 9 (Stockyard).
63.   (454) Iron object, possibly part of a staple. O2, Pit O3 (Stockyard).
64.   (243) Iron object; possibly a cup handle. Trial trench 2, layer 3c.
65.   (410) Chain and staple. O3, Oven 4. (From corn-drying oven in Stockyard).
66.   (173) Bucket handle. C1, layer 7 (south of Bath-house).
67.   (120) Half of a balance yoke (?). C2, layer 2 (Room 9) (cold bath).
68.   (433) Bracket.
69.) (158) Flat sectioned strips; two of many examples found on the site and probably 'stock'
70.) (45)   from which small objects would be forged. C2, layer 3, and A1, layer 5 (Bath-house fill).
71.   (424) Curved sheet studded with rivets. M1, layer 9 (Stockyard). Found lying on road surface between main gate postholes.

Chilgrove 2

72.   (189) Fragment of wrought iron, probably part of a pair of blacksmith's tongs. H4, layer 22 (Building 2, floor of aisled barn).
73.   (203) Ring and staple. J1, layer 18 (Ditch 1).
74.   (175) Part of hippo-sandal. K1, layer 7 (Ditch 1).
75.   (98) Part of a hippo-sandal, possibly an intermediate form. D1, layer 15 (Building 2).
76.   (455) Decorative fitting.
77.   (591) (a and b) Cotter pins. K6, layer 4 (below destruction levels of Building 3).
78.   (534) Pot hanger. L3, Pit L1.
79.   (281) Split pin. L1, layer 2 (below ploughsoil).
80.   (198) Axle pin. J1, layer 17 (outside Building 1, below ploughsoil).
81.   (305) 'D'-shaped buckle. H4, layer 18 (Building 2).
82.   (194) Lashing hook probably from a wagon. H4, layer 31 (Building 2).
83.   (464) Small axle pin. K6, layer 16 (building debris above Building 3).
84.   (631) Fitting, probably a handle.

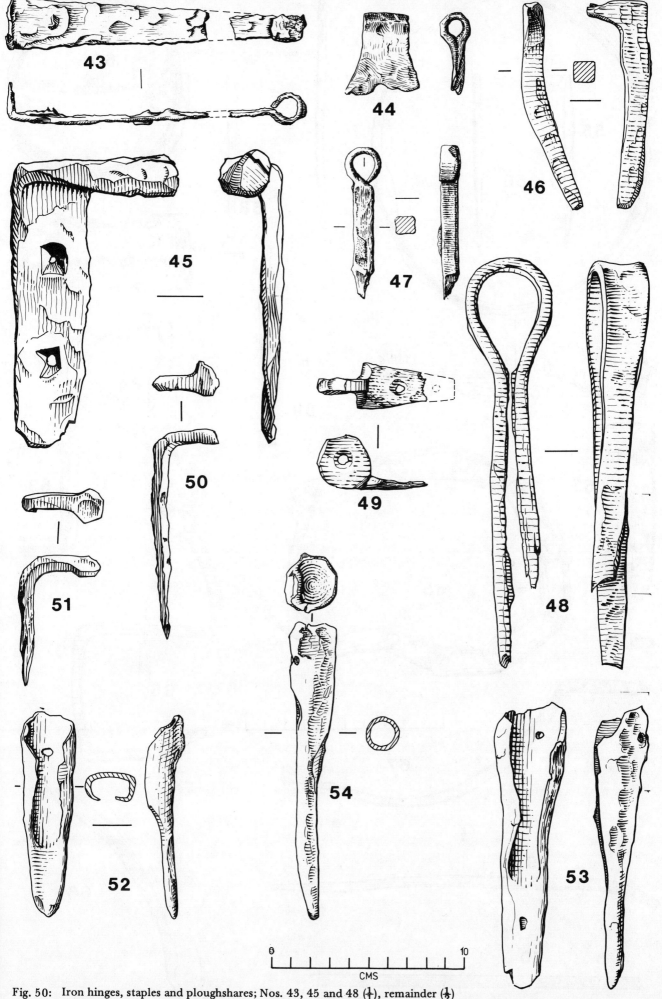

Fig. 50: Iron hinges, staples and ploughshares; Nos. 43, 45 and 48 ($\frac{1}{1}$), remainder ($\frac{1}{2}$)

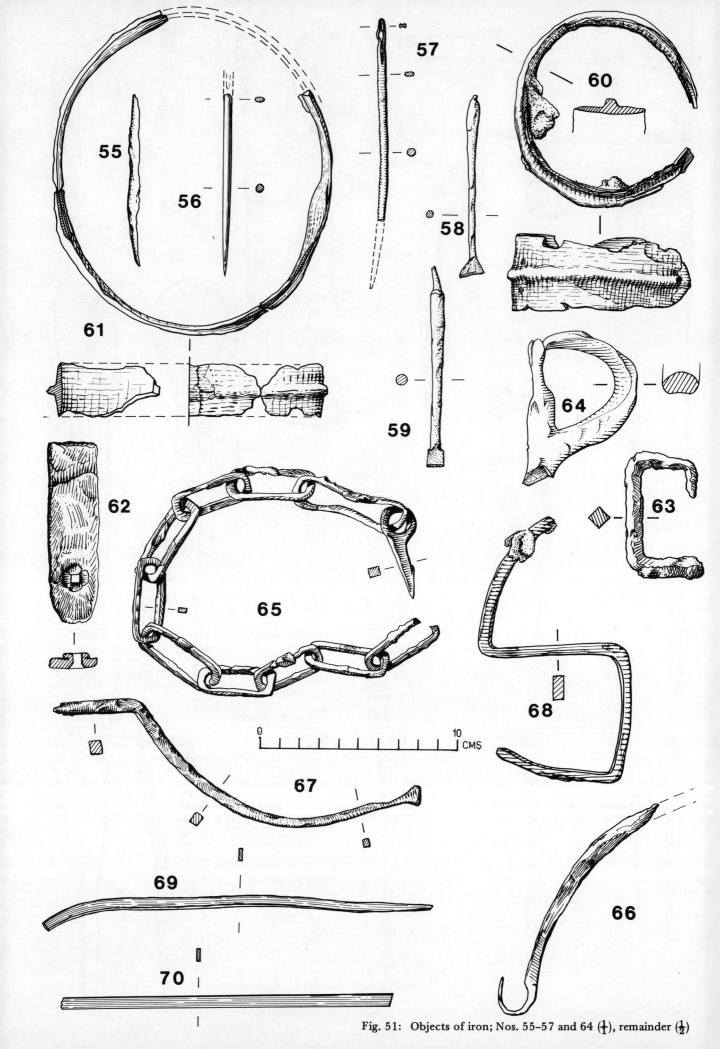

Fig. 51: Objects of iron; Nos. 55-57 and 64 ($\frac{1}{1}$), remainder ($\frac{1}{2}$)

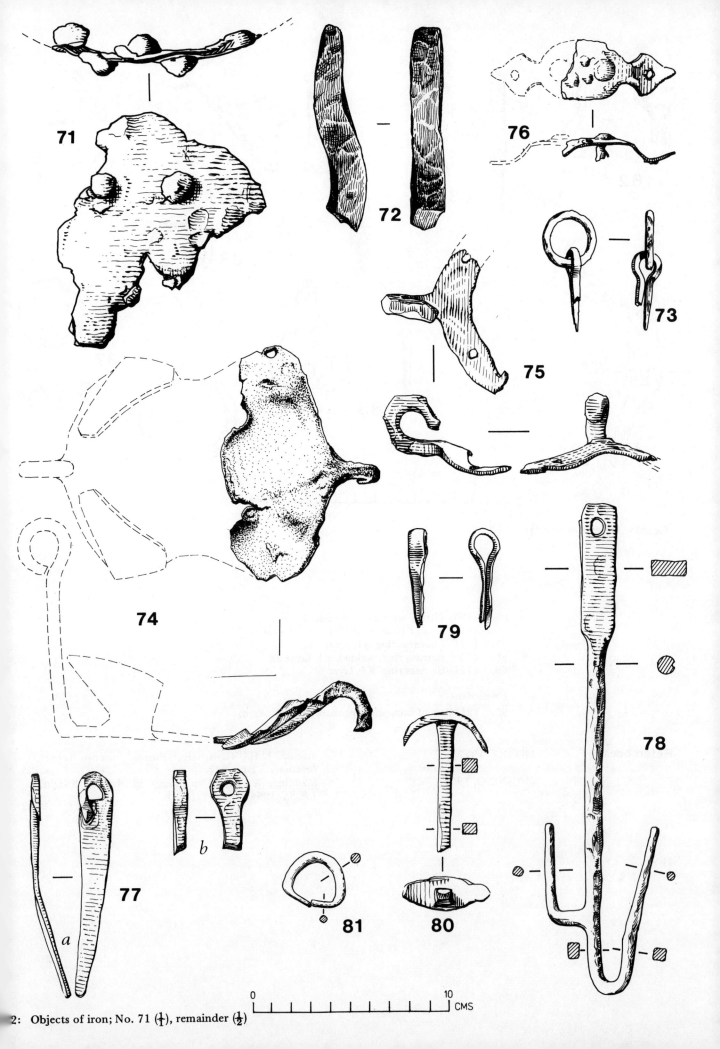

71

72

76

73

75

74

79

78

77

b

81

80

a

0   10
CMS

2:   Objects of iron; No. 71 (¼), remainder (½)

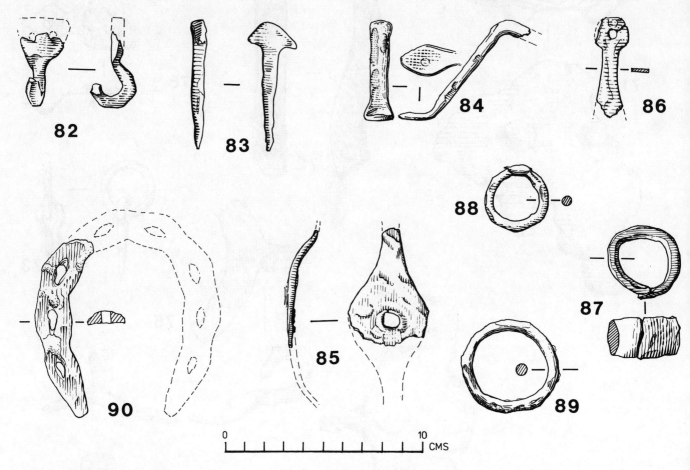

Fig. 53: Objects of iron ($\frac{1}{2}$)

85. (495) Fitting with a punched hole.
86. (217) Small fitting, probably part of a latch.
87. (221) ? harness ring. J1, layer 18.
88. (309) Harness ring, welded. F1, layer 14.
89. (477) Harness ring. K5, layer 6.

Upmarden
90. (21) Part of horseshoe, probably post-Roman.

References

MONEY 1977

Money, J. H., 'Garden Hill, Sussex', Interim Report, *Britannia* VIII, 1977.

MANNING 1964

Manning, W. H., 'The plough in Roman Britain', *J.R.S.*, 1964.

Bone (Fig. 54)

Bone pins

Chilgrove 1

1.   (200) Hairpin. F1, Pit F2 (south of Bath-house).
2.   (234) Hairpin. F1, Pit F7 (south of Bath-house).
3.   (296) Hairpin. L1 (Room 5).
4.   (184) Spindle. Trial trench 2, layer 3.

Chilgrove 2

5.   (206) Hairpin. J1, layer 13 (Building 1).
6.   (260) Hairpin. H4, layer 43 (Building 2).
7.   (535) Head of hairpin. L3, Pit L1.
8.   (358) Hairpin. E1, layer 19.

Miscellaneous bone objects

Chilgrove 1

9.   (330) Counter. E2.

Chilgrove 2

10.   (294) Spindle whorl. H4, layer 47 (Building 2).
11.   (304) Part of lap-rivetted bangle. H4, layer 28 (Building 2).

Shale and Jet (Fig. 55)

Chilgrove 1

1.   (507) Shale ring. M6, layer 2 (Stockyard). Could be Early Iron Age (Period 1).
2.   (236) Shale bracelet. Pit F7, layer 5 (south of Bath-house).
3.   (1) Jet counter. Trial trench 1, layer 5.

Chilgrove 2

4.   (68) Part of a shale bangle, approximately 63 mm. inside diameter. K3, layer 6 (Ditch 1).
5.   (426) Part of a jet bangle. H4, layer 63 (Building 2).
6.   (272) Jet pin, showing signs of having been re-sharpened. J1, layer 21 (outside Building 1).
7.   (453) Part of jet pin. K6, layer 19 (Building 3).

Glass (Figs. 56 and 57)

Chilgrove 1

1.   (88) Rim of glass bowl. D2, layer 2 (above floor of Room 2).
2.   (271) Handle of glass cup approximately 80 mm. diameter outside. (From the top fill in the Bath-house.)
3.   (67) Part of a moulded glass handle. A2, layer 3f (Bath-house fill).

Chilgrove 2

4.   (220) Three fragments from a ribbed glass vessel, probably from a conical beaker. J1, layer 18 (Ditch 1).
5.   (506) Fragment from a decorated bowl. K6, layer 31 (Building 3).
6.   (67) Fragment from a beaker. K3, layer 6 (Ditch 1).
7.   (505) Fragments of a cut-glass bowl engraved with the figure of Silenus, presumably seated upon an ass, as the ear of the beast can be seen below the figure's right hand. Diameter of rim approximately 270 mm. K6, layer 31 (Building 3).
8.   (444) Part of a glass bowl with incised decoration; rim diameter approximately 118 mm. K5, layer 6 (below ploughsoil).
9.   (263) Rim of bowl, approximate diameter 190 mm. H3, layer 2 (below ploughsoil).
10.   (63) Fragments of a cone beaker. H3, layer 1, ploughsoil.
11.   (307) Rim of vessel. H4, layer 47 (Building 2).
12.   (266) Base of a bowl. J3, layer 2 (below ploughsoil).
13.   (214) Bead. J1, layer 18 (Ditch 1).

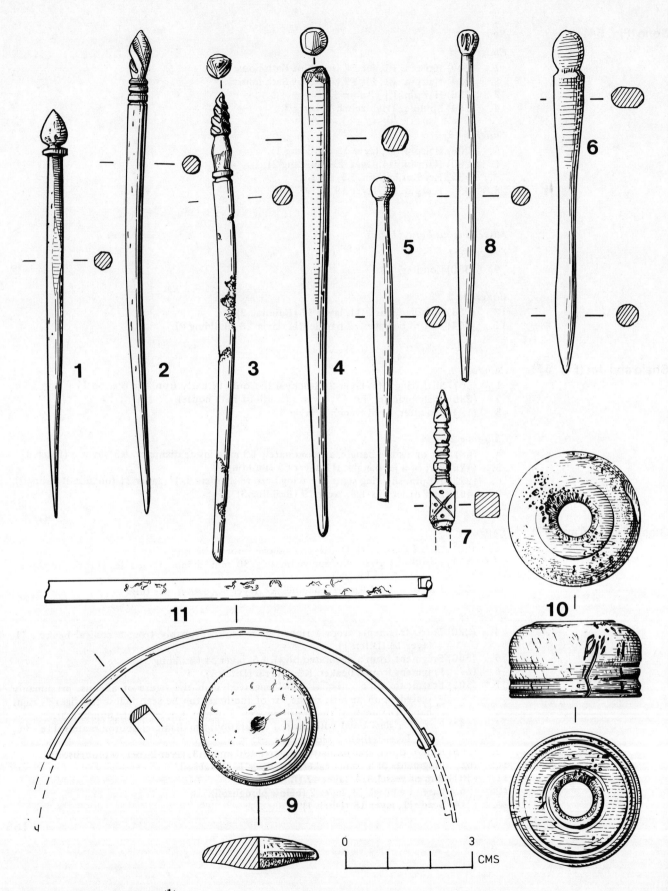

Fig. 54: Objects of bone ($\tfrac{1}{1}$)

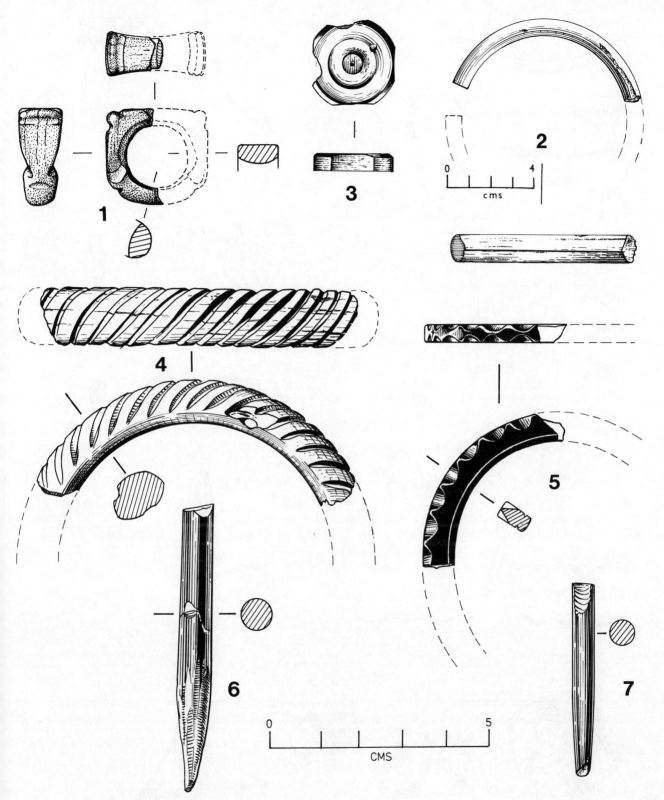

Fig. 55:   Objects of shale and jet; No. 2 ($\frac{1}{2}$), remainder ($\frac{1}{1}$)

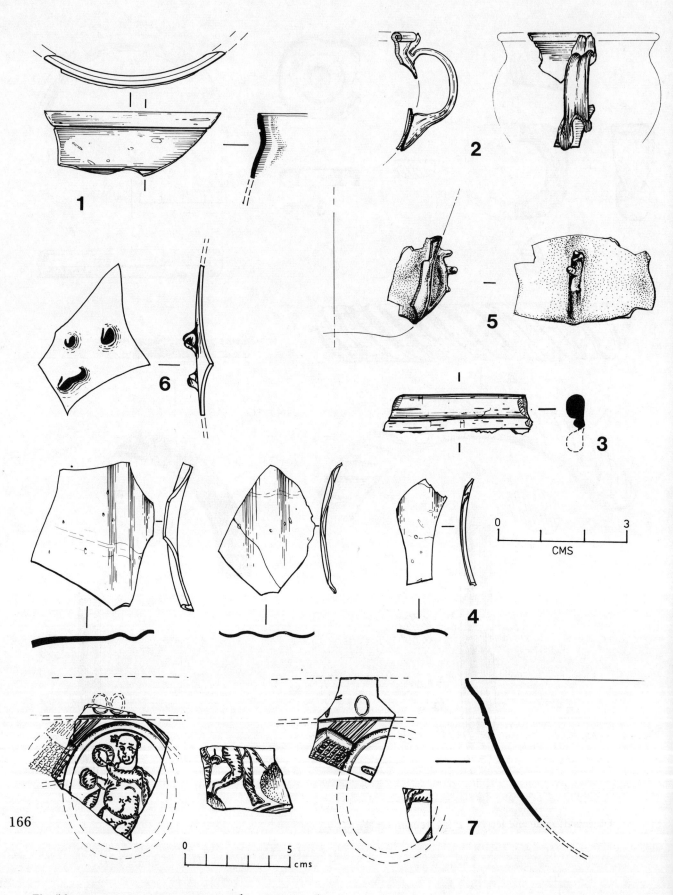

166

Fig. 56: Roman glass; Nos. 2, 5 and 7 ($\frac{1}{2}$), remainder ($\frac{1}{1}$)

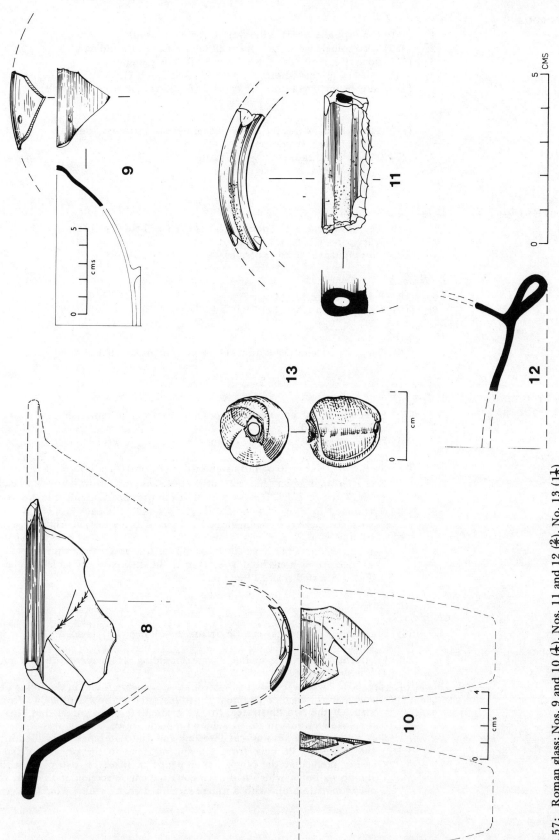

Fig. 57: Roman glass; Nos. 9 and 10 ($\frac{1}{3}$), Nos. 11 and 12 ($\frac{2}{3}$), No. 13 ($1\frac{1}{3}$)

167

Miscellaneous (Fig. 58)

Chilgrove 2

1. (449) Lead spindle whorl. K6, layer 16 (below topsoil).
2. (389) Lead spingle whorl. H4, layer 28 (above floor of Building 2).
3. (515) Pottery spindle whorl. K6, layer 32 (below ploughsoil).
4. (81) Pottery spindle whorl. J2, layer 3 (above Ditch 1).
5. (113) Butt-seamed lead tube. B3, layer 2 (Building 2, destruction levels).

Upmarden

6. (7)   Fired brick with incised point-impressed markings, possibly part of a sundial. M1, layer 9 (Hypocaust).
7. (27) Flint arrow head. P5, layer 1 (garden soil).
8. (28) ? Arrow head. P5, layer 1 (garden soil).

Objects of Stone (Fig. 59)

Chilgrove 1

1. (240) Neolithic stone axe. Trial trench 2, Pit 1 (see below, p. 178).
2. (217) Whetstone. C1, Pit C4 (south of Bath-house).
3. (265) Fine-grained sandstone used as a hone. (Unstratified.)

Chilgrove 2

4. (193) Pebble counter. L1, layer 2.
5. (191) Greensand spindle whorl. K1, layer 9 (Ditch 1).

Upmarden

6. (36) Part of a circular chalk disc. M4, layer 1 (in apse of Bath-house).

Masonry Fragments (Figs. 60—63)

Chilgrove 1

7. (75) Fragment of carved sandstone, possibly part of the capital of a pillar. D2 (unstratified). (Fig. 60.)
8. (90) Part of a sandstone fluted column. From D2, layer 2a (above floor of Room 7). (Fig. 61.)
9.   Section of ridge capping in fine-grained sandstone (Fig. 60).
10.   Part of a small pillar (Fig. 62), originally symmetrical, which was ploughed up by Mr. Tribe in 1963. It has a dowel slot in the base, and one side has been roughly trimmed to allow it to be fixed against a wall. The back corner has been relieved so as to clear the coving along the base of the wall. The pillar, which was split by the plough in recent years, is carved from a fine-grained sandstone. In its modified form the most likely use for it was as a support for a decorative piece or perhaps a household god. It may be the base on which the statuette of Fortuna rested (Plate 11 and p. 181).

Chilgrove 2

11. (66) Fragment of Purbeck marble frame moulding. F3, layer 2, below ploughsoil (Fig. 60).
12. (262) Fragment of Purbeck marble frame moulding. H3, layer 2 (below ploughsoil). (Fig. 61.)
13 and 14. (Fig. 63). Two large slabs of dressed limestone were found in the filling of the well, and a third, smaller fragment (not illustrated here) was probably from another slab. Of the two illustrated, No. 14 is complete. Both are rebated, socketted and dressed in a similar manner and are the same width.

    No. 13 has a keyway cut into one end and two holes are drilled into each of the long sides 26 cms. from the opposite end to the keyway. Viewed thus, it seems likely that the block was designed to pivot on two pins set firmly into the dowel holes, which had been cut to a square section at the top. This would accommodate a pin with a square-sectioned shank which would prevent it from

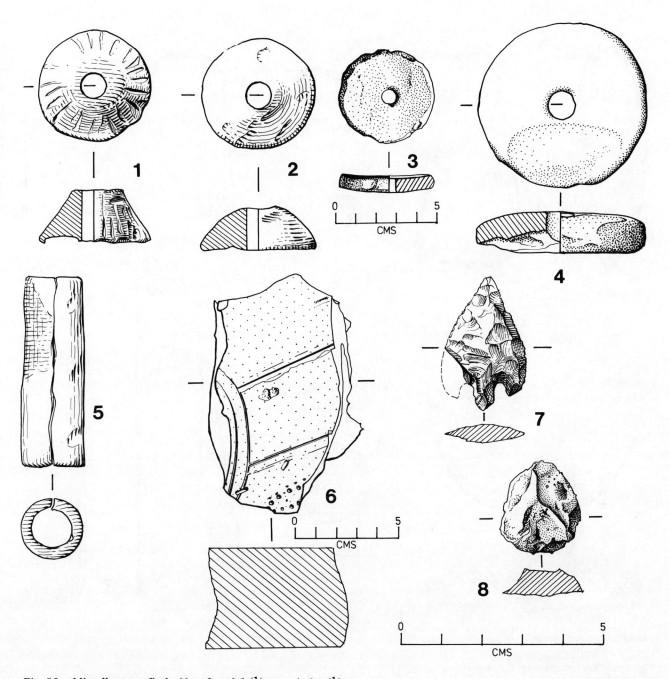

Fig. 58: Miscellaneous finds; Nos. 3 and 6 (½), remainder (¼)

169

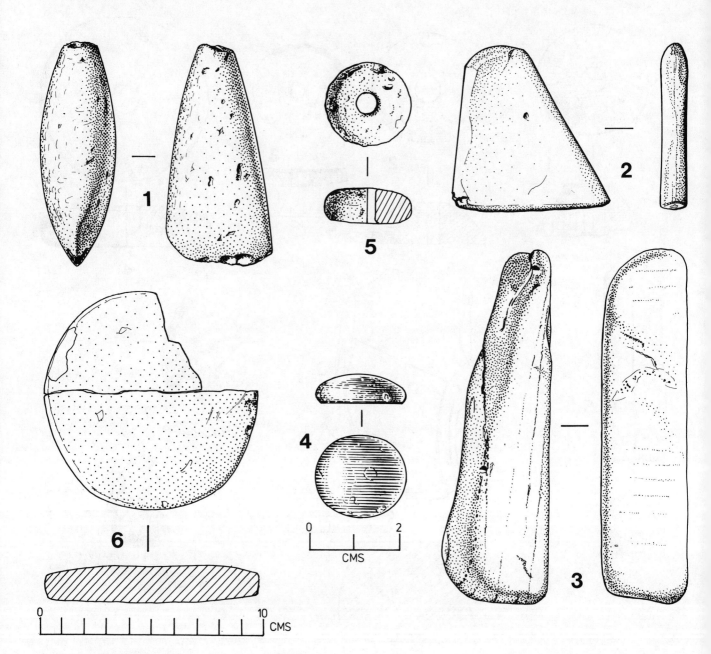

Fig. 59: Objects of stone; No. 4 ($\frac{1}{1}$), remainder ($\frac{1}{2}$)

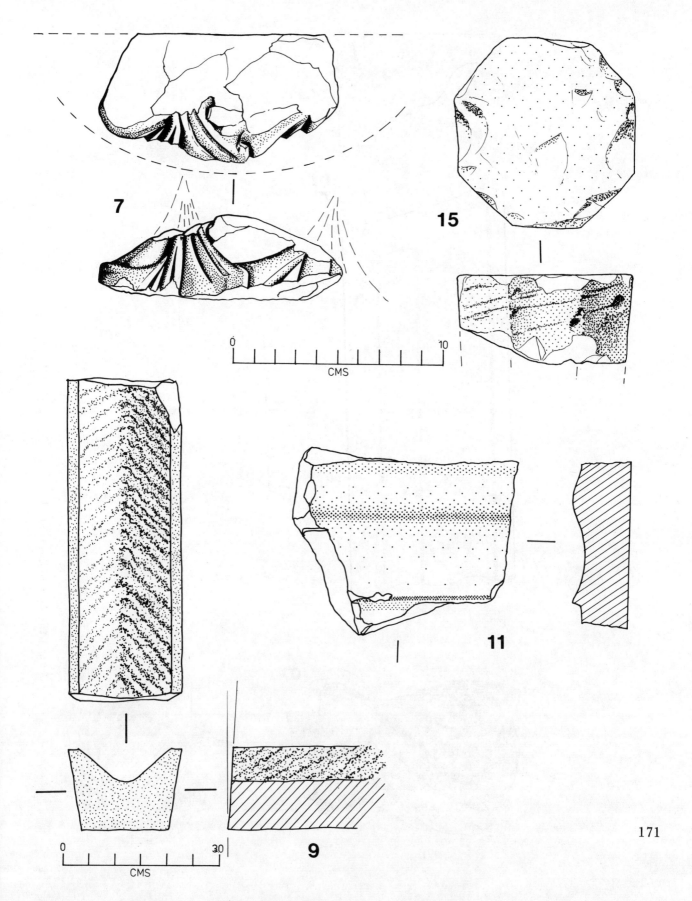

7

15

11

9

0 — CMS — 10

0 — CMS — 30

Fig. 60: Masonry fragments; No. 9 ($\frac{1}{8}$), remainder ($\frac{1}{2}$)

172

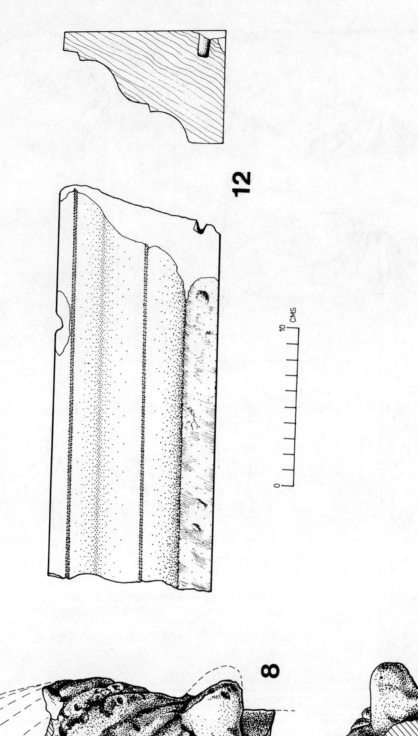

12

8

CMS
10
0

Fig. 61: Masonry fragments (⅓)

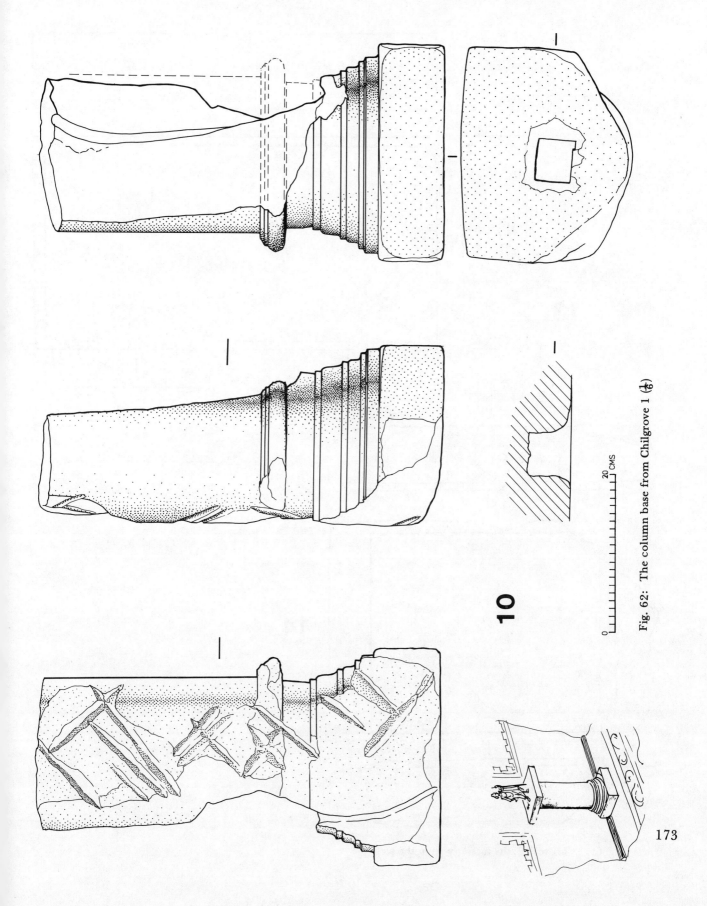

Fig. 62: The column base from Chilgrove 1 (1/6)

173

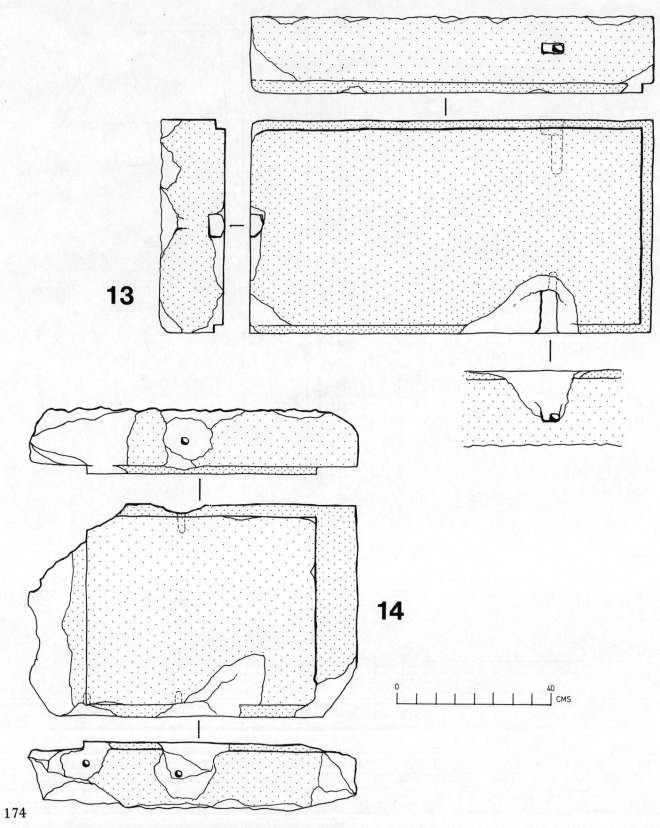

13

14

0   40
|___|__|__|__|__|__|__|___|
                     CMS

Fig. 63:   Chilgrove 2; the masonry from the well ($\frac{1}{12}$)

turning within the hole. The ends of the pins must have pivotted within an external housing on either side of the block, and it can be seen that it would function as a flap which could be raised by inserting a bar into the keyway at the end and lifting.

No. 14 is smaller than No. 13 and has a wider rebate at the top and bottom, with the rebates on the long sides being slightly wider than those on No. 13. It has been drilled to take four round pins and would be rigidly held when these were inserted. In both cases the blocks were broken from their fixtures in antiquity when the iron pins were still robust enough to break the stone. The purpose of these blocks remains obscure. They may have been part of the well-head fittings, but it is difficult to envisage their function. Certainly they must have been part of a larger assemblage, but whether the missing pieces rest at the bottom of the well awaiting discovery, or whether they were robbed and removed from the site, can only be conjectured. It is possible that they may have been brought to the site in the condition they were found in and used in the bath-house construction.

Upmarden

15. (13) (Fig. 60). Fragment of octagonal capping of greensand. Area 5, Trial trench 1.

Flue Tiles (Figs. 64 and 65)

Chilgrove 1

A number of complete box flue tiles were found in the corner of Room 7, where they had collapsed. They had probably been used as voussoirs to support an arch over the doorway into the room. Three specimens are illustrated here, showing three different types of piercing and styles of combing. (See also Plate 9.)

1. Rectangular slot. 6 cms. by 2.4 cms. (42 by 22.4 by 11.6 cms.)
2. Two triangles apex to apex, 10 by 5.4 cms. (44 by 21 by 11.6 cms.).
3. Oval aperture 5.6 by 4 cms. (45 by 24 by 12.2 cms.).
4 and 5. Two half sections of box flue cut at an angle at one end so that they could be used as keys in an arch when being used as voussoirs or to fit the inclined angle of the roof when used as a flue. These were also from Room 7.

Upmarden

6. Part of a serrated flue tile, one of three examples found, made so as to fit together with a mating second tile. No examples were noted at the Chilgrove villas, but one has been identified by the writer at the Garden Hill Excavations. The design was apparently to simplify production and firing, and assembly on site would have been no more difficult than using the fully enclosed tiles. (See Fig. 65 for reconstruction drawing.

7. One of two fragments of roller-impressed flue tile, one from the garden soil (M2, layer 1), and one from the bath-house (M1, layer 9). Both are similar and may be from the same tile. The pattern is Lowther's diamond and lattice (*Lowther*, (Fig. 46).

While these tiles are common in Chichester this is the only example from the three villas.

Reference

Lowther, A. W. G. 'A Study of the patterns on Roman flue tiles and their distribution. Research Paper No. 1 of the Surrey Archaeological Society.'

Stone Roofing Tiles (Fig. 66)

Both Chilgrove 1 and 2 were roofed in part at least, with Horsham stone tiles during Period 4, and large quantities were found where they had fallen, with the nails still intact. One is illustrated here.

The source of these tiles known today is in the Horsham region, but it is likely that the Chilgrove villas were supplied from nearer at hand, possibly from the Midhurst area, where similar sandstone outcrops.

8. Horsham stone tile, measuring 42 by 28 cms., which has been re-drilled either for a second fixing or because the first nail bent when being driven.

175

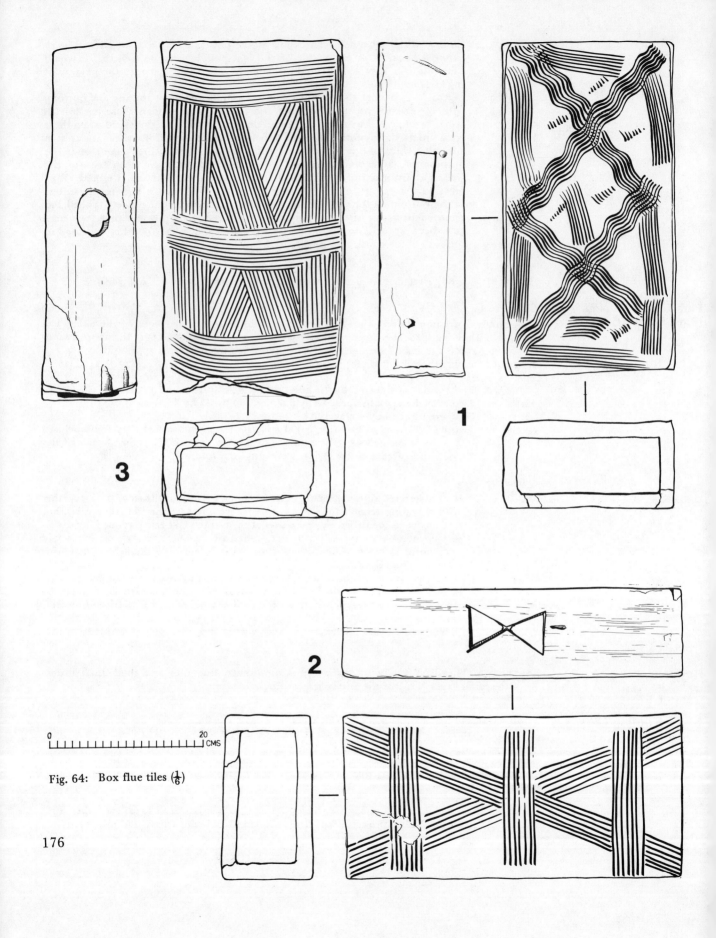

0 |||||||||||||||||||||| 20
                      CMS

Fig. 64: Box flue tiles ($\frac{1}{6}$)

176

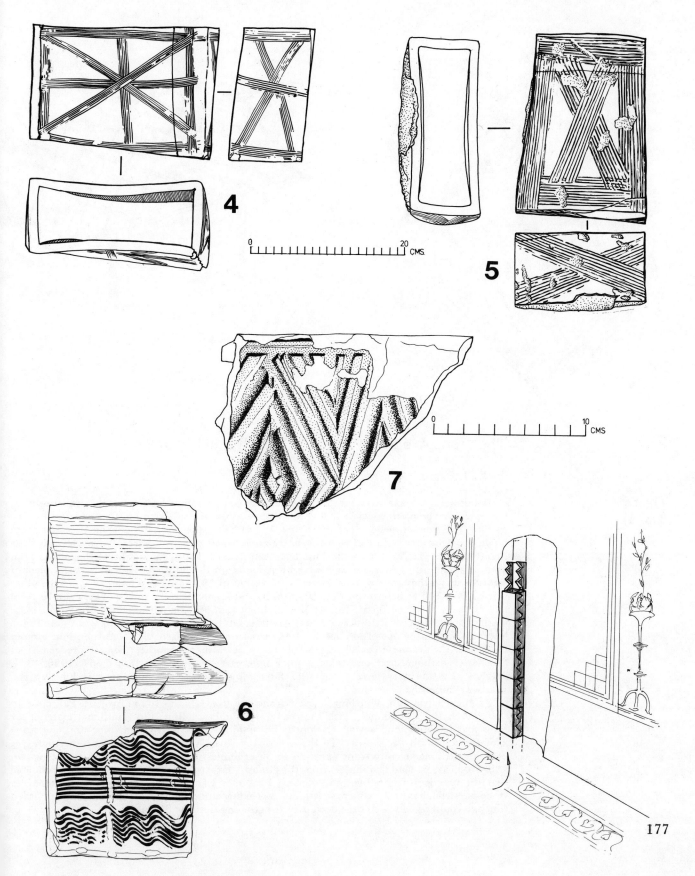

4

0 |||||||||||||||||||| 20 CMS.

5

0 ||||||||| 10 CMS.

7

6

177

Fig. 65:   Flue tiles; No. 7 ($\frac{1}{3}$), remainder ($\frac{1}{6}$)

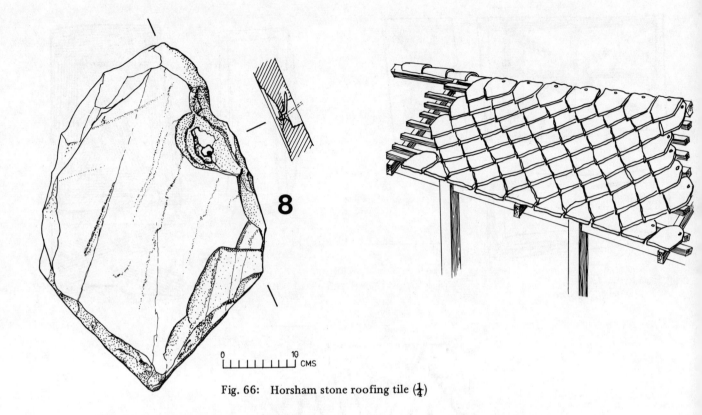

8

Fig. 66: Horsham stone roofing tile ($\frac{1}{4}$)

The Stone Axe from Pit 1, Trial Trench 2 at Chilgrove 1

by K. J. Evans

Fig. 59 (No. 1)

Neolithic stone axe of a greenish medium to coarse-grained igneous rock, probably from Cornwall. A complete specimen, it is small to medium size (9.7 cm.) with a wide oval cross-section, the sides showing signs of rolling. It has had much use, the cutting edge was worn down more on one side and it has been re-ground and polished. Part of the edge has been slightly damaged. The tip of the butt has been pecked, which may indicate that it has been used as a hammer. Few stone axes have been found on the South Downs and coastal plain of West Sussex, although two, both larger, were found in 1923 only two miles away on the other side of Bow Hill at Stoughton (Sx. 107, Sx. 91, on Manor Farm). An axe of very similar form and size was ploughed up at Rowner, Billingshurst (Sx. 56), six miles away in the Weald, close to the upper reaches of the River Arun. Another similar specimen (Sx. 109) was found in the lower Arun valley at Toddington, Littlehampton. The pattern of distribution around Chichester, with one (Sx. 80) from the shore at Bosham, another (Sx. 7) dredged from Chichester harbour, and one from a pit a mile east of Chichester (*S.A.C.* 67, 1926, 217), suggests that the axes were brought to Sussex by traders or immigrants travelling by sea, coastwise rather than overland.

At High Salvington, Worthing, a greenstone axe (Sx. 50) was found by J. H. Pull close to the Church Hill flint mines. With the ready availability of flint, the traditional material for tools and weapons, and a well-developed flint-mining industry, it is surprising that any stone axes are found on the Downs. To the east of the River Adur, where no flint mines have yet been located, many more stone axes (25 to 30 examples) have been discovered, including two (Alfriston, Sx. 5; Patcham, Sx. 9) from the Group 1 factory (Cornwall, Penwith). It is probable that the practice of grinding and polishing flint axes was adopted after seeing the imported stone axes which introduced a new fashion. A grinding stone found at Ford with half a polished flint axe could equally well have been used for grinding stone or flint axes.

The stone axe was not just a prestige object; the worn edge of the Chilgrove specimen testifies to the use made of it. However, it is possible that generations later these smooth stone objects were 'collected' by the British and Roman inhabitants and kept as ritual objects (e.g., thunderstones). A very small greenstone axe (Sx. 53) was found during excavations on the site of the Romano-British bath-house on Highdown Hill in an Iron Age pit.

The Chilgrove axe has been assigned the number Sx. 142 in the Sussex Implement Petrology List.*

*See S.N.Q. XVII, 1968, pp. 15–21, for published list of stone implements with their respective reference and locations.

The Worked Flints from Site 1

by Richard Bradley

Fig. 67

A total of 59 worked flints were recovered in the excavation and came either from the cobbling of the Roman stockyard or from the overlying ploughsoil. None were stratified in pre-Roman contexts. All of the flints are characterised by heavily-eroded cortex and range in patination from white to blue-grey or grey-black. No significance is to be attached to these distinctions, and it is probable that all made use of the flint rubble of the valley floor. It is unlikely that any chronological importance can be given to the findings of all these items in Roman contexts and the industry as a whole may well have been introduced to the site together with the material for the stockyard. There is no evidence that any of the flakes had been struck with a metal implement. Almost all of the material has, however, been damaged either by the plough or by Roman use of the site. The limited number of flints represented makes the assemblage unsuitable for metrical analysis.

Cores

Two examples, both with flakes struck in two directions from a single edge, Clark's 'chopper' type.[1] It is unlikely that these had been re-used. (3.)

Waste

Eight flakes and two blades show no sign of utilisation, while a further 15 flakes and seven blades are too badly damaged by the plough for possible re-touch or wear to be recognised upon the edges.

Utilised

Eight flakes and four blades show limited areas of re-touch. The condition of the flints will not permit any division between those used for scraping and those used for cutting, although blades were more commonly used for the latter task (1, 31).

Implements

Twelve implements are included in this group, though the majority are again damaged. Details are as follows:

Scrapers. Ten roughly re-touched scrapers, one on a primary flake and five retaining large areas of cortex. All are struck from the base and re-touched at the distal end. Seven examples are also re-touched along one edge, while a single example shows working at both edges. All are upon flakes rather than blades, though three symmetrical examples have a length; breadth ratio of 2:1. In one case the bulb of percussion has been removed. Scrapers with true prepared bases are normally a feature of the middle and late Neolithic[2] though the implement itself uses a normal blade technique (7, 26, 28).

Hollow Scraper. Hollow scraper with small areas of pressure flaking on either face (18).

Borer? One partially cortical flake with a re-touched tip may have served as a borer or piercer in view of the severe abrasion upon its end, though, if so, it must have become blunted by use (14).

Backed blade. A short fragment of the tip of a steeply blunted blade. The bulbar segment has been lost, probably with the plough (56).

179

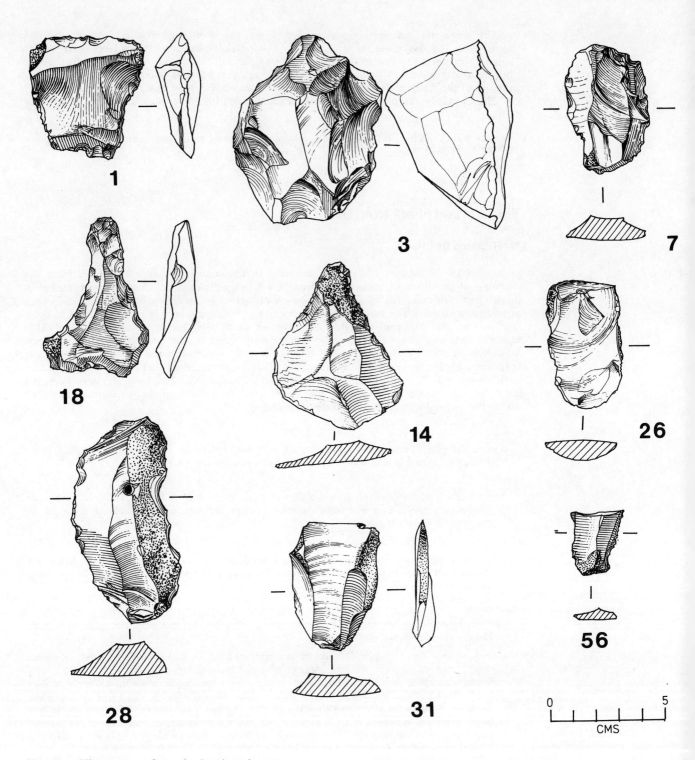

Fig. 67: Flint scrapers from the Stockyard

CMS

Comments

Few comments can be made on such a small assemblage, especially since it is in a secondary context. The industry seems to have been based on narrow flakes and blades, and a Mesolithic or earlier Neolithic date might be appropriate. There are too few items for a firm decision to be made. The high proportion of scrapers can be matched in either period. The hollow scraper is equally ambiguous, but could well belong to the later Neolithic. Finally, it cannot be assumed that every item is prehistoric and Roman use of this material is reliably attested in Dorset.[3]

Notes

1. J. D. G. Clark: 'A Microlithic industry from the Cambridgeshire Fenland'. *Proc. Prehist Soc.,* 21 (1955), 7.
2. J. D. G. Clark: 'Excavations at the Neolithic site at Hurst Fen, Mildenhall, Suffolk.' *Proc. Prehist Soc.,* 26 (1960), 220.
3. R. Bradley in N. J. Sunter: 'Excavations at Norden, Corfe' (forthcoming).

The Statuette of Fortuna

by J. M. C. Toynbee

Plate 11

This fragmentary sculpture which was found unstratified in August 1964, measures 8½ins. across the front and 4¾ins. from back to front. It is worked in Caen Stone,[1] perhaps from a piece left over from a block that was imported into Roman Britain for building purposes. The subject is a female figure, of which everything above the level of the knees is lost,[2] seated facing the spectator on a chair, the front and right-hand leg of which are decorated with triple fluting. The carving is carried out partly in the round and partly in very high relief; and it is likely that the whole of the back of the figure was flat and unworked, the statuette being intended to be set against a wall or in a niche. The base supporting the figure is four inches deep and into its face is recessed an oblong, rectangular panel, with a neatly chamfered frame, which was obviously meant to receive an inscription that was never cut.[3] There can be little doubt that the sculpture was votive in character, designed most probably for a domestic shrine.

The religious personage portrayed wears shoes, a long tunic reaching to the insteps, and a cloak which is wrapt across the knees, while one end of it falls in a vertical, zig-zag fold between them. She can be identified by the object on the ground beside her right foot. This is a large globe, with two crossed bands passing round it; and on top of it are the remains of another object which in that position can only have been a rudder. The figure is, in fact, that of the goddess Fortuna, whose distinctive attribute in Roman art is a rudder, shown either by itself, or combined either with a globe or with a wheel, or combined with both. Here no trace of a wheel can be detected either beside Fortuna's left foot or elsewhere in the group. But in most of the best authenticated representations of the seated Fortuna in official Roman art, those on the reverses of imperial coins of the second century A.D., where she is nearly always clearly labelled FORT(unae) RED(duci) ('In honour of Fortune who brings the emperor safely back to Rome from abroad'), the goddess holds a rudder resting on a globe and has no wheel beside her.[4] Types that show the wheel as well,[5] or the wheel and the rudder, but no globe,[6] are rarer. The absence on the Chilgrove group of a wheel, the object most commonly associated in the popular mind with Fortuna, is thus no argument against the equation of our figure with her.

In all the seated Fortuna coin-types of the second century, as well as in most of the types of the first and second centuries that depict her standing,[7] the goddess holds a cornucopia in her left hand and has a diadem on her head. It is therefore virtually certain that the Chilgrove Fortuna held in her vanished left hand that symbol of prosperity; and it is also very possible that she wore a head-dress of that form. These suppositions win support from the better-preserved provincial carvings of Fortuna that survive.

181

The closest parallel from Britain to the Chilgrove sculpture known to me is the statuette found at Lanchester and now in the Durham Cathedral Library.[8] Here again Fortuna is seated on a chair and is worked partly in the round and partly in high relief. The head is lost, but the rest of the goddess is relatively well preserved. She wears shoes, a long tunic girded below the breasts, and a cloak wrapt across her knees, although in this case no vertical fold of that garment hangs down between them. In her left hand is the stem of a cornucopia, and her right hands holds the remnant of a rudder that must once have rested on the globe beside her left foot. Beside her right foot is a wheel. Two reliefs of British provenance show Fortuna standing. On an altar from Chesters, inscribed D(e)AE FORT(unae) CONSERVATRICI, she is very crudely carved, but recognisable by her cornucopia and her globe or wheel;[9] while an equally naive figure in a niche from Castlecary on the Scottish Wall has a cornucopia and a rudder resting on a wheel.[10] On neither of these reliefs does Fortuna wear a diadem. Among the comparatively frequent sculptural representations of Fortuna from Roman Gaul and Germany published in Esperandieu's corpus[11] is a number of seated statuettes of the Chilgrove class, most of them unfortunately headless.[12] But of two with the head intact, one shows certainly,[13] the other probably,[14] a diadem; and Fortuna wears a diadem on two reliefs.[15] In one statuette[16] and on two reliefs[17] she is veiled and apparently without a diadem. Our Fortuna could, then, have been either diademed or veiled; but the coin evidence cited above favours the former alternative. Nearly all of the continental provincial sculptures in which the left hand of the goddess is preserved show in it a cornucopia. In all of them Fortuna has a rudder, often resting on, or placed near, a globe; and in some of them she has a wheel as well.

A feature of the Chilgrove Fortuna's globe calls for special mention—the two cross bands carved in low relief that encircle it. These would appear to represent the rings of the armillary sphere, that is, Ptolemy's equinoctial rings (κρικοί ισημόρινοι).[18]

They are found on a number of other renderings of globes in Roman art, for instance, in a painting of the Muse Urania from the House of the Vettii in Pompeii,[19] on the 'astronomer' mosaic in the Roman Villa at Brading in the Isle of Wight,[20] on a coin-type of Domitian which depicts a dead baby prince seated on a globe,[21] on two Mithraic reliefs,[22] and on Fortuna's globe on the Rheinzabern relief.[23] The five or six bands seen encircling the globe at the feet of the right-hand Victory on the Bath Gorgon pediment[24] probably represent the astrolabe.

As regards the Chilgrove figure dress, her tunic and her cloak are the standard garments for Fortuna and her shoes are of a type commonly worn by goddesses on works of art from the Romano-Celtic provinces, for example, by Fortuna herself on the Lanchester statuette (see above), on a relief from Jagsthausen in Germany,[26] and in a statuette from Weinsberg, also in Germany,[27] and by the Mother Goddesses on two reliefs from Cirencester.[28] On both of these Gloucestershire sculptures there is also to be seen the vertical, zig-zag fold of drapery, already noted in the case of our Fortuna, falling between the figure's knees: and the same feature occurs on the Fortuna statuette from Grand.[29] Her drapery now provides the sole criterion for judging of the style and technique of the Chilgrove goddess. The folds of both the tunic and the cloak are carefully, boldly and pictorially cut, suggesting plastically modelled limbs beneath them. The statuette would seem to be the work of a very competent provincial sculptor, perhaps a Gaul who was domiciled in Britain. On the other hand, the possibility cannot be excluded that the piece was carved in Gaul and imported into Britain in its finished state. Its execution could have taken place at any time within the second, or early third, century. No evidence has so far come to hand for a closer dating.

Notes

1. Kindly identified by Mr. F. G. Dimes of the Geological Survey and Museum, South Kensington.

2. No trace of the missing portion has so far come to light, although the site has been most carefully searched for it. It may be that the sculpture was deliberately smashed in early Christian times.

3. If there was once a painted inscription no vestige of it survives today.

4. H. Mattingly, *Coins of the Roman Empire in the British Museum*, iii, 1936, p. 305, No. 516, Plate 57, 4 (Hadrian: Æ; p. 310, No. 547, Plate 58, 3 (Hadrian: Æ); p. 446, No. 1368, Plate 83, 12 (Hadrian: Æ); p. 455, No. 1415 (Hadrian Æ); *ibid.*, iv, 1940, p. 411, No. 199, Plate 57, 2 (Marcus Aurelius and Lucius Verus: AV); p. 548, No. 1027, Plate 74, 15 (Marcus Aurelius and Lucius Verus: Æ); p. 718, No. 161, Plate 95, 5 (Commodus: Æ); p. 734, No. 244, Plate 97, 2 (Commodus: Æ); p. 817, No. 618, Plate 108, 2 (Commodus: Æ).

5. e.g., *ibid.*, iv, p. 481, No. 659, Plate 66, 15 (Marcus Aurelius and Commodus: Æ).

6. e.g., *ibid.*, iv, p. 506, No. 796, Plate 69, 18 (Marcus Aurelius and Commodus: Æ).

7. e.g., *ibid.*, ii, 1930, p. 140, No. 630, Plate 24, 13 (Vespasian; Æ); p. 404, No. 467, Plate 80, 7 (Domitian: Æ); *ibid.*, 111, p. 2, No. 11, Plate 1, 6 (Nerva: Æ); p. 5, Nol 36, Plate 1, 19 (Nerva: AV); p. 321, No. 635, Plate 59, 13 (Hadrian: Æ), etc.

8. J. Liversidge, *Furniture in Roman Britain*, 1955, Fig. 31.

9. E. A. Wallis Budge, *An Account of the Roman Antiquities Preserved in the Museum at Chesters, Northumberland*, 1907, pp. 306–7, Fig. on p. 113.

10. G. Macdonald, *The Roman Wall in Scotland*, ed. 2, 1934, p. 446, Plate 77, Fig. 1.

11. E. Espérandieu, *Recueil general des bas-reliefs, statues et bustes de la Gaule romaine*, 1907–38; *La Germanie romaine*, 1931.

12. e.g., *ibid.*, *Gaule*, vi, p. 82, No. 4462 (Naix); p. 227, No. 4936 (Trier); p. 234, No. 4950 (Trier); p. 267, No. 5028 (Trier); p. 281, No. 5067 (Trier), p. 427, No. 5248 (Bitburg); viii, p. 47, No. 5945 (Ratskirchen), *Germanie*, p. 458, No. 729 (Nassenfels).

13. *Ibid.*, *Gaule*, vi, p. 204, No. 4899 (Grand).

14. *Ibid.*, *Gaule*, viii, p. 331, No. 4613 (Cologne).

15. *Ibid.*, *Gaule*, vii, p. 267, No. 5727 (Mainz); viii, p. 31, No. 5924 (Rheinzabern).

16. *Ibid.*, *Germanie*, p. 241, No. 375 (Karlsruhe).

17. *Ibid.*, *Gaule*, v. p. 361, No. 4247 (Luxembourg).

18. C. Daremberg and E. Saglio, *Dictionnaire des antiques grecques et romaines*, s.v., astronomia, p. 488, Fig. 583.

19. S. Reinach, *Repertoire de peintures grecques et romaines*, 1922, p. 154, Fig. 7.

20. J. M. C. Toynbee, *Art in Roman Britain*, 1963, Plate 233.

21. Mattingly, *op. cit.*, ii, p. 311, Nos. 61, 63, Plates 61, 6, 7.

22. M. J. Vermaseren, *Mithras, the Secret God*, 1963, p. 111, Fig. 45; p. 119, Fig. 49.

23. See Note 15.

24. J. M. C. Toynbee, *Art in Britain under the Romans*, 1964, Plate 36, b.

25. Daremberg and Saglio, *op. cit.*, p. 489, Fig. 584.

26. *Germania Romana*, ed. 2, iv, 1928, Plate 18, Fig. 1.

27. *Ibid.*, Plate 18, Fig. 2.

28. J. M. C. Toynbee, *Art in Roman Britain*, 1963, Plates 75, 84.

29. See Note 13.

The Iron Age Pottery from Chilgrove 1

by Barry Cunliffe

The small group of sherds illustrated here* represents a cohesive group best dated to the early part of the first century B.C., or perhaps a little earlier before wheel-turned vessels of Southern Atrebatic type appeared. The basic forms, the straight-sided or slightly barrel-shaped saucepans and the jars with simple beaded rims appear on a number of local sites including the Trundle (*Curwen* 1929, 1931), Selsey Bill (*White* 1934), and Torberry (*Cunliffe* 1976). They correspond to the characteristics of a style-zone which covers the area broadly between the Rivers Test and Arun.

Considerable interest attaches to the sherd of the Glastonbury ware bowl (Fig. 00), which belongs to Peacock's Group 1 (*Peacock* 1969). These vessels were evidently made on the Lizard Peninsular in Cornwall and exported for considerable distances into Somerset, Dorset, and as far east as Mill Plain and Hengistbury Head in Hampshire. The present Chilgrove find is the most easterly occurrence of the type so far recorded, being more than 200 miles from its place of origin!

*I would like to thank Miss Jane Holdsworth for drawing the sherds illustrated in Fig. 68.

Fig. 68

Description of the Illustrated Sherds (Fig. 68)

1. Bowl with upright neck and rolled-out rim. The body is decorated in a zone which probably extends from the base of the neck to the maximum girth leaving the lower part of the vessel undecorated. The pattern consists of depressed circular areas linked together with oblique grooves between which are areas shaded with close-spaced shallow tooled lines. This kind of ornament is strictly a development of the recurring spiral motif common among the ceramic art of south-west Britain.

    The fabric is dark brown and contains grits of felspar. The surface is fired to a blackish brown and smoothed.

    The sherd was examined by Dr. D. P. S. Peacock who confirmed that it belonged to his Group 1 Glastonbury ware (*Peacock* 1969, 44–6), the mineral content of which shows that vessels in this group were made of clay derived from decomposed gabbro which outcrops only on the Lizard peninsula in Cornwall.
2. Saucepan pot. Smooth black ware with fine flint grits. Fired black; surface smoothed and shallow tooled.
3. Saucepan pot. Smooth black ware with fine flint grits. Fired black; surface smoothed and shallow tooled.
4. Saucepan pot. Smooth black ware with fine flint grits. Fired black; surface smoothed and shallow tooled.
5. Saucepan pot. Black ware with fine flint grits. Fired black; surface smoothed and shallow tooled.
6. Barrel-shaped saucepan pot. Black ware with fine flint grit. Fired black; surface smoothed and shallow tooled.
7. Saucepan pot. Smooth brownish ware with fine flint grits. Fired black; surface smoothed and decorated with shallow tooled lines and small dots.
8. Jar with beaded rim. Brown ware with medium flint grits. Fired to black externally; surface smoothed and shallow tooled.
9. Jar with beaded rim. Smooth brown ware with sparse flint grits. Fired to reddish brown and decorated with deeply impressed vertical lines.
10. Bead rimmed jar. Hard grey ware. Fired to black; surface highly burnished.
11. Bead rimmed jar. Coarse ware with medium flint grits. Fired to reddish brown.
12. Jar. Smooth black ware with sparse flint grits. Fired to black and burnished.
13. Bead rimmed jar. Red-brown ware with medium flint grits. Fired to reddish brown; surface smoothed.
14. Everted rimmed jar. Grey sandy ware. Fired to reddish brown on the surface.
15. Proto bead rimmed storage jar. Grey-brown ware with medium flint grit. Fired to brown on the surface and regularly burnished.

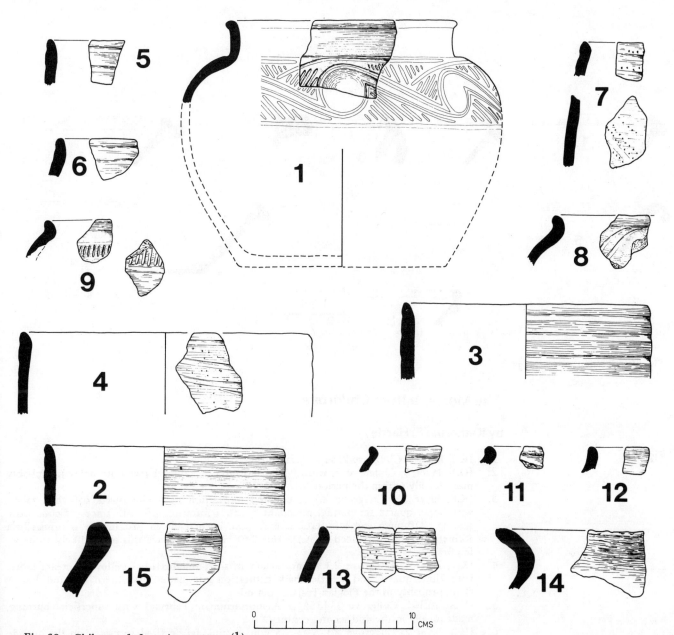

Fig. 68: Chilgrove 1, Iron Age pottery (⅓)

References

CURWEN 1929 — Curwen, E. C., 'Excavations in the Trundle', *S.A.C.* LXX, 33–85, 1929.

CURWEN 1931 — Curwen, E. C., 'Excavations in the Trundle', *S.A.C.* LXXII, 100–150, 1931.

PEACOCK 1969 — Peacock, D. P. S., 'A Contribution to the Study of Glastonbury ware from South-Western Britain', *Ant. J.* XLIX, 41–61, 1969.

WHITE 1934 — White, G. M., 'Prehistoric remains from Selsey Bill', *Ant. J.* XIV, 40–52, 1934.

CUNLIFFE 1976 — Cunliffe, B. W., 'Iron age Sites in Central Southern England', C.B.A. Research Report No. 16, 1976.

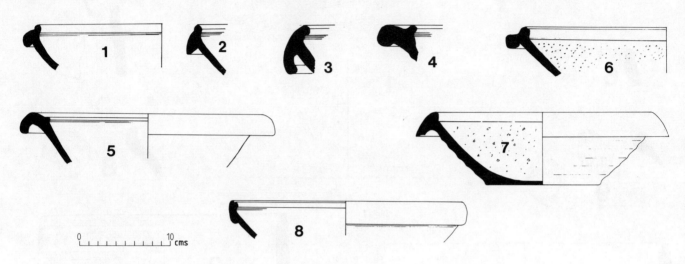

Fig. 69: Roman mortaria ($\frac{1}{4}$)

The Mortaria from Chilgrove

by Katherine F. Hartley

Fig. 69

1. (K.1, layer 7, Chilgrove 2; superficial burning.)
2. (O.1, layer 3, Chilgrove 1; worn.) Two mortaria in Fabric 1 (see note below). Probably made locally within the period A.D. 160–250.
3. (K.6, layer 32, Chilgrove 2.) A collared mortarium in fine-textured, off-white fabric with some quartz tempering; abundant quartz trituration grit with traces of concentric scoring. Although some imitations may have been made in Britain this is primarily a Rhineland type, produced *c.* A.D. 150–240, and on balance this seems likely to be an import.
4. (K.7, layer 4, Chilgrove 2.) A mortarium in soft, fine-textured yellowish cream fabric with flint, quartz and a little chalk trituration grit made in southern England and/or Gaul, probably in the Flavian-Trajanic period.
5. (Unstratified, Chilgrove 1 [362].) A mortarium in Fabric 1 with superficial burning, made locally in the mid-second century.
6. (H.3, layer 2, Chilgrove 2.) A mortarium in pink fabric fired to cream on the outside surface; made in the Oxford potteries (*Young* 1977, Type M 22; see *Atkinson* 1941, Fig. 5, No. 78 for an exact parallel), A.D. 240–400+.
7. (H.4, Pit H.1, Chilgrove 1 [358].) Worn.
8. (J.2, layer 2 [345], Chilgrove 1.) Two wall-sided mortaria in a variant of Fabric 1, which could well have been made in the same local workshop as Nos. 1, 2 and 5. A.D. 170–250.

   Note.—*Fabric 1.* A slightly granular, greyish-white fabric containing much finely fragmented grit, mostly quartz; the trituration grit is often very sparse and includes quartz, flint and sometimes red-brown material. There is sometimes a slightly darker slip. The fabric is closely similar visually to that made at Brockley Hill, Middlesex, but the quartz tempering is of a finer grade. Nos. 1, 2 and 5 are in this fabric. In Nos. 7 and 8 the fabric is of a sandwich type; brownish-cream with greyish cream core; No. 7 has tile and pink quartz in the tempering and differs from the rest in having abundant flint, red-brown and quartz trituration grit.

This fabric is only known in the south where it has been noted especially at Chichester (*Down* 1978, 250, No. 29, and 252, Nos. 48–53), Rapsley and Fishbourne. It can be attributed to a workshop somewhere in the vicinity.

References

ATKINSON 1941 — Atkinson, R. J. C., 'A Romano-British Potters' Field at Cowley, Oxon.', *Oxoniensia* VI, 9–21, 1941.

DOWN 1978 — Down, A., *Chichester Excavations* 3, Chichester, 1978.

YOUNG 1977 — Young, C. J., *Oxfordshire Roman Pottery*, British Archaeological Reports 43, Oxford, 1977.

Fig. 70

CHILGROVE 1: THE POTTERY FROM THE BATH-HOUSE FILL

A1 and A2, layer 5, A3, layer 3a, A4, layer 2, and C1/2, layers 2 and 3 were layers of dark organic fill which had been thrown into the demolished bath-house on top of the building rubble. They represent part of a deliberate clearance of the site, presumably to level off an inconvenient crater, and were covered by a layer of hillwash and soil brought down the slope by later ploughing (Fig. 17). While some of the wares are residual, a large amount must represent the pottery in use immediately before the site was abandoned. The Alice Holt wares were identified and dated by Mr. Malcolm Lyne, to whom thanks are due, while the colour-coated wares were studied by Dr. C. J. Young (see page 194).

1. (A1, layer 5). Bowl in fine white fabric reduced to grey with traces of white slip on and below the cordon and the rim. Alice Holt ware. Unusual form, but late, 330–390 A D.
2. (A1, layer 5). Collared jar, fine grey fabric. Traces of what might be a creamy white slip on shoulder and over rim. Alice Holt ware c. 300–390 A.D.
3. (A1, layer 5). Jar in dark grey fabric. Alice Holt ware c. 250–350 A.D.
4. (A1, layer 5). Narrow-mouthed jar with grooved neck. Traces of white slip below the neck. Grey fabric; some sand filling.
5. (A1, layer 5). Vessel in fine sandy fabric. Metallic dark grey slip on shoulder over lip. Alice Holt c. 250–390 A.D.
6. (A1, layer 5). Flagon in similar fabric to 5. Metallic grey slip over rim. Alice Holt ware c. 300–390 A.D.
7. (A1, layer 5). Rim of a flagon in fine grey ware.
8. (A1, layer 5). Body sherd of a large vessel—? flagon— with a line of wavy combed decoration and a zone of metallic grey slip below. The fabric is fine light grey with a fair amount of sand, and oxidised to a pinky buff. ? Alice Holt.
9. (C2, layer 2). Club-rimmed bowl. Brown sandy fabric, reduced to dark metallic grey. Alice Holt, 330–390 A.D.
10. (C2, layer 2). Similar form and fabric to 9, but rim has been folded back and there are traces of metallic grey slip over the rim. Alice Holt ware 330–390 A.D.
11. (C2, layer 3). Strainer; similar fabric to 9 and 10, reduced black. Probably Alice Holt ware.
12. (C2, layer 2). Jar in a soft brown fabric heavily loaded with coarse sand. Reduced black.
13. (C2, layer 2). Large bowl; 13½ins. inside diameter. A very fine light grey fabric. Traces of metallic grey slip on rim.
14. (C2, layer 3). Small beaker, fine grey fabric, exterior white slip over upper half of vessel.
15. (C2, layer 3). Flanged bowl. Dark grey fabric oxidised to a light brown. Coarse sand filling. Alice Holt c. 330–390 A.D.
16. (C2, layer 3). Straight-walled bowl in a hard grey fabric.
17. (C2, layer 3). Bowl in a soft fine orange fabric. Exterior surface is lumpy and uneven, but this may be due to the erosion of the soft fabric.
18. (C2, layer 3). Mortarium in hard grey fabric, patchily oxidised to a dirty buff. Flint trituration grit.
19. (A2, layer 5). shallow straight-walled vessel. Fine grey ware. Metallic grey slip inside and over rim.

187

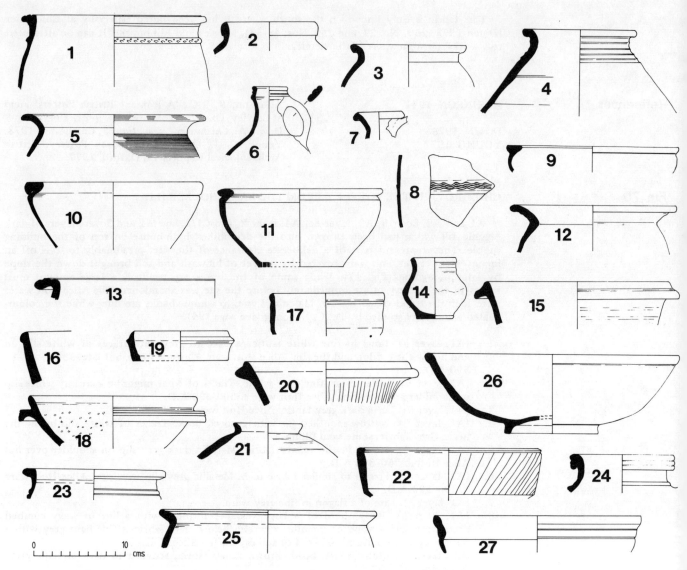

Fig. 70:   Chilgrove 1; the pottery from the bath house ($\frac{1}{4}$)

20.   (A2, layer 5). Flanged bowl. Soft black fabric, oxidised reddish-buff.
21.   (A4, layer 8e). Narrow-mouthed jar in hard light grey sandy ware.
22.   (C1, layer 2). Bowl in hard light grey sandy fabric.
23.   (A3, layer 3a). Bowl; fine grey ware. Traces of slate grey exterior slip. Alice Holt ware, c. 330–390 A.D.
24.   (A2, layer 5). Narrow-necked jar in hard fine grey ware. Alice Holt c. 300–390 A.D.
25.   (C1, layer 8). Bowl with rilled rim; fine grey fabric.
26.   (A4, layer 2). Bowl; imitation Dr. 31. Grey sandy fabric oxidised reddish-buff.
27.   (A4, layer 2). Bowl in a fine creamy buff fabric. Traces of a red-brown slip.

THE FINE WARES FROM THE BATH-HOUSE FILL

A total of 72 sherds, probably representing a minimum of 52 vessels were found in the bath-house fill. These are roughly summarised below:

Kiln				Numbers (all types)		Latest Dated Sherds
Central Gaulish	..	..	..	1		Second century
New Forest	..	..	..	56 (*Fulford* 1975)	..	.. Type 57 *c.* 330–400 A.D.
Oxford	..	..	..	15 (*Young* 1977)	..	.. Type C 48 ⎫
						Type M 22 ⎬ up to
						Type C 97 ⎨ A.D. 400+
						Type C 45 ⎭

The proportion of Oxford wares in this small sample is 21 per cent. as against 78.8 per cent. for New Forest, although for the whole site the proportions are: New Forest 66 per cent.; Oxford, 17 per cent; with the balance being made up by wares from Central Gaul, the Rheinland etc.

CHILGROVE 2—THE POTTERY FROM THE BOUNDARY DITCHES (Fig. 71)

Only a few scraps of samian came from the earliest silt layers in Ditch 1 and these are briefly mentioned on page 83. The remainder of the wares illustrated here came from the layer of organic rubbish which represented domestic tipping from Building 1 after Ditch 1 had gone out of use. Ditch 2 at the east end of the site is contemporary with Ditch 1 and the majority of the pottery came from L3, layer 4 (Fig. 30, Section F–F) and represents a similar accumulation of domestic debris from nearby buildings.

Ditch 1
28. Platter, approximately 16ins. in diameter; grey sandy ware.
29. Flanged bowl, approximately 9ins. in diameter, black under-fired fabric with coarse sand tempering, oxidised dirty buff inside.
30. Platter in grey ware; fine sandy fabric.
31. Flanged bowl, approximately 9ins. diameter; light grey sandy ware.
32. Jar in fine light-grey sandy ware, *cf. Chichester* 3, Fig. 10, 20, 47.
33. Fine light-grey sandy fabric.
34. Grey ware.
35. Mortarium, softish white fabric.
36. Small flanged bowl, soft grey ware with coarse sand filling.
37. Neck of a flagon; fine sandy ware oxidised pale buff.
38. Hard grey sandy fabric.
39. Shallow dish, 7ins. diameter. Soft brown ware with sand tempering; reduced black, burnished inside.
40. Dish in light sandy grey ware.
41. Grey ware,
42. Soft brown fabric with coarse sand filling, reduced black.

Ditch 2
43. Neck of a jar in fine grey ware.
44. Small beaker sherd in fine grey ware.
45. Sandy grey ware.
46. Dish in hard grey fabric.
47. Small necked jar in fine reddish sandy ware.
48. Shallow dish; reddish-brown sandy ware with some flint inclusions; fairly soft.
49. Flanged bowl, soft black fabric with coarse sand filling.
50. Grey ware.
51. Dark grey sandy ware.
52. Bowl in a soft brown-grey laminated fabric, traces of black slip inside and out.

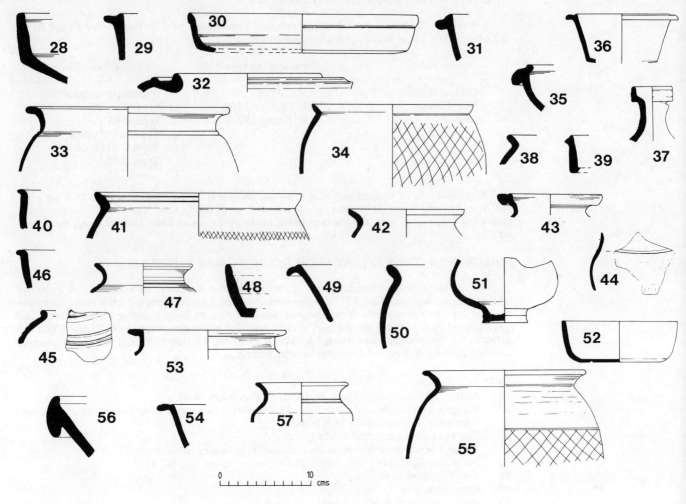

Fig. 71: Chilgrove 2; pottery from the boundary ditches ($\frac{1}{4}$)

53. Fine grey ware.
54. Flanged bowl, 10ins. diameter; black fabric tempered with coarse sand and oxidised reddish-buff.
55. Bowl in identical fabric to 12.
56. Wall-sided mortarium in dirty pale greyish-buff ware with quartz and red-brown trituration grits, *cf. Chichester* 3, Fig. 10, 16, 45.
57. Small jar, fine grey ware, burnished exterior finish reduced to slate grey.

The samian and coloured-coated wares from the ditches are summarised below:

Ditch 1	..	..	Central Gaulish	..	..	..	11
			Rheinland	..	..	..	13
			Nene Valley	..	..	..	3
			New Forest	..	..	..	16
			Oxford	..	..	..	4
			Samian	..	..	..	3 (all Antonine)
Ditch 2	..	..	Central Gaulish	..	..	..	11
			Rheinland	..	..	..	3
			New Forest	..	..	..	10
			Samian	..	..	..	7 (all Antonine)

Of the late colour-coated wares, none of the New Forest wares need be later than late third century, and of the four Oxford sherds, only two are dateable and these came from the eroded top fill of the ditch and were found after a winter's weathering. They are both Type C 26 (*Young* 1977) with a date bracket of *c.* 270–400 A.D. It can be seen that by the time the late Roman fine wares had arrived on site the ditches were almost completely filled by weathering and rubbish tipping.

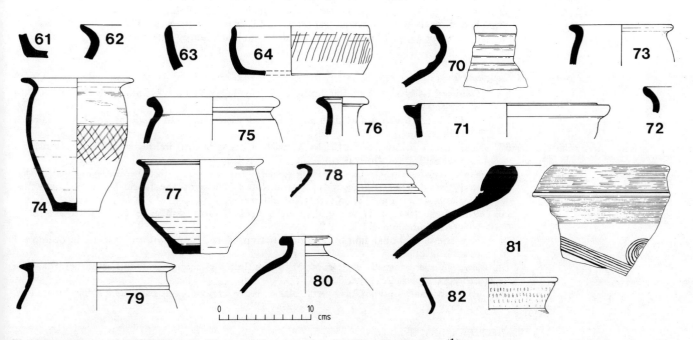

Fig. 72:   Chilgrove 1 and 2; Nos. 61–73, grogged wares, Nos. 74–82, miscellaneous ($\frac{1}{4}$)

191

Fig. 72

GROGGED WARES

A number of soft under-fired wares were found in the top levels of both Chilgrove sites. In general, the fabric is reduced brown or black and is grogged with small fragments, some of which might be chalk, varying from 2 mm. to 4 mm. across. Some also have coarse sand filling and others have traces of organic material which has burnt out in the firing. The sherds vary from medium hard to soft and friable, and the surface is sometimes lumpy. They are easily distinguished from the Early Iron Age sherds from Chilgrove 1 by the almost complete absence of the flint tempering which is a salient feature of the Iron Age wares. The latter wares are also usually well burnished, whereas the grogged wares are not.

It is likely that they were made on site and since those identified have all come from late fourth-century layers or the ploughsoil above, it is possible that they are home-made pots produced at a time when few, if any, standard coarse wares were obtainable from the local market. Alternatively, they may derive from occasional batches of wares made on site when supplies of domestic pots ran out before the next market day. The *ad hoc* manufacture of coarse pottery was probably well within the competence of someone on the farm staff throughout the life of the villas, and it would be unwise to attribute these wares solely to a late or sub-Roman phase, attractive though this theory might be.

Chilgrove 1

58. Body sherd, fabric reduced to dark brown; some coarse sand filling. A3, 2A (above bath-house). (Not illustrated),
59. Body sherd from large vessel in similar fabric to 1. F2, layer 1B (south of bath-house). (Not illustrated.)
60. Body sherd from a beaker, partially oxidised reddish-brown. Some sand filling. Pit F2 (south of bath-house). (Not illustrated.)
61. Base sherd, approximately 7ins. diameter; similar fabric to 1. F1 (ploughsoil).
62. Rim of cooking pot, similar fabric to 1. L1, layer 2 (Building 1).
63. Rim of shallow bowl, similar fabric to 1. A1, layer 5 (bath-house filling).
64. Shallow bowl, soft brown fabric, similar to 6; black lumpy exterior.

Chilgrove 2

65. Oxidised body sherd; similar fabric to 1. H4, layer 51 (above floor of Building 2). (Not illustrated.)
66. Body sherd, much abraded, heavily loaded with small and medium grits. K7, layer 3. (Not illustrated.)
67. Base sherd in similar fabric to 1, with a cross incised in the ware before firing. K3 (ploughsoil). (Not illustrated.)
68. Small sherd, oxidised dark reddish-brown, similar to 8. K3 (ploughsoil). (Not illustrated.)
69. Body sherd from cooking pot. In addition to the grog the fabric has some small flint grits and sand filling. J2, layer 7. (Not illustrated.)
70. Rim sherd from a vessel with grooved neck. Fabric similar to 1, oxidised externally to a reddish-brown. B3, layer 2.
71. Rim sherd in similar fabric to 1, one of four sherds found within Hearth 4 in Building 3 (bath-house).
72. Two sherds, grogged, with some medium flint inclusions, fired rather harder than the other examples. D2, layer 2.
73. Rim of small bowl, fabric very black, some organic tempering which has burnt out. F2, layer 2.

MISCELLANEOUS

Fig. 72

Chilgrove 1

74. (F1, Pit F3.) Almost complete beaker. Soft brown fabric. Heavily loaded with coarse sand, burnished above zone of lattice decoration and over rim.
75. (Unstratified.) Jar in soft dirty white sandy fabric. Dark reddish-brown slip inside and out.

76. (C1, layer 1.) Neck of flagon. Hard fine sandy grey ware, oxidised reddish-buff.
77. (F1, Pit F3.) Bowl in dirty grey sandy fabric.
78. (Trial Trench 2, layer 3c.) Bowl in hard fine grey sandy ware. Alice Holt, *c.* 150–250 A.D.)
79. (E2, layer 1.) Bowl in fine sandy brownish grey ware. Traces of exterior metallic grey slip. Alice Holt, *c.* 330–390 A.D.
80. (D1, layer 2.) Narrow-mouthed jar. Soft brown sandy fabric. Metallic grey slip.

Chilgrove 2
81. (D2, layer 5.) Storage jar with grooved collar rim; fine light grey sandy ware, metallic grey slip on rim and above zone of combed decoration.
82. (J2, layer 9e.) Rim of a vessel in fine grey sandy ware. There may have been an exterior whitish slip, faint traces of which are perceptible in the pecked decoration.

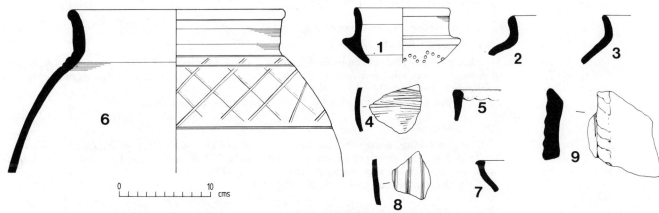

Fig. 73:   Pitlands Farm, Upmarden; late Saxon and medieval wares ($\frac{1}{4}$)

Fig. 73   POST-ROMAN POTTERY FROM UPMARDEN

Late Saxon—Saxo-Norman
1. (N1/2, Pit N1.) Shallow bowl ? lamp. Gritty dark grey fabric with some sand, oxidised reddish-buff outside. Heavily sooted on the inside. The stick-end decoration and fabric suggests an 11th-century date.
2. (N1/2, Pit N1.) Rim of a cooking pot in similar fabric and colour to 1.
3. (N1/2, Pit N1.) Similar ware to 2.
4. (N5, Pit N1.) Two body sherds from a cooking pot. The fabric is soft dark grey to black with a lot of coarse sand filling. The rilling suggests that the sherds are from a 'Porchester type' vessel—(*Cunliffe* 1974, 125–135)—and would imply a pre-Conquest date.
5. (N1, Pit N5.) Rim from a cooking pot with finger impressed decoration. Similar fabric to 3.
6. (N5, Pit N1.) Large storage jar. Grey fabric oxidised reddish-buff. The ware is grey, with some large flint grits and random chalk inclusions. The lattice decoration is unusual in the Chichester area for a vessel of this type and date.

Medieval
7. Sherd from a shallow vessel or perhaps a lid. Grey fabric with coarse sand tempering, oxidised brown.
8. (B, layer 2.) Body sherd from a green glazed jug with vertical combed decoration. 13th/14th century in date. Fine grey sandy ware oxidised buff inside.
9. (P6, layer 2.) Sherd from a chimney vent. Coarse reddish fabric, heavily flint gritted.

The Roman Fine Ware

by Christopher J. Young

Introduction

This report summarises the Roman fine wares found at Chilgrove 1 and 2, and at Upmarden, except for the samian and mortaria which are reported on elsewhere (Oxford and New Forest mortaria have been included in the ware lists for the sake of completeness). The amount of pottery submitted for report was relatively small (less than 1,000 sherds from all three sites) and has been quantified by ware and form within context. The method of quantification used was a sherd count. The full catalogue is deposited with the finds in accordance with the recommendations of the Frere report (*D.O.E.* 1975).

Because the quantity of pottery was small there were some difficulties in defining the minor fabric groups; larger groups of material would be needed to determine which differences and similarities are signficant of ware groupings within the Miscellaneous category.

SUMMARY OF THE FINE WARES

The following wares were present:

Central Gaulish 'rhenish ware'

Fine pinkish-red ware (similar to central Gaulish samian) with black glossy slip. All sherds present are from enclosed vessels. This ware was made at the central Gaulish samian potteries, probably *c.* 150–200 (*Greene* 1978, 18–19).
Chilgrove 1: 13 sherds; Chilgrove 2: 47 sherds; Upmarden: 1 sherd.

Trier 'rhenish ware'

Fine, hard ware, normally laminated dark-red and grey with black glossy slip. This ware was made at Trier. All sherds are from enclosed vessels. The ware was probably made from the late second to the mid-third centuries (*Greene* 1978, 18–19).
Chilgrove 1: 2 sherds; Chilgrove 2: 46 sherds.

'Rhenish ware' of uncertain origin

Sherds which could have come from either of the two main centres were found at both the Chilgrove sites.
Chilgrove 1: 3 sherds; Chilgrove 2: 3 sherds.

Fine white rough cast wares

Very fine white ware, no visible tempering with black colour-coat, rough cast with clay pellets. This ware is distinguished from other white wares by its extreme fineness. It is most probably an import, perhaps from the Rhineland. All the sherds found are from beakers.
Chilgrove 2: 9 sherds.

Other rough cast wares

A variety of other rough cast sherds were found at both the Chilgrove sites. The fabrics varied from orange through red to red-brown, sometimes with a grey core. The colour-coats were various shades of brown or black, rough cast with either sand or clay pellets. It is likely that several different sources are represented, but the quantities studied were too small to allow of any real divisions. It is likely that some of those with the finer fabrics and colour-coats are imports.
Chilgrove 1: 2 sherds; Chilgrove 2: 16 sherds.

Colchester colour-coated ware

A small number of sherds in a fine brown ware with a dark colour-coat was found at Chilgrove 2. Of known production centres, they are closest to Colchester, but this identification is not certain. All sherds were from enclosed vessels, one with white barbotine. They are most likely to date to the late second and early third centuries.
Chilgrove 2: 4 sherds.

194

Nene valley type ware

A number of sherds were of a fine white fabric with small red inclusions and a dark brown or black colour-coat. They are very similar to known products of the Nene valley kilns, but similar wares were made elsewhere in Britain and on the continent, and attribution cannot be certain. Such wares were current in Britain from the mid-second century onwards and dating must depend on the forms. Those which could be dated fell within the late second or early third centuries. Types represented included castor boxes (*cf. Hartley* 1960, Fig. 4, 17), hunt cups (*cf. Hartley* 1960, Fig. 4, 1), bag beaker, and other enclosed vessels.

Chilgrove 1: 2 sherds; Chilgrove 2: 13 sherds; Upmarden: 1 sherd.

New Forest wares

These wares date to the late third and fourth centuries, and have been classified by *Fulford* (1975 a) and were common at all three sites. A wide variety of forms were found:

Fabric 1a: Chilgrove 1: types 7, 11/15, 12, 18, 30, 41, 45, 53, 1 sherd each; type 27, 41 sherds; type 42, 3 sherds; type 44, 10 sherds; type 47, 2 sherds; type 57, 4 sherds; 4 enclosed-vessel rims of uncertain form; 14 sherds of enclosed-vessel bases; 23 enclosed-vessel body sherds; 4 painted body sherds; 34 body sherds and 5 base sherds of uncertain form, but probably from enclosed vessels.

Chilgrove 2: types 18, 24, 28, one sherd each; type 27, 17 sherds; type 30, 3 sherds; type 44, 12 sherds; 11 enclosed-vessel rims of uncertain form; 2 enclosed-vessel bases; 22 enclosed-vessel body sherds; 1 flagon handle; 1 jug spout; 15 base, 5 painted body, and 58 body sherds probably from enclosed vessels; 4 bowl-body sherds.

Upmarden: type 28, 1 sherd; type 27, 4 sherds; 2 enclosed-vessel body sherds.

Fabric 1b: Chilgrove 1: types 27, 53, 60, 1 sherd each; type 63, 3 sherds; type 67, 2 sherds; 2 enclosed-vessel base sherds; 3 bowl-base sherds; 1 base sherd, 2 body sherds, probably from bowls.;

Chilgrove 2: type 67, 3 sherds; type 70, 8 sherds; type 73, 3 sherds; 1 bowl base, 10 bowl-body sherds; 2 base sherds, 14 body sherds, probably from bowls; 2 mortaria body sherds. sherds.

Upmarden: 1 bowl base sherd.

Fabric 2a: Chilgrove 1: types 91, 102, 106, 1 sherd each; types 90, 2 sherds; types 102, 103, 3 sherds each; 1 mortarium rim, form uncertain; 2 mortaria body sherds.

Chilgrove 2: types 86, 102, 103, 104, 1 sherd each; type 89, 8 sherds; 1 mortarium body sherd.

Upmarden: types 89, 102, 1 sherd each.

Fabric 2b: Chilgrove 1: type 89, 1 sherd.

Fabric 2c: Chilgrove 2: type 89, 1 sherd.

Oxford wares: these were common at all three sites in the late Roman period and are noted here according to the recently-published classification (*Young* 1977).

White colour-coated ware: Upmarden: WC7, 1 sherd; mortarium of uncertain form.

Red colour-coated ware: Chilgrove 1: C14, C30, C45, C47, C100, 1 sherd each; C22, 2 sherds; C23, 3 sherds; C48, 4 sherds; C50, 2 sherds; C51, 5 sherds; C68, 2 sherds; C75, 2 sherds; C97, 3 sherds; 2 enclosed body sherds; 2 sherds of flagon handle; 1 bowl base; 4 bowl body sherds; 2 painted body sherds and 3 body sherds of uncertain form; 1 mortarium base sherd, 1 mortarium body sherd.

Chilgrove 2: C18, C22, C24, C26, C32, C 53, C55, C64, C71, C74, C77, C82, C99, 1 sherd each; C8, C23, C46, C83, 2 sherds each; C75, C100, 3 sherds each; C44, C45, C68, C78, 4 sherds each; C51, 33 sherds; C81, 5 sherds; C97, C115, 9 sherds each; 3 base sherds, 11 body sherds (2 painted) of enclosed vessels; 24 base sherds, 103 body sherds of bowls; 1 rim sherd, 2 base sherds and 12 body sherds (1 painted) of uncertain form; 4 body sherds and 1 mortaria base.

Parchment ware

Chilgrove 1: P24, 1 sherd; Chilgrove 2: P24, 10 sherds.

White-ware mortaria

Chilgrove 1: M22, M23, 1 sherd each; 1 body sherd; Chilgrove 2: M22, 2 sherds; 1 unidentified rim; 4 body sherds.

Local red-slip ware

This ware was first recognised in Chichester (*Fulford* and *Young* 1978, 257) and has a sandy red fabric, with small black and white inclusions, sometimes with a grey core. Most sherds have a red colour-coat. All identifiable sherds from the Chilgrove sites appear to come from bowls, the forms present being imitation Dr 31 and Dr 38 and straight-sided dog bowls. At Chichester this ware was exclusively late Roman, and it is probable that this is yet another of the small fine-ware products now known to have existed in the fourth century.

Chilgrove 1: 10 sherds; Chilgrove 2: 7 sherds.

Other ? local ware

Five sherds, probably all from the same vessel, were found at Chilgrove 2, of a highly distinctive colour-coat ware. It is hard, sandy, with large white inclusions. In colour it is pink-orange with a thin grey skin on the exterior surface. The colour-coat is black.

The form was a bulbous beaker with white-painted decoration similar to the Oxford type C27 (*Young* 1977, Fig. 55). The source of this ware is unknown, but examples have been found also at Portchester (M.G. *Fulford*, pers. comm.).

Miscellaneous

At both Chilgrove sites a number of sherds were found which did not readily fall into any of the established categories. All had orange or brown fabrics often with a grey core, and red to brown or black colour-coats. They are difficult to classify, particularly since the quantity found at each site was relatively small, and have therefore been classed as miscellaneous. It will not be possible to do more than this until larger quantities of material are available. Dating also is uncertain.

Forms present included disc-rimmed flagons (*cf. Young* 1977, Fig. 53, C4), and bulbous beakers, either plain, rouletted, or with white-painted decoration (*cf. Young* 1977, Fig. 55, C22, C23, C27 for general appearance), which all tend to be late Roman rather than earlier, and bag beakers which tend to be earlier.

Discussion

Table 1 summarises the sources of fine-ware supply to the three sites and can be used as a basis for consideration not only of the importance of the various sources of supply, but also to compare differences between the two Chilgrove sites. The quantity of pottery from Upmarden is so small as to be insignificant. Even with the two Chilgrove sites it must be remembered that the quantities are relatively small, and hence some of the minor variations noted may not be significant or could even be misleading.

It is now accepted that the pattern of fine-ware supply altered radically between the end of the second and the middle of the third centuries; it is therefore appropriate to consider the supply of fine wares before and after *c.* 250 separately.

(a) *Pre-250*

The biggest proportion of fine wares of this period was of so-called 'rhenish' wares from both Central Gaul and the Trier regions. These are not earlier than the mid-second century. The few sherds from Colchester are of the same date range, and the Nene valley-type wares cannot be earlier than the later second century, though some of the sherds could of course be much later. The only closely datable Nene valley form here, though, is a hunt-cup which dates before the mid-third century. All the other sherds could be of the same date, and, in view of the dominance of Oxfordshire and New Forest wares after 250, it is assumed for the purposes of this discussion that they are. The quantities are in any case very small. The only material probably dating earlier than the mid-second century are the various rough cast wares (*Greene* 1978, 17–18), and these form a very small proportion of the fine wares as a whole (*c.* 2 per cent. at Chilgrove 1; 3 per cent. at Chilgrove 2).

Thus, very little fine ware seems to have reached either site before the mid-second century. Thereafter the major sources of supply were the two producers of rhenish ware. The proportion from British suppliers was very low indeed. Indeed, compared with the later Roman period the quantities of fine ware from any source are low. In part this distinction is apparent rather than real since the need for table wares was met by samian, which is considered elsewhere. If, however, the earlier fine wares (all enclosed vessels) are compared with the similar vessels from the late Roman period, the quantities of late Roman enclosed vessels are very much larger (see Table 2). This perhaps reflects the relative poverty of the earlier phases of the two villas.

(b) *Post-250*

Table 2 shows the late Roman fine wares found at Chilgrove 1 and 2 classified according to origin and major vessel categories—enclosed vessels (beakers, flagons, etc.), tablewares and mortaria (shown here for the sake of completeness). The main suppliers were clearly the major industries of the New Forest and Oxfordshire. It is of interest, though, to note the presence of products of what must be local minor industries. These are being recognised increasingly (e.g., Pevensey ware: *Fulford* 1973), but as yet are imperfectly known. At both Chilgrove villas, however, they were of minor importance only.

If comparison is made of the relative proportions of the wares of the two major industries and of vessel categories, very interesting differences between the two sites emerge. Firstly it is clear that the bulk of the New Forest products were enclosed vessels, while the bulk of the Oxford products were tablewares. Reference to the ware lists given above shows also that the New Forest fabric 1b, the hard purple-colour-coated ware made only by that industry, was the predominant New Forest ware at both sites. This reflects the normal pattern of New Forest distribution (*cf. Fulford* 1975a, 118, *Swan* 1973).

Apart from this it is notable that at Chilgrove 2 Oxford wares and table wares were both much more prolific than at Chilgrove 1. The increased popularity of Oxford wares at Chilgrove 2 probably reflects the longer period of fourth-century occupation at that site—at Portchester, Oxfordshire wares became more common in the later fourth century (*Fulford* 1975 b). The difference in the proportions of enclosed vessels and tablewares at the two sites is more difficult to explain. It may reflect different catering habits at the two sites, or at Chilgrove 1 tablewares may have been supplied from a different source and be found among the grey wares or, perhaps, may not even have been pottery. It is also possible that at Chilgrove 2 other materials, such as glass, may have been used for drinking vessels.

TABLE 1

SHERD COUNT OF ROMAN FINE WARES (figures in parenthesis are percentages)

	Central Gaulish 'rhenish' ware	Trier 'rhenish' ware	C G/Trier 'rhenish' ware	Fine white rough cast ware	Other rough cast wares	Colchester c/c ware	Nene valley-type ware	New Forest wares	Oxford wares	Local red-slip ware	Other local ware	Miscellaneous	TOTALS
Chilgrove 1	13 (5)	2 (1)	3 (1)	— (—)	2 (1)	— (—)	2 (1)	183 (66)	48 (17)	10 (3)	— (—)	15 (5)	278 (100)
Chilgrove 2	47 (7)	46 (7)	3 (—)	9 (1)	16 (2)	4 (—)	13 (2)	222 (34)	277 (42)	7 (1)	5 (1)	23 (3)	658 (100)
Upmarden	1 (7)	— (—)	— (—)	— (—)	— (—)	— (—)	1 7	10 (66)	3 (20)	— (—)	— (—)	— (—)	15 (100)

TABLE 2

Late Roman fine wares at Chilgrove 1 and 2, classified by origin and vessel category. (Quantification by sherd count; figures in parenthesis are percentages of total number of sherds.)

	Chilgrove 1				Chilgrove 2			
	New Forest	Oxon	Other	Total per vessel category	New Forest	Oxon	Other	Total per vessel category
Enclosed vessels	150 (62)	11 (4.5)	—	161 (66.5)	150 (29)	23 (5)	5 (1)	178 (35)
Tablewares	23 (10)	23 (10)	10 (4)	56 (24)	66 (13)	214 (42)	7 (1)	287 (56)
Mortaria	10 (4)	9 (3.5)	—	19 (7.5)	6 (1)	25 (5)	—	31 (6)
Unidentified	—	5 (2)	—	5 (2)	—	15 (3)	—	15 (3)
Total per ware	183 (76)	48 (20)	10 (4)	241 (100)	222 (44)	277 (55)	8 (1)	511 (100)

References

CUNLIFFE 1974 — Cunliffe, B. W., 'Some late Saxon stamped pottery from Southern England', *Medieval Pottery from Excavations*, eds. Evison, V. I., Hodges, H. and Hurst, J. G.

D.O.E. 1975 — Department of the Environment, *Principles of Publication in Rescue Archaeology*, London, 1975.

FULFORD 1973 — Fulford, M. G., 'A fourth-century colour-coated fabric and its types in South-East England', *S.A.C. 111*, 41–4.

FULFORD 1975a — Fulford, M. G., *New Forest Roman Pottery*, B.A.R. No. 17, Oxford, 1975.

FULFORD 1975b — Fulford, M. G., 'The Pottery', in Cunliffe, B. W., *Excavations at Portchester Castle*, Vol. I, Roman, 1975.

FULFORD and YOUNG 1978 — Fulford, M. G. and Young, C. J., 'A discussion of the later Roman Fine Wares', in Down, A., *Chichester Excavations 3*, Phillimore, Chichester, 1978.

GREENE 1978 — Greene, K., 'Imported fine wares in Britain to A.D. 250; a guide to identification', in Arthur, P. and Marsh, G., *Early Fine Wares in Roman Britain*, B.A.R. No. 57, Oxford, 1978.

HARTLEY 1960 — Hartley, B. R., *Notes on the Roman Pottery Industry in the Nene Valley*, Peterborough, 1960.

SWAN 1973 — Swan, V. G., 'Aspects of the New Forest late-Roman Pottery Industry', in Detsicas, A. P. (ed.), *Current Research in Romano-British Coarse Pottery*, C.B.A. Research Report No. 10, London, 1973.

YOUNG 1977 — Young, C. J., *The Roman Pottery Industry of the Oxford Region*, B.A.R. No. 43, Oxford, 1977.

Abbreviations

S.A.C.   Sussex Archaeological Collections.
B.A.R.   British Archaeological Reports.

The Samian Stamps from Chilgrove

by B. R. Hartley

1. CLEME(N)S II 4a on form 33, CLEMIIS.
   One of the less-common stamps of a Lezoux potter who is associated with Priscus III in the making of decorated moulds. His work occurs at sites in northern Britain re-occupied *c.* A.D. 160. His forms include 31R, 38 and 79, *c.* A.D. 160–190.
2. CUCCILUS i 7a, CVCCILLVS.F (form not noted).
   A stamp of a Lezoux potter whose work occurs in Antonine Scotland and the Wroxeter Gutter. This particular stamp was used occasionally on form 27.*c.* A.D. 150–170.
3. DONATUS III 1d on form 31, [D] ONATVSF.
   The dating evidence for Donatus, as for many other Rheinzabern potters rests on his forms. Since he made 31R, 32, 40, etc., he cannot have belonged to the earlier groups of potters there. *c.* A.D. 180–260.
4. TITURO 1a on form 33, TITVRONISFO.
   Tituro worked at Lezoux, as this stamp attests. It also occurs in the Wroxeter Gutter and at sites in the north reoccupied *c.* A.D. 160. It appears frequently on forms 31R, 79 and 80. *c.* A.D. 150–180.
5. TITURO 5b on form 33, TITVRONIS.
   There is no site dating for this stamp, but since it appears on forms 79, 80 and Ludowici Tg and Tx, a range *c.* A.D. 150–180 is certain.

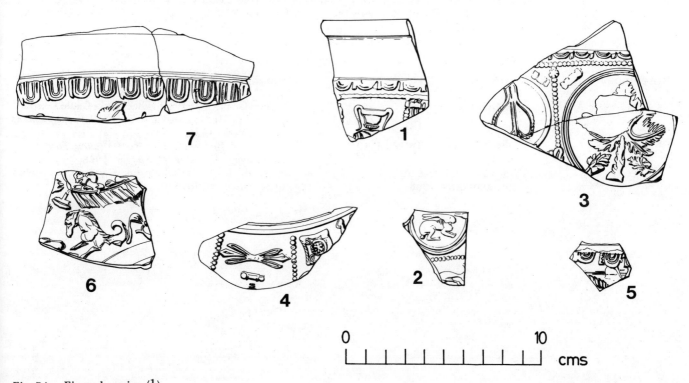

Fig. 74: Figured samian (½)

The Samian Ware

by G. B. Dannell

Fig. 74

Chilgrove 1

1. Form 37. The closest parallel for the fragmentary ovolo seems to be Rogers' B.211, taking into account the placing of the tongue, and the size. The crater is close to Rogers' T7. It is not impossible that this is the work of PRISCVS, and that the ovolo is an earlier version of B186. *c.* A.D. 155–180, Lezoux. Trial Trench 1, layer 5.
2. Form 30. Panel with a hare, O. 2061. Antonine, Lezoux. H5, layer 4.
3. Form 37. DOECCVS style, his ovolo (*Stanfield* and *Simpson,* Fig. 44, 1). The leaves are all in his work, *ibid.* 27, 39; *Rogers'* H167, and *Dannell,* 1971, Fig. 136, 108). The tree trunk is not known for him. *c.* A D. 160–190, Lezoux. B2, layer 3.

Chilgrove 2

4. Form 37. 'Cushion' motif, *Rogers'* U3. To the right an astragalus above an opposed pair of leaf-motifs, similar to Rogers' G225. The latter is used by DOECCVS and IVLLINVS. *c.* A.D. 160–190. Lezoux. K6, layer 30.
5. Form 37. Neither Rogers or Stanfield and Simpson show this ovolo, which is on a very small bowl, with thin walls. The fabric looks as if it belongs to the mid-Antonine period. *c.* A.D. 150–180 ? Lezoux. L2, layer 2.
6. Form 37. A vessel in the LIBERTVS style, with his galley (*cf. Stanfield* and *Simpson,* Plate 53, 626), and seahorse (*ibid.* 54, 643). *c.* A.D. 120–150, Lezoux. L3, layer 3.
7. Form 37. A rather worn version of the ovolo used by B. F. ATTONI (Ricken-Ludowici V1. Taf. 262/23), with the head of lioness D792. *c.* A.D. 160–195. Rheinzabern. K5, layer 1.

References

DANNELL 1971	Dannell, G., in B. W. Cunliffe, *Excavations at Fishbourne,* Vol. II, The Finds. London, 1971.
ROGERS 1974	Rogers, G. B., 'Poteries Sigillees de la Gaule Centrale, Vol. 1, Les Motifs non Figures', XXVIIIe *supplement a Gallia,* Paris, 1974.
RICKEN and LUDOWICI 1948	Ricken and Ludowici, *Der Rommischen Topfer von Rheinzabern. Kattolog VI, Speyer,* 1948.
STANFIELD and SIMPSON 1958	Stanfield, J. A. and Simpson, G., *Central Gaulish Potters,* London, 1958.

List of Subscribers

Mrs. A. Adams
Major J. F. Ainsworth
Mr. J. E. Andrews
Paul Arthur, B.A.
Mr. J. G. Ayling
John E. Ayto

Dr. Rodney M. Baguley, B.A., Ph.D., D.Litt.,
    F.S.A.Scot., F.R.S.A.I.
Dr. H. M. Barnes
Jean and David Barnes
Barr-Hamilton, Alec
Mr. Tom Beaumont
Martin Bell
Miss J. A. Bestow
Dr. and Mrs. D. G. Bird
B. G. Boddy
Mrs. Peter Booker
Robert G. Britnell
A. M. Burnet
C. G. Busbridge
Dr. N. F. H. Butcher, M.A.

Geoffrey Claridge
Mrs. E. M. Clarke
A. S. Esmonde Cleary
Gillian Clegg
E. A. Crossland, I.S.O.
Michael Coker
John L. Cole
A. H. Collins, M.A., F.S.A.
Jeffrey Collins
J. R. Collis
Miss D. M. Cox

Dan and Rhon Daniel
P. G. Day
A. P. Detsicas
Mary Dickinson
J. C. Dove
Patricia Drummond
P. J. Drury

Dr. P. W. Edbury
Pamela Edwards
Susan C. Eeles
Mr. J. E. Eschbaecher

Mr. John Farrimond
H. R. Fawcett
Frederick E. Ford, A.R.I.B.A.
David J. Freke
S. S. Frere
Dr. M. G. Fulford, F.S.A.

Miss Joan Gates
K. W. E. Gravett
Mr. T. K. Green
F. W. Greenaway, Mr.
Roger Goodburn
Dr. John Leveson Gower
M. L. Grenfell

R. C. Hammond, B.Sc., D.Phil.
Rosamond Hanworth
Mrs. Guy T. Harden
Harry I. Hodges
E. W. Holden, F.S.A.
Dorothy Howell-Thomas
Dr. R. F. Hunnisett
Gerry Hutchinson

M. G. Jarrett
W. T. Jones, F.S.A.

Mr. M. J. Karn
Martin Knight

Mr. and Mrs. A. W. Lane
Leva, C., c/o Cira. 1180 Brussels
K. G. Lintott
Miss Joan Liversidge

Mr. R. J. Maskelyne
Mr. and Mrs. T. J. McCann
A. G. Eric Millington
Mrs. J. N. Mills
Mr. E. N. Montague
R. R. and S. Morgan
Julian Munby
Dr. K. M. E. Murray

E. W. O'Shea

Keith Parfitt, B.A.
The Rev. Dr. Thomas M. Parker, D.D., F.S.A.,
    F.R.Hist.S.
Miss J. G. Pilmer
J. L. Piper
M. W. Pitts
J. E. Pratt

Reflex 1946
Mrs. R. Reilly
Dr. W. J. Rodwell
D. R. Rudling
Ms. Jane Russell

Edward Sammes
Sylvia Saunders-Jacobs

Alan G. Scott
Caroline Scott
David J. Screen
C. G. Searle
Mr. W. Shannon
James L. Shields
Maurice J. Smith
Louis E. Smith
Mr. Grahame Soffe
K. Stanford
Sally G. Stow
Michael L. Stuart
Surrey Archaeological Society
Mrs. Vivien G. Swan, B.A., F.S.A.
Mr. M. B. Swatridge

Tim Tatton-Brown
H. L. Tewkesbury

Phillip Thompson
Mrs. R. M. Tittensor
Malcolm Todd

Miss W. Underhay
Mr. and Mrs. R. Upton

Mollie Vernon

C. M. Walker
A. J. K. Webb, B.A.(Hons.)
Dr. Graham Webster
Basil Wedmore
West London Archaeological Field Group
Jeanne Wyatt